KW-363-968

Basic Gardening

Basic Gardening

Edited by Clay Jones

ORBIS PUBLISHING·LONDON

Acknowledgements

A-Z Collection: 31, 32, 44, 46, 50, 52, 55, 60, 64, 65, 113, 133, 144, 145, 147
Bernard Alfieri: 25, 52, 95, 132, 147, 151
Alphabet & Image: 45
Heather Angel: 26, 48, 111, 112
Barnaby's Picture Library: 150
Bees Ltd: 23
C. Bevilacqua: 22
Pat Brindley: 19, 22, 40, 44, 45, 46, 47, 51, 53, 55, 56, 57, 60
Ron Boardman, Fisons Ltd: 160
S.T. Buczaki: 168, 169
R.J. Corbin: 24, 42, 43, 62, 100, 101, 102, 103, 116, 124, 125, 128, 135, 136, 137, 138, 141, 142, 143, 145, 146
Crown Copyright: 64, 65
Ernest Crowson: 36, 53
Samuel Dobie & Sons Ltd: 23, 151
Flymo Ltd: 108
Geest Horticultural Group: 24
Halls Homes & Greenhouses Ltd: 154, 155
J. Hamilton: 96
Hozelock Ltd: 109, 146
ICI: 152, 171
Michael Leale: 117, 123
May & Baker: 161, 163, 171
Murphy Chemicals Ltd: 168, 171
National Vegetable Research Station: 164
Oxford Scientific Films: 164, 169
PBI: 169
Shell International Petroleum: 161, 163
Donald Smith: 51
Harry Smith: 11, 25, 26, 30, 31, 32, 36, 37, 43, 48, 49, 56, 61, 99, 109, 116, 127, 138, 139, 140, 147, 153, 163
Peter Stiles: 97
Sutton Seeds: 85
Brian Tysterman: 62
W.J. Unwin Ltd: 23
Weed Research Organization: 161
D. Wilderidge: 37, 39
Wolfe Ltd: 146

© Orbis Publishing Limited, London 1978
Originally published in 1978 as *Gardening in Springtime*
Reprinted in this edition 1982

Printed and bound in Spain by Graficromo, S.A. — Cordobá

ISBN: 0-85613-457-0

CONTENTS

INTRODUCTION

In simple terms, gardening is defined as the care and cultivation of plants. For the professional it is a full-time job, but for the amateur it is a part-time occupation that has to compete, in terms of time and expenditure, with his chosen profession and with his other leisure activities.

Even for the amateur, gardening can be more than a hobby; it can be a way of life. It is certainly therapeutic. It takes you out into the open air and it involves healthy and gentle exercise in a pleasant environment. In the garden you also have the opportunity for total mental relaxation away from the cares and worries of modern living. All plants live their lives in concert with Nature. They respond to the varying seasons and they accept and adjust to their surroundings without striving to change them. Nevertheless, plants, like ourselves, are competitive. They vie for sun and space, and it is the fittest that survive in a free society.

The successful gardener is the one who knows enough about his subject to enjoy it to the full. As with anything else, insufficient knowledge results in failure, frustration and sometimes real danger. Unless he knows the requirements for successful germination, for instance, the seeds he sows may rot in the ground and, unless he uses chemical gardening aids wisely and correctly, the gardener can do irreparable harm to his plants and even, perhaps, to himself.

For despite its close association with Nature, gardening is not natural. Left to its own devices an area of ground will adopt its own ecological pattern. It will become populated first by grasses and simple, lowly annual plants. In time they will be ousted by stronger perennials, that in turn will eventually be compelled to give way to the mighty forest trees. Gardening, therefore, involves exercising a modicum of control over Nature's tendency to let things run riot, whilst at the same time endeavouring to work with her rather than against her. To succeed, the gardener needs to know and understand his plants – how they grow, indeed why they grow, and what their individual preferences are. There are, for example, plants that actually like growing in partial or total shade, whilst others will only grow and flower in the eye of the sun. Then again some plants revel in moist marshy ground, whilst others prefer dry, arid banks or shallow, rocky soils. Still other plants flourish on chalky ground, whereas the merest hint of lime in the soil spells death to many. Just as there are 'horses for courses'. so there are 'plants for places'. It is very much easier and more rewarding to grow a plant where it finds conditions to its liking, instead of trying to defy the very laws of Nature.

Armed with an adequate fount of knowledge, the gardener's other pressing need is for time. There is nothing more discouraging than to be constantly slaving away, trying to keep pace with the various jobs that have to be done in their due season. To enjoy gardening is to have enough time to do things leisurely. At the very beginning, therefore, you would be well advised to equate time and space. For the retired gardener, time is not at a premium. If he so wishes he can devote himself to growing, planting and caring for large and varied beds of half-hardy annuals that are pretty but time consuming. The average amateur gardener needs a garden that he can care for in his spare time, whilst still indulging in one or more other hobbies.

All this is possible with careful pre-planning. A vegetable plot is not too demanding of time; it needs digging, feeding, sowing, planting and weeding. It is only the weeding that is repetitive and by using chemical weedkillers, or merely by regular hoeing, the time spent need not be more than an hour per week, often less. Using mechanically-propelled machines, lawns are mown quickly and easily once a week when the grass is growing. It is only when the lawn is pock-marked with small, fussy little flower beds that mowing becomes tedious and time-wasting.

To save time, make full use of flowering trees and shrubs; there are hundreds to choose from. With careful selection it is possible to have colour in the garden whenever you want with shrubs alone. In fact by choosing only one genus – the heathers – and selecting the appropriate varieties, you can have flower and foliage colour all the year round. Shrubs, moreover, and heathers, in particular, are great weed smotherers. They grow so close together and provide such deep shade, at soil level, that weeds are unable to survive beneath them. Furthermore, evergreen shrubs give a background of colour right through the winter with the added bonus that most of them burst into flower in spring and summer. Finally, many shrubs may be planted as living fences that need very little maintenance and are virtually everlasting. A hedge of *Berberis darwinii* or *B. stenophylla* is thorny and impenetrable; it keeps its leaves through the winter and it becomes a wall of brilliant orange colour in spring. Admittedly shrubs and trees are comparatively expensive and although the initial cash outlay may be high, the resulting labour economy, combined with floral and foliar effect, is well worth the money.

To relieve the monotony of having shrubs alone, you can have a choice of planting perennials, biennials or annuals, either in their own beds, or in open spaces between the shrubs. Perennials, in all shapes, sizes and colours, have a fairly long life and need only be lifted, divided and replanted, to rejuvenate them, once in every four or five years. Biennials and annuals, on the other hand, are sown afresh every year and, as such, are more demanding than perennials. Every gardener, however, likes to change the scene from year to year and the annuals provide the opportunity to 'ring the changes'.

For the gardener without a greenhouse, and with insufficient funds to buy hundreds of 'bedding-plants' every year, the answer is to plant hardy annuals. Seeds of lovely things such as godetias, larkspurs, sweet peas and calendulas may be sown in the open ground towards mid-to-late spring (late March and early April). They will begin to bloom in mid summer (June) and will continue to carpet the garden with colour right through the remainder of the season.

Roses are dear to every gardener's heart and deserve a place in all our gardens. Choice of varieties must be based on personal preference, but, for a labour-saving garden where maximum colour is required, the floribundas are without equal. Some of the shrub roses, too, are among the loveliest of our garden plants and fit in extremely well among other shrubs. But if what is wanted is the traditional English rose, with its perfectly formed, immaculate blooms, the choice must be the hybrid tea. Keeping the rose bed free of weeds is no problem. There are several suitable weedkillers that kill the weeds and do not harm the roses, or, instead, the bed can be mulched with weedkiller-free lawn mowings.

There are those who complain that gardening is an expensive hobby. It need not be. Friends and neighbours will readily provide cuttings and offshoots, and seeds are still reasonably inexpensive. Fertilizers are costly and getting costlier, but here again considerable savings can be made by using rich compost made from garden and kitchen waste. Tools are expensive and it is all too easy to practise false economy by buying a whole range of cheap implements. This is one area where it pays to buy the best even though it costs a bit more. In the long run a good garden tool will last longer and do a much better job than a less expensive version.

Knowledge and the right tools, these are the basic ingredients of good gardening. This book is a well of information, part of that bottomless sea of knowledge which is the fascination of the horticultural art. Time spent in the pursuit and practice of gardening knowledge and expertise is sheer, unadulterated pleasure.

March, 1978 Clay Jones

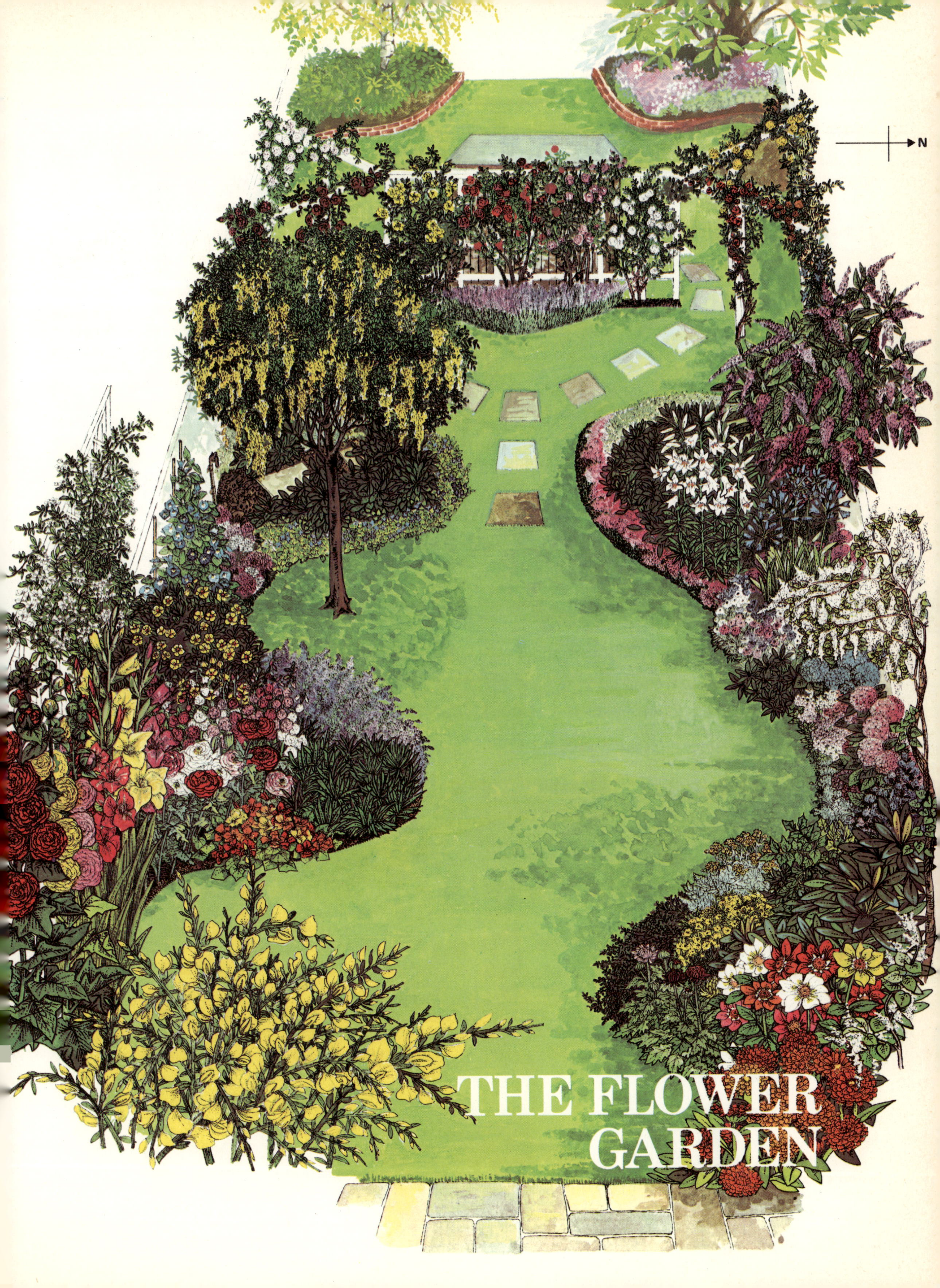

THE FLOWER GARDEN

THE FLOWER GARDEN

We have created this special 'Flower Garden' so that you can follow its development and maintenance during the twelve vital weeks in the gardener's calendar, from February through to March. You can incorporate the unusual design features into your own existing garden and our week-by-week expert advice will help you to achieve the same visually exciting results. For those of you who would like to fill your gardens with vegetables and fruit as well as flowering plants and shrubs, we illustrate (on pages 66–67) a companion design based on the need to grow your own food.

This long, narrow plot, typical of so many back gardens, calls for an imaginative layout, so we have steered away from the tunnel-like effect of narrow side borders and a central rectangle of grass or paving and created instead a series of curving lines and irregular shapes. In this way the eye is attracted by informal groupings of flowering plants and shrubs (which avoid the considerable upkeep required by more formal herbaceous borders), while the rose-covered trellis acts as a natural break in the length.

We have filled the garden with easy-to-care-for evergreens, flowering shrubs and trees, seasonal bulbs and roses for the paired pergolas. Annuals planted at appropriate times of the year and flowering plants in tubs on the patio provide additional patches of instant colour, as and where they are needed.

The paved patio runs the whole width of the garden, providing a convenient eating-out and relaxation area near the house on sunny days and somewhere to scrape the mud off your boots on the wet ones. There is room for a lean-to greenhouse to be erected against the north wall if you feel tempted to invest in one, and facing the end wall of the garden, screened by the rose-covered trellis, is a sizable shed for all those tools, toys and miscellaneous garden furniture.

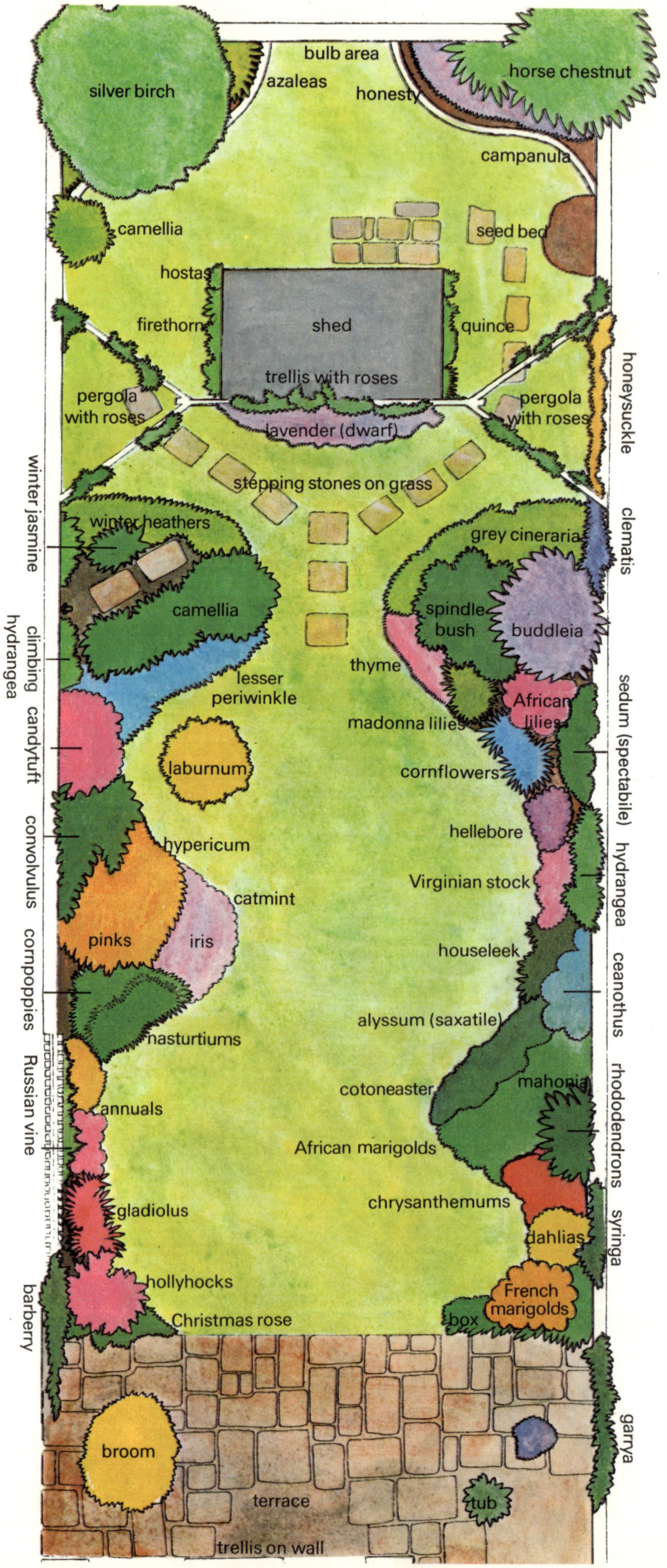

Ground plan, showing the main features of the Flower Garden plot, which measures 22 metres (72 feet) long by 7·5 metres (25 feet) wide

Spartium (Spanish broom) is a shrub that thrives near the sea on light, sandy soil. It can be grown elsewhere, but you will not get such good blooms

Turfing or seeding?
For the lawn, with its attractive curved edges, we opted for turf – which need not be such an expensive outlay as you might imagine (unless you hanker after the bowling-green effect of a really luxury lawn). The great advantage of turf is that it gives you a quicker result than if you had settled for sowing from seed.

Food for compost
If you have not already got a compost heap, start saving vegetable waste as soon as you can. The compost is vital to the well-being of your garden – as important as a fridge is to a cook. If possible, keep *two* waste bins in the kitchen – one solely for vegetable matter which can be added to your compost. Avoid saving very smelly things like fish bones, though – and meat bones take far too long to break down.

Know your weeds
There are several weeds that produce colourful displays and fill a border quite prettily, but their spreading roots may be doing untold damage beneath the surface. It is important to be able to tell the difference between growing weeds and good plant stock. Forthcoming sections in the book will help you to distinguish the 'good' weeds from the 'bad' ones – and how to control them.

Inheriting the earth
If you are already the owner of a well-cared-for garden, you are spared the trials, and may lose the pleasures, of creating a totally new one. But you still have plenty of room to exercise your talents by redesigning the planting areas, choosing new shrubs – even reshaping the lawn, and our week-by-week advice will tell you how to do all this.

A little caution is called for, however, if you have recently acquired a garden of unknown quantity. Do not rush ahead with a complete replanting job as there are many perennials that die down and remain dormant underneath the earth for months at a time, and you may not know that they are there. One of the most enjoyable experiences here is being happily surprised as a small shoot in late spring grows unaccountably tall and blossoms, for instance, into a hollyhock come mid summer. If you keep a note in your garden file of the plants that appear out of seemingly bare earth as you identify them, it will be of enormous help to you in any redesigning plans you may have.

Some plants grow happily anywhere, such as cotoneaster (shown here) and berberis. Both these shrubs are tolerant of all soils, including chalk or limestone

ACID OR ALKALINE?

Before planting it is necessary to know if your soil is acid (peaty) or alkaline (limey). Some plants, such as heathers and rhododendrons, like acidity; a few, such as clematis and viburnum, like alkalinity; but most prefer a slightly acid-neutral soil.

Soil acidity or alkalinity is expressed in terms of its pH value. This can be measured by using a proprietary soil-testing kit.

Something like pure water is neither acid nor alkaline and has a neutral pH of 7. The higher the pH reading, the higher the alkalinity; the lower the reading, the more acid. pH 6.5 (slightly acid) is the level at which most plants flourish best.

If too acid, lime should be added; if too alkaline, an acid substance such as peat should be dug in.

Calluna (ling, often called heather). These shrubs grow best in peaty (acid) soil. Similar conditions can be created by importing the right type of acid soil

During this watchful period you must not neglect basic maintenance such as pruning and so on, as this is of vital importance.

Know your neighbours
Different districts have their own peculiar quirks, and so indeed do individual gardens in the same street. Useful local knowledge can be gathered from conversations over the garden wall. You'll soon find out what grows well in your area by this method and by looking at other nearby gardens.

You'll also be told of great disasters of the past, and so learn by the mistakes of others, and of great successes which you may well emulate.

Don't be afraid to stop and speak to someone working his patch – gardeners are great talkers, and as often as not you'll end up by having cuttings of admired plants bestowed on you.

Starting from scratch?
If you have just moved into a new house with an as yet unplanned space for a garden, this means that you have the opportunity to create your own design from nothing. With the ideas and expert advice supplied throughout this book you will be able to transform a site into a thriving, colourful garden.

Overleaf we will tell you how to tackle the vital chores involved in getting your garden into shape.

SOIL CHART Recognize your soil type and make the best of it

TYPES	PROBLEMS	ADVANTAGES	HOW TO IMPROVE
CLAY Smooth, not gritty, often wet, sticky and slimy in winter and brick-like in summer	The very small particles stick together when wet, making a solid, almost airless mass. Heavy and difficult to dig and break down. Cold – takes a long time to warm up in spring. Dries out slowly, unevenly and in clods. Seeds germinate poorly (because of lack of air) and plant roots have difficulty in growing (because it is so heavy and solid).	Usually rich in plant food. Can hold water well in dry summers. Is receptive to the addition of plant and animal organic matter, which will decompose by physical, chemical and bacterial activity in the soil. This completely decomposed material is called humus. **Humus** is rich in plant foods, gives the soil 'body' and encourages the retention of food, water and air. In particular, it helps to make clay more workable by breaking down the mass.	Unless already alkaline (chalky), spread garden lime – 375g per sq m (12 oz per sq yd) – all over dug soil in autumn and let the weather work it in. Otherwise fork in during February. Lime makes it easier to dig and cultivate. For lasting improvement dig in large quantities of organic (animal and plant) matter in early spring for several years. This will rot down in the soil and gradually improve its structure and colour. Preferably use 'strawy' farmyard manure, otherwise plenty of peat and garden compost. Continue organic treatment every year, liming every 2–3 years. Do not mix lime with other fertilizers; apply 1 month before, or 2–3 months after, other soil conditioners. If clay is very heavy, artificial drainage may be required.
SAND Light and dry, gritty, crumbly and rough to handle	Poor in plant food. Unable to retain moisture; rainwater passes right through, leaching (washing out) plant foods into the subsoil out of reach of plant roots. Can be very acid due to leaching of lime.	Easy to work at any time of year. Warms up quickly after winter so cultivation can begin early in spring. Plenty of air in soil, allowing plant roots to grow strongly and deeply. Excellent for vegetables, especially root crops, when sufficient organic matter is added to retain water.	Manure, peat and compost must be dug in deeply to increase the soil's organic content. This will add plant foods and increase food- and moisture-retaining abilities. Treatment must be repeated yearly. Also add general fertilizer before sowing or planting in spring and autumn. A light sprinkling of lime should be added every other year if soil is acid. Watering with nitrogenous fertilizer is advantageous throughout the growing season. Artificial watering will probably be necessary during dry spring and summer periods.
CHALK OR LIMESTONE Variable, often shallow, topsoil with recognizable lumps of chalk or limestone, especially in lower soil	Lacks humus and plant food. Difficult to work when wet. Tends to dry out quickly in summer. The calcium in chalk or limestone soil inhibits plants from using many plant foods, and deficiencies may result. Chalky soil is alkaline, and not tolerated by most plants.	Generally light, easy to work, free-draining and warms up quickly in spring. Good for rock garden plants.	Add large quantities of farmyard manure, compost or other organic matter, preferably to the top layer of soil, each spring and autumn. This will break down (into humus) in the soil, improving its condition. Give top-dressings of general fertilizers throughout the growing season.
PEAT Dark brown or black, spongy to touch	Usually waterlogged and may need artificial drainage. May be very acid and sour. Often deficient in plant foods.	Contains plenty of organic matter as it consists mainly of organic material not yet fully decomposed. Easily worked. Too acid for most garden plants but very fertile when drained and limed.	If soil is waterlogged, then a soakaway or drainage pipes may be needed. Liming helps drainage and counteracts acidity. Add lime at 250g per sq m (8 oz per sq yd) every 2–3 years. Add regular, fairly heavy, dressings of general-purpose fertilizers in spring, summer and autumn.
LOAM Dark, crumbly, easy to clean from fingers	Should not be any problem as long as the drainage is satisfactory and the humus and plant food content is maintained.	Ideal garden soil, with a balanced mixture of sand, humus and clay. If humus content is maintained, a well-drained, well-aerated soil rich in plant food will result. Warm enough for early cultivation.	The improvements depend on the proportions of clay and sand in the loam. Sandy loam will require the regular spring and autumn addition of organic matter and fertilizers. Clayey loam may need regular addition of 375g per sq m (12 oz per sq yd) every 2–3 years. Heavy loams will benefit from being roughly dug over in autumn.

GIVING SHAPE TO YOUR GARDEN

A paved patio makes a good setting for the table and chairs that would otherwise be sinking into the lawn and it provides an interesting change of texture and colour as well as a useful area for walking about in wintertime without getting deep into mud. In addition, you can grow a colourful variety of plants all the year round here in tubs and containers.

In our Flower Garden we have a variety of plants chosen for their spring colour and one of the most important areas for this, as it is viewed close at hand from the windows of the house, is the paved patio area.

Here a hamamelis (witch hazel) grows up the trellis to the right of the sliding glass doors. Its fragrant yellow, strap-like flowers will bloom for at least another month. Unaffected by frost and with golden-yellow leaves in autumn, this is one of the most attractive of shrubs to train against a trellis.

On the north wall near the house the garrya, which is a good green shrub, still bears a few of its fascinating, catkin-like flowers. Around the kitchen window both the wisteria and the honeysuckle may require some pruning back of old wood now so that they don't get out of hand and cover the window later.

Vinca (periwinkle) and aubrietia make pleasing patches of green in gaps in the paving. Any moss on the paved area should be cleared away, either by hand or with a mosskiller. *Cytisus praecox* (broom), already arching its stems, grows out of a gap specially left in the paving. An underplanting of tulip species would look most effective here.

The containers hold a mixture of colourful plants during the summer months, and in the spring a mixture of bulbs such as tulips, daffodils, muscari and hyacinths planted the previous autumn. (After flowering, remove the bulbs, plant them out elsewhere in the garden and replant the containers with the summer bedding plants.)

Evergreens and bulbs
Looking farther down the garden, a mixture of evergreens cheers the duller areas: some heathers, camellias and winter jasmine are in flower, while at the far end there's a riot of colour in the bulb area. To help the bulbs build up food storage reserves for next year's display, pick off the dead flowerheads regularly.

While wandering around on fine days, take the opportunity to clear away leaves and debris accumulated during the winter months, cut out dead or broken stems and branches from any plants damaged by snow or gales, and tread down any soil areas which have been raised by frost.

The lawn
If parts of the lawn have also been raised by frost you should roll it slightly to consolidate the soil. While doing this take the opportunity to check whether there are any soggy or waterlogged areas remaining. If there are, stick either a garden fork or a hollow-tined lawn fork into the lawn every 10–15 cm (4–6 in) to the full depth of the prongs so as to aerate the grass and improve drainage.

Ordering in time
Apart from these regular seasonal tasks there is the all-important planning and ordering to be done if you are thinking of altering or redesigning some of your garden. Make sure to order early, while the varieties you have so carefully inspected at the local garden centre, or marked in catalogues, are still in stock.

Starting your garden from scratch

When faced with a derelict patch instead of a garden, you must first of all clear the site by removing all the litter and rubbish that is lying about. Some of the bricks, stones and timbers may be useful later on, so pile them into a corner.

If the amount of rubbish is not too great, you can put it into strong polythene bags but don't overfill them, or they become too heavy to move around. For large loads of rubbish you will have to hire a skip for which you will need a licence from the local council.

The next clearance job is to remove all unwanted plants from the garden site, including such things as brambles, weeds, tree stumps and even old, weedy turf.

If you come across any plants worth keeping at this stage, leave them where they are or carefully dig them up, with plenty of soil around the roots, and plant them in a prepared trench that has been well dug over until they can be put into final positions.

Drawing up the ground plan
Having done all this, you can then see more easily how to set about the next task, which is to draw up a rough plan of the available area.

You will need a long measuring tape (borrowed or hired if necessary), a ball of coarse twine, some stakes, a sheet of strong paper clipped to a board and a pencil. Begin by taking the measurements of existing structures such as the walls.

Don't forget to mark on your ground plan where the points of the compass fall, so sun-loving and shade-preferring plants can be given the positions they need. Any existing features should also be marked in, such as the three trees in our garden – laburnum, silver birch and horse chestnut.

Now transfer the details from this first rough drawing to a sheet of graph paper, using a simple scale. Be sure to allow for the whole garden to be shown on a single sheet. On this ground plan you should have accurate measurements of structures and existing plants.

Outlining special features
First of all decide what special features you want in your garden and list them on a separate sheet of paper. In this design for instance, the paved patio, the shaping of the borders and lawn areas, the shed with its rose-covered trellis and matching pergolas are all important, some for practical reasons, others for helping to break up this long, narrow garden. The sample garden feature plan at right shows how these are indicated on the graph paper, with the essential measurements needed to transfer your plan into reality outdoors.

Whatever you plan at this stage, don't get carried away and make your garden too complicated and overfull. It is always more effective if the design is kept relatively simple and interest maintained throughout the year by your plants.

Once you have finalized your plan in general outline, get the building-type work done before you start making preparations for planting. If you construct the paved patio near the house first, you will have a solid base from which to carry out other work as well as a resting place for sunny days.

Preparing the patio area
From your graph of the garden you will be able to calculate the quantities of materials you require. We chose York stone, for its old-world character and lasting quality, but there are many suitable alternatives, such as pre-cast slabs in various colours and textures.

Before laying the paving, it is essential to peg out and level the site, taking care not to bridge the damp proof course and under-floor ventilation bricks of the house wall.

As the lawn comes right up to the terrace, it makes for easy mowing if you set the paving a little lower than the intended final level of the lawn surface. (If the paving is higher than the lawn, mowing becomes very difficult and you will have to use shears to cut the grass along the edge.) The grass here will help to hide any unevenness in the front edge of the paved patio.

Dig in comfort – at the correct angle

Siting the shed
The next important feature is the shed, centred within the garden's width but towards the far end so as to give a visual break to the length of the site. It is hidden from the house by a screen of trellis-climbing plants and other perennials in a shaped bed below.

Our shed measures some 3 × 2m (10 ft × 6 ft 6 in) and the door and window face west, with access via the stepping-stone path. If you decide on an easy-to-erect prefabricated one, the only essential is that it should be on a level base, preferably of brick, concrete or wooden sleepers. If possible, allow an air space below to prevent the floor timbers from rotting. You will need to fix guttering and a water barrel or soakaway to collect rain water and prevent puddles forming around the base.

Digging a new garden

Unfortunately, all the heavy work – digging the site and levelling by raking – comes at the beginning. This is also the time to buy in, and spread where necessary, any extra topsoil you need to mix in with the existing soil. Dig it over to at least the depth of the spade blade or fork tines (prongs). This rule applies to the whole garden.

Digging can be very hard work, and it is advisable not to do too much at one time; take it at your own pace, and dig correctly to minimize aches and pains. It doesn't matter how dry the soil is, but don't try to dig when it is very wet.

If the soil seems to be compacted (very hard and heavy) or very light, such as sandy or chalky, it would be a good idea to dig in some compost, manure, peat or similar soil-conditioning material.

Decide in which direction you are going to dig; in this garden, for instance, it is best to start from the far end and work backwards, trench by trench, to the paved patio. In this way you will avoid treading on the dug soil.

Digging in comfort

Always stand face on to the line of soil to be dug, and never try to dig too large a lump of soil at any one time. The least tiring way to dig is to stand close to the upright spade or fork, and if you are right-handed place your right foot on the cross-piece over the blade or tines, with your left hand on the handle and right one about halfway down. Press the head of the tool into the ground to its full depth by putting your weight onto the foot on the cross-piece. Then place your right elbow on your right knee and use this knee as a fulcrum (leverage point) to lift the soil free from the ground and turn it over and forwards. Another way is to use the edge of the undug soil on which you are standing as the lifting and pivoting point. If the soil is very compacted you may have to cut the edge of each spadeful by pressing the implement in at right angles before digging the soil.

If manual digging seems too arduous a task, you can hire a powered cultivator (from your local hire service shop) which turns the soil over quickly, rather like a miniature plough.

If time allows, it pays to leave the soil for a week or so to settle naturally. Then, when the weather is fine and the ground not too wet, you should go over the whole site with a rake and roughly level it. If you want slightly raised soil anywhere, as round the silver birch and horse chestnut at the far end of the garden, now is the time to see that it is in position.

Planning for planting

Between bouts of digging, and while the soil is settling, make notes of what plants you intend to grow, and where they are to be placed in the garden. This will enable you to estimate the cost and order in advance.

First draw the shape of each of the planting areas onto separate sheets of graph paper, as this enables you to use a large scale. Then, with the aid of plant, bulb and seed catalogues, select your plants and list them on a sheet of paper. Alongside each plant put down what type it is (perennial, bulb, etc.), the variety, what height and width it will mature to, what colour its flowers and leaves are, when it is at its most colourful, whether it likes sun or shade, and any other points of interest about it. Armed with this information you are then ready to transfer your choice to each planting area graph.

In our Flower Garden, mixed borders of different types of plants predominate, giving variety, interest and plenty of colour all the year round, yet requiring the minimum of upkeep. The plant plan here shows how the border against the north wall (which faces south and is therefore sunny) has been planned, indicating the position of the selected plants and how many of each you need. Don't forget that the taller plants should be at the back and the smaller ones at the front of the border, with an intermingling zone in the centre.

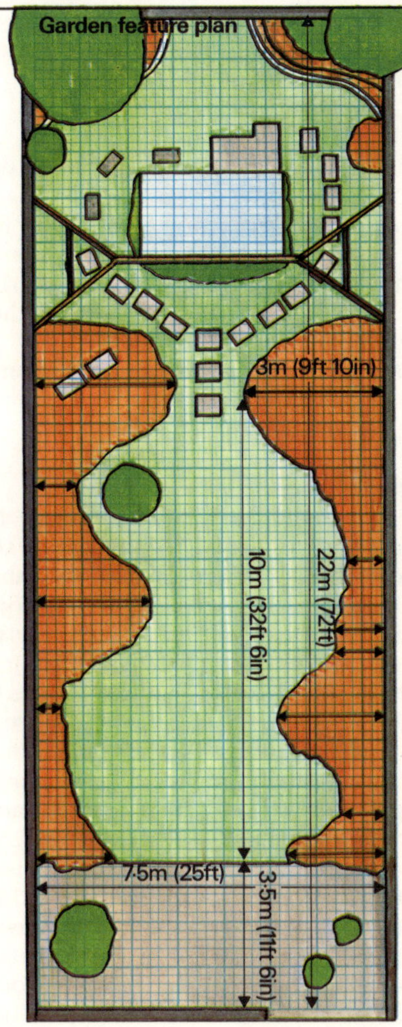

Draw up your ground plan on graph paper, marking in essential features, and measure up the north border to help you work out your plant plan

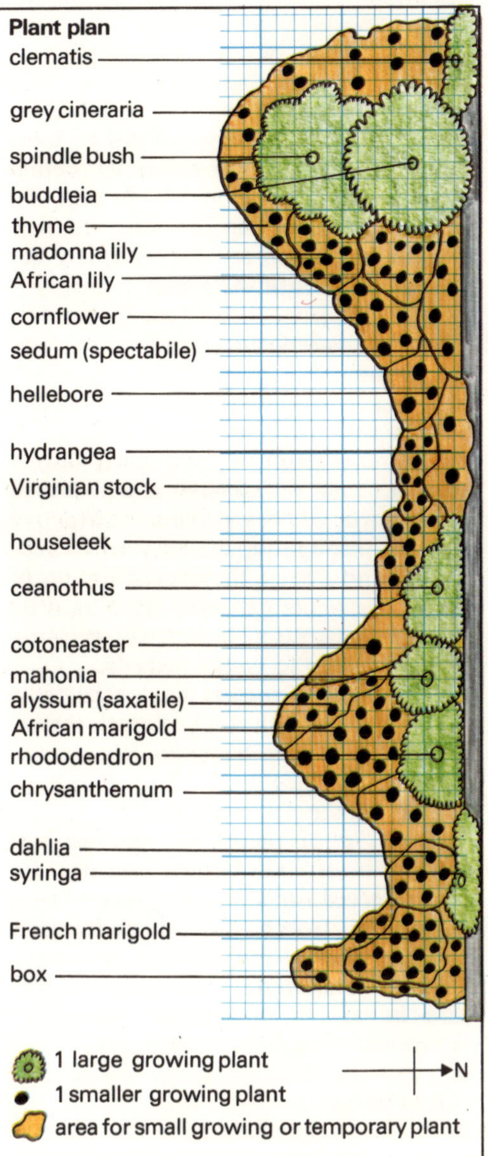

Some first steps in garden design

Once you have finalized your basic garden feature and plant plans on graph paper (following our examples given on page 15), it is time to make more detailed lists of plants you want and to put your planning into practice.

Marking out borders and features

Clip your plans to a board and protect them with transparent plastic. With your garden feature plan worked out to scale, you already have your basic measurements. You now need to measure out these positions on site. For this you require a long measuring tape, canes and stakes, wooden mallet, and a large ball of string.

At each of the marked points you hammer in a stake. When you want curves (for the border) use canes at intervals of about 1m (3 ft) between the stakes. When these are positioned (see the north border plan here), take the ball of string and tie one end to one of the end stakes. Then twine string round all intermediate marking canes and main stakes until you reach the other end of the border.

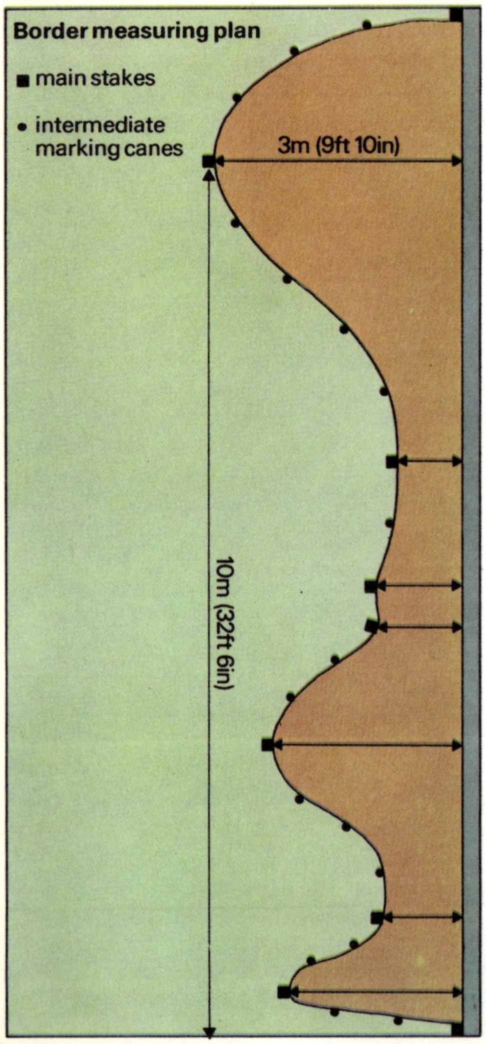

Continue marking each of the edge lines of the borders, shed, pergola, trellis and raised borders in this way. These lines will be essential when turfing the lawn and other grassed areas. The final edges of the flower borders will be formed when you cut the turves.

Planning plants for the borders

You will have seen from the illustration of the established Flower Garden on page 9 that we selected a wide variety of plants. To help you make your choice we list ours here under the following groupings: trees, shrubs, climbers, herbaceous perennials, bulbs including corms, tubers and rhizomes, annuals and biennials. We will, of course, be adding to these as the garden develops.

Trees

In our Flower Garden we were fortunate enough to have some mature trees *in situ:* aesculus (horse chestnut), *Betula pendula* (silver birch) and laburnum. To assist in breaking up the long, narrow plot we added three smaller trees, decorative in themselves.

Our selection: acer (small maple); *Euonymus europaeus* (spindle tree); syringa (lilac).

Shrubs

Be they evergreen or deciduous, shrubs help to create perspective and depth in mixed borders. They also make attractive features throughout the year when tub-grown, and add to the overall design of the garden while generally needing little care and attention. The lower-growing types also help to control weeds.

Our selection: aucuba; azalea; berberis (barberry); buddleia (butterfly bush); buxus (box); camellia; ceanothus; chaenomeles (quince); choisya (Mexican orange blossom); cotoneaster; cytisus (broom); erica (heathers and heaths); euonymus (spindle bush); garrya (in area reserved for a lean-to greenhouse); hamamelis (witch hazel); hydrangea; hypericum (St John's wort); lavendula (lavender); mahonia; olearia; pyracantha (fire-thorn); rhododendron; skimmia; viburnum; vinca (periwinkle).

Climbers

Both climbers, and shrubs that can be treated as climbers, are ideal for clothing bare walls or helping to hide unsightly objects as well as being highly decorative. In our garden they cover the trellis and pergolas that help to break up the length of the site and give it a broader appearance.

Our selection: clematis; jasminum (jasmine); lonicera (honeysuckle); polygonum (Russian vine); rosa (rose).

Herbaceous perennials

In a mixed border herbaceous perennials give colour at different periods in spring, summer and autumn, and provide cut flowers for the house. Unfortunately, they die down during the winter months, so use shrubs to help hide the bare patches.

Our selection: agapanthus lily (African lily); *Alyssum saxatile*; *Anemone japonica* (wind flower); campanula; chrysanthemum; grey cineraria; dianthus (pinks); helleborus (hellebore); *Helleborus niger* (Christmas rose); hosta (plantain lily); nepeta (catmint); pyrethrum; sempervivum (houseleek); thymus (thyme).

Bulbs

The bulb area (to be at the far end of our garden) should be a riot of colour each spring and provide plenty of flowers for early picking. Allow space for bulbous plants, including corms, tubers and rhizomes, in a mixed border as well, as they give long seasons of flowering.

Our selection in the mixed borders: *Lilium candidum* (madonna lily); gladiolus (sword lily); dahlias; iris.

Annuals

To give splashes of colour during the summer months, and to fill gaps in the borders, annuals are ideal plants – either the hardy forms sown straight into their final positions, or half-hardy ones planted out in late spring. (See page 23 for a further choice of half-hardies.)

Our selection: centaurea (cornflower); convolvulus; iberis (candytuft); malcolmia (Virginian stock); papaver (poppy); tagetes (African and French marigolds); tropaeolum (nasturtium).

Biennials

Raised from seed one year to flower the next, biennials have a useful part to play as temporary gap-fillers. In some cases, as with lunaria (honesty) plants, they will seed themselves each spring, flower in summer, and produce unusually decorative seed pods to enliven your winter flower arrangements.

In situ: althaea (hollyhock); luneria (honesty).

ANNUALS FOR COLOUR

What could be nicer or more cheerful than a mass of colourful mixed annuals to liven up your border during the summer and autumn months?

Annuals – hardy, half-hardy or tender – are old favourites that have a place in every garden. On the following pages we tell you how to sow hardy annuals and help you make your choice, but meanwhile there are certain things to be done in the garden at this time – mid spring.

First clear the mixed flower border of dead leaves and weeds. Then give a dressing of a general purpose fertilizer such as Growmore, at the rate recommended by the manufacturers, that will help new spring shoot and root growth. Hoe this in lightly, taking care not to disturb the roots near the plants. A layer of mulching material – peat, bark fibre, compost, hop manure and suchlike – will help to improve soil conditions, retain moisture during drought periods and suppress weeds; if any of the latter do appear, they are easy to pull out of the mulch layer.

Plant gladiolus corms now in warm parts of the border, where they will get sun and be protected by other plants. With a hand trowel, dig out a hole 10cm (4 in) deep (or a little deeper if there is still danger of frost), put in a small handful of silver or coarser garden sand and then place the corm, root disc downwards, on the sand and replace the soil. For most effective results, plant the corms in clusters of 5–10, each about 12cm (5 in) apart. Mark each batch with a label or stake so you remember where they are.

While planting the gladiolus, take the opportunity to fork over the soil (to a depth of the tines) where chrysanthemums and dahlias are to be planted next month. Mixing in some bonemeal (at the manufacturer's recommended rate) will help the plants make a good start in life.

PRUNING

Most pruning can be started in early spring (February) in warmer areas, as much as four or five weeks earlier than would be possible in colder regions. Judge by weather conditions rather than the calendar: in cold frosty weather delay pruning until late spring (April).

Roses

This is the usual time to prune established hybrid tea and floribunda bushes, established repeat-flowering shrub roses and climbers, standards and miniatures. Single-flowering climbers and weeping standards are *not* pruned, though any dead or out-of-place stems should be cut out in autumn.

If roses are not cut back every year they become unshapely and suffer from diseased and dead wood. This causes them to produce smaller, shorter-lasting blooms and weak, sparse shoots. Pruning encourages healthy and shapely future growth. Don't be afraid to attack your roses with the secateurs in a ruthless fashion. You will be rewarded by a continuous, successful show of flowers.

Really sharp secateurs are important: blunt instruments will pinch the stems and make a messy cut. Each cut should be made 6mm (¼ in) above a dormant bud, sloping down to the other side of the stem so that the top end of the cut is level with the top of the bud. Pruning at an angle prevents water collecting on the cut which could lead to disease or cause it to become frozen in winter, damaging the wood. Choose a bud growing outwards so that the new growth does not turn inwards and clutter up the centre of the plant, encouraging the breeding of pests and diseases in the summer, and adversely affecting foliage and flowers.

Any frost-damaged, dead or diseased wood should be cut out. You will notice that when healthy wood is cut it is a creamy-green colour. If it appears brown when cut, then it is diseased or frost-damaged, so make some further cuts until you reach healthy wood, or cut the stem out completely. Dead or frost-damaged wood is much lighter in weight than good, healthy wood and the thorns become brittle and turn brown.

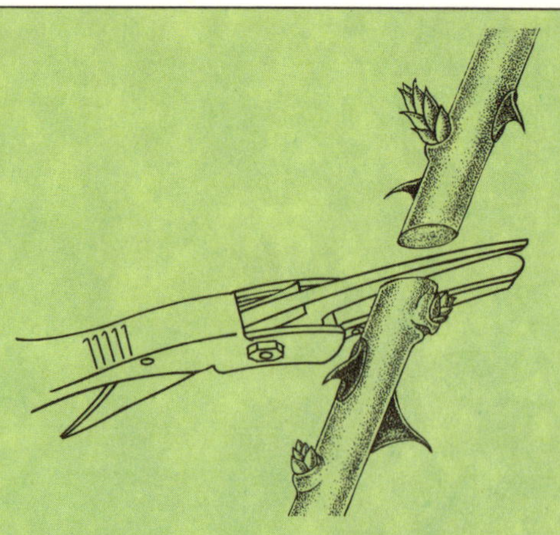

Top end of cut is level with top of bud

If the leaves are late dropping after a gentle autumn, frozen rain caught in the angle of leaf stalk and stem is liable to damage the dormant bud and again trigger off disease, so watch

Creating an annual border

When making a new garden it is virtually impossible to produce a finished result in one year, unless you are going to spend a small fortune on buying container-grown plants of a fairly large size.

It is generally best to plan first for your major trees, shrubs and perennial plants and to get them into position. For the first year or two, while these are growing to their more mature size, fill up the gaps between with annual plants which will give welcome splashes of colour during the summer months. It may even be that in your first year of a new garden you will not be able, for various reasons of timing, design and final selection decisions, to do much permanent planting. In such cases the borders can consist entirely of annuals for the first summer. For an explanation of the different types of annuals, see our Plant Categories section on pages 22–23.

However, as there is going to be plenty of ground work to be done in the first year of preparation, it is not very practical to add to your chores by raising half-hardy and tender annuals yourself, as these need to be grown under heated glass (greenhouse, frame or propagation unit). Buy some packets of hardy annual seeds instead, and sow these from mid spring to early summer (March to May) directly into the borders where you wish them to flower. In addition, you can always purchase, quite cheaply, boxes of young half-hardy annuals for planting out in early summer when all danger of frost is over.

It is best to select from some of the more popular hardy annuals likely to be found in most seed catalogues, shops or garden centres. Choose ones that will give you a variety of heights and colours.

Sowing hardy annuals

When the soil is not too wet and sticky it should be dug over lightly with a fork, and weeds removed, then trodden down to firm it. To do this, simply walk up and down with your footsteps close together. Then rake it lightly backwards and forwards so that the surface soil is as crumbly and flat as possible. If the soil is not in very good condition (lumpy and hard, for instance) add a 13mm (½ in) layer of moist peat and a handful of a general fertilizer, such as Growmore, per square metre (or square yard) while raking.

The seeds are best sown in fairly bold patches, with the taller-growing annuals towards the back of the borders and the lowest along the front edges. An easy way to plan a layout is to get a stick and draw the outline of the clumps on the soil. Then scatter the seeds as thinly as possible over the soil in the designated areas. Very fine seeds will require a sprinkling of fine soil over them (some topsoil through a sieve is easiest) but the larger seeds can be covered by careful raking. The biggest seeds of all, like sweet peas and nasturtiums, can be sown separately by pushing each one down about 2–3cm (1 in) into the soil – each seed approximately 15cm (6 in) apart.

The seeds should germinate and start poking their noses through the earth any time in the next four weeks. When the seedlings are large enough to take hold of, thin them out by pulling some out completely – roots as well – so that those left behind are about 10–30cm (4–12 in) apart, according to the instructions on the packet and their ultimate height. After that, except for removing weeds, watering with a sprinkler in very dry weather and dealing with pests, there should be nothing to stop a fine display of colour through the summer. (Incidentally, removing the dead flowerheads promptly will help to encourage the plants to keep on producing more and more blooms.)

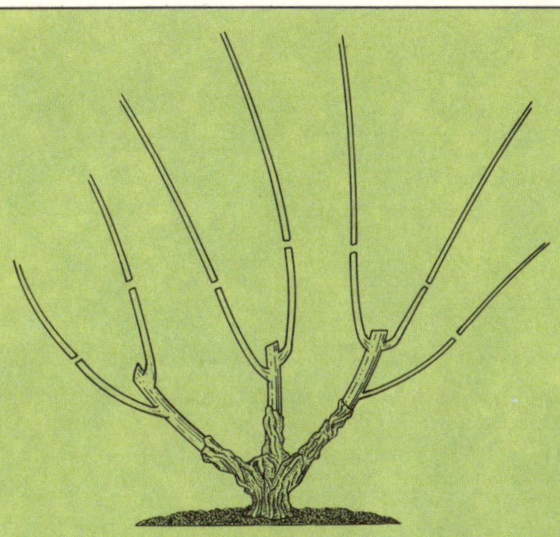

Prune new buddleia shoots hard back

out for small brown patches in otherwise healthy, green stems. These are signs of disease, so prune well below them. Cut thin, twiggy shoots right back to the main stem, but thicker, healthy stems less ruthlessly. In colder areas paint the cut with a protective compound to stop disease and rotting.

When you are pruning roses wear a tough pair of old gloves or it becomes a painful exercise. Throw the cuttings onto a large sheet of polythene or paper, cutting the larger trimmings in half. It is then a simple matter to tip them onto a bonfire heap.

Trees and shrubs
Newly-planted trees will do better if their side branches are cut back by a good 30 per cent, if this has not already been done by the plant nursery.

Prune laburnum after it has flowered, never before, not forgetting to cut down from an outward-facing bud. The shrubs that need pruning most here are the hydrangeas, buddleia, ceanothus, winter-flowering jasmine, wisteria, lonicera (honeysuckle) and large-flowered clematis.

Do not be afraid to cut back quite drastically as the emerging plant will be stronger and healthier as a result. Cut back to healthy buds on growth made the previous season. The wisteria, lonicera and large-flowered clematis can be pruned less vigorously, with just the over-crowded and unwanted shoots being removed, if you prefer.

If you want to add *half-hardy* annuals, such as althaea (hollyhocks), antirrhinums, petunias, verbena, nicotiana (tobacco plants), nemesia, zinnias, tagetes (African and French marigolds), these should be planted out in early summer.

Down with slugs
These pests are the main enemy of your flower border. They must be destroyed or they will, in turn, destroy the plants. The small, grey slug loves to munch his way through the leaves, especially if the weather is warm. Operating mostly at night, slugs leave a tell-tale trail of white, mucous film behind them. This is the sign of all types of slugs, and snails too. Put down proprietary slug pellets; remember to carry out this eliminating operation regularly.

Beware birds – and cats!
Both birds and cats love newly seed-sown areas of the garden and to prevent them wreaking havoc among your annuals anchor down some nylon netting over the beds, and place a lot of twiggy sticks and branches, or gorse, over the areas. Remove these protective barriers when you thin out the seedlings. Alternatively, treat these areas with a proprietary animal repellent that will help to deter both birds and rodents.

Laying the stepping stones
York stone slabs were selected for the stepping stones here. Once the positions of the flower beds, trellis and pergolas have been marked out it is easy to estimate the number of slabs required. Laying them is also a simple matter and it is advisable to position them before making the lawn. (On page 33 we tell you how to turf the lawn area.)

Stepping stones should be level and the best way to achieve this is to remove approximately 5cm (2 in) of soil, put down a layer of coarse sand to replace it and lay the paving slab in position. Then, using a spirit level, ensure it is level by raising or lowering it by adding or removing sand. It is particularly important to ensure the slabs by the shed door are all level, not only with the ground but also with each other, so there are no jutting-up edges to trip over. When the lawn turfs are laid, these should come slightly above the level of the slabs, thus making it easy to cut the grass with a lawn-mower. If the slabs are above the turfs, then it will involve the onerous task of cutting grass round the paved areas with hand shears. The turfs will be about 3·5cm ($1\frac{1}{2}$ in) thick and you can always adjust the paving slabs later so that they are at the correct height to the grass.

POPULAR HARDY ANNUALS

alyssum (madwort)
amaranthus (love-lies-bleeding)
Anchusa Blue Bird
bartonia/*Mentzelia lindleyi*
calendula (pot marigold)
centaurea (cornflower)
chrysanthemum (annual varieties)
clarkia
delphinium, annual (larkspur)
dianthus (annual pinks)
eschscholtzia (Californian poppy)
godetia gypsophila
helianthus (sunflower)
iberis (candytuft)
lathyrus (sweet pea)
lavatera (mallow)
linum (flax)
lupinus (annual lupin)
lychnis (silene)
malcolmia (Virginian stock)
nemophila (Californian bluebell)
nigella (love-in-a-mist)
Papaver rhoeas (shirley poppy)
Phacelia campanularia
reseda (mignonette)
Salvia horminum
tropaeolum (nasturtium)

Popular hardy annuals: (top) annual chrysanthemums and tropaeolum

DESIGNING A MIXED BORDER

With this section of a mixed border we go on to illustrate an interesting way of using a blank area by exploiting the changing heights, textures and colours of the plants, allowing them to display their various attributes and perform different functions in the overall scheme.
For example, the tree provides constant interest from ground level up to two or more metres (seven feet) and acts as a frame to one side of the 'picture'.
Your eye then moves from the top of the tree, along the climber on the trellis that gives a feeling of privacy, to the shrubs and herbaceous plants below.
The front section of low-growing ground cover plants helps to break the hardness of the lawn edge.

Making something new out of a blank area is very stimulating, and what better than a mixed border like ours? It adds interest to your gardening life while you keep up with the following general maintenance that ensures that desirable, well-cared-for look.

Spring-cleaning the garden

A general clear-up is essential after the ravages of winter as dead leaves and general debris are bound to have accumulated, becoming more and more unsightly.

The first thing to do is to go round all trees and shrubs and cut out any dead, broken, damaged or twiggy branches. This will help prevent disease setting in and make them more sightly when in leaf and flower. Don't forget to check hedges and remove accumulated rubbish from their bases. Herbaceous plants that weren't cut back in the late autumn should be cut now to tidy up the plants and enable them to make fresh and healthy spring growth.

Cleaning up the mixed borders

Your next job is to clean up the mixed flower borders by raking them lightly from the back to the front and collecting your rakings onto a sheet of sacking or polythene for easy tipping into a wheelbarrow or bucket.

If you can, sort out the rubbish as you clear it, the leaves and soft, twiggy stems can be added to the compost heap, but the remainder should be disposed of by burning or putting in the garbage bin.

Key to mixed border

1 euonymus (europaeus)
2 choisya
3 cotoneaster
4 aucuba
5 viburnum
6 olearia
7 campanula
8 clematis
9 pyrethrum
10 skimmia
11 anemone (japonica)
12 acer
13 vinca

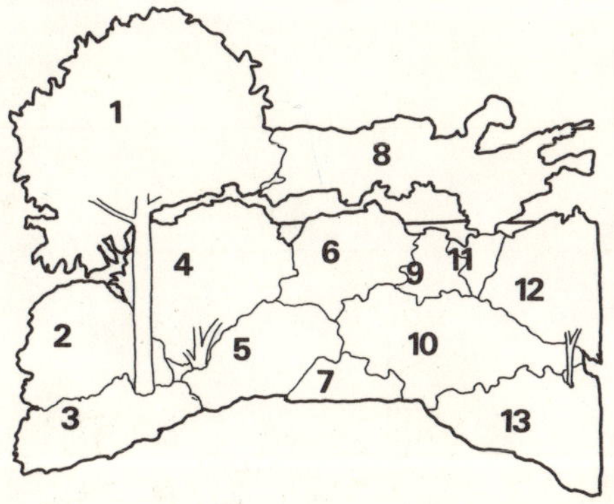

The lawn

As your lawn may be looking a bit untidy now, give it a good brushing to remove rubbish and any wormcasts. Then apply a proprietary wormkiller of low toxicity at the rate recommended by the manufacturers and, with luck, this will prevent unsightly pieces of soil disfiguring the overall greenness for the rest of the year. It may be that a further dressing of the wormkiller will be required to make certain the job is done thoroughly.

Provided the ground isn't too wet, it will do no harm to give the lawn a light rolling – if you haven't already done so – to level any bumps caused by frost raising the soil. After this rake the lawn with a metal rake so that the blades of grass stand upright again and don't remain permanently flattened. It will soon be time to start the mowing season when the grass will repay you for this bit of attention.

Planting new trees

If you are putting in any new trees, shrubs or herbaceous plants, now is as good a time as any (weather and soil conditions permitting) to start preparing the sites for them. The bigger the plant will ultimately grow, the larger the area to be prepared. As a rough guide, the final root area of any plant is assumed to spread over the same area of soil that the leaves cover above ground.

Dig the soil thoroughly and add to it some humus-forming material such as compost, peat, spent hops, farmyard manure or suchlike. A handful or two of bonemeal fertilizer won't come amiss either as it helps the roots of the new plants to get away to a good start in their new positions. Leave the soil rough at this stage, don't level it down.

Know your plant categories

Plants are allotted to convenient categories according to their hardiness and the following descriptions will help you to understand these classifications
All plants exhibit varying degrees of hardiness, or tolerance towards cold and damp, and this tolerance is directly related to the climates of their countries of origin.
Overleaf we explain the differences between trees, shrubs and climbers and divide the confusing bulb group into bulbs, corms, rhizomes and tubers.

A lot of the terms used to describe plant categories are usually abbreviated in catalogues and plant references, and we give these initials following the full name, where appropriate.

Hardy perennials HP

This term denotes plants that will live and grow outside from year to year in all but extreme climates. Although this group includes shrubs and trees, the term 'hardy perennial' commonly refers to hardy herbaceous border perennials.

Examples of: (right) half-hardy perennials, pelargoniums; (far right) tender or greenhouse perennial, the house plant dizygotheca; (below) hardy perennials, the true geranium psilostemon

Herbaceous perennials

These overwinter by using various forms of rootstock. The top growth dies down in the autumn and more new shoots emerge the following spring. This group of plants may be propagated from seed, although it is advisable to increase them by dividing the roots or taking cuttings. Familiar examples are delphinium, dianthus pinks, phlox and geum (avens).

Half-hardy perennials HHP

This group includes some of the well-known summer bedding plants, for example pelargonium and begonia. Dahlias, chrysanthemums and some bulbous plants like gladiolus are also represented here. Although some of these plants will survive outside during mild winters, they stand a much better chance of living if they are taken out of the ground and over-wintered in a dry place where temperatures remain above freezing.

Certain 'tender' or 'greenhouse' perennials also fall into this category. An example of this is abutilon, which is often used as a 'dot' plant in summer bedding schemes, but originates in a warmer climate and requires a high winter temperature to ensure survival. Other plants, such as antirrhinum (snapdragon), petunia and nemesia, although often referred to as half-hardy annuals and indeed treated as such by being raised from seed each year, are also in fact half-hardy perennials.

Tender/Greenhouse perennials GP

Natives of hot and often humid zones, these plants require constant protected cultivation, although some of them may be placed outdoors in sunny positions during good summer weather. A few members of this group are used in elaborate summer bedding schemes.

Annuals A

All annuals are characterized by completing their life cycle within a twelve-month period. They germinate, grow, flower and produce seed all during the favourable growing period.

Hardy annuals HA

Hardy annuals are the familiar flowering plants of the summer cottage gardens. Plants such as calendula (pot marigold), clarkia, godetia and centaurea (cornflower) may be grown from a spring sowing in open ground and will be flowering profusely in early summer.

(Above) hardy annuals, calendula (pot marigold), not to be confused with tagetes (French and African marigold)
(Below) half-hardy annuals, double zinnias

Seeds of hardy annuals may be sown during autumn and the young plants will stand the winter outside to give an extra early flower show during the following spring. Lathyrus (sweet pea) is often treated in this way.

Half-hardy annuals HHA
The colourful bedding plants, half-hardy annuals, brighten many gardens in summer. They are natives of warm climates and so will not reproduce naturally outdoors in countries that experience cold, wet winters. The gardener has to intervene in the plant's natural cycle and either collect seed in autumn and store it in a dry warm place in winter, or purchase fresh seed every spring. To obtain maximum showiness from these plants, seedlings should be raised in a warm environment, such as a greenhouse or heated frame, and planted out when all danger of frost is passed. Tagetes (African marigolds), zinnias and lobelia are familiar examples in this group. Seed of half-hardy annuals may be sown outdoors when all danger of frost is passed, but generally this method does not give such a good show of blooms.

Tender annuals
Although generally requiring constant greenhouse cultivation, tender annuals can safely go outdoors at the height of summer when they are already in bloom. Schizanthus (butterfly flower), cineraria and celosia are all good examples.

(Below) tender annual example, a group of greenhouse-grown dwarf cinerarias

Typical biennial (above) cheiranthus, the colourful and scented wallflower

Biennials B
These plants grow one year to flower the next. Cheiranthus (wallflower), *Dianthus barbatus* (sweet William), bellis (daisy) and myosotis (forget-me-not) are all familiar spring bedding plants which are biennials. They are all hardy and seed is sown in early summer so that the plants will be large enough to plant out in their spring flowering quarters during the autumn. There are several greenhouse biennials, such as calceolaria. In addition, some tender perennials such as cyclamen are often treated as biennials.

Left: Lathyrus odoratus *Gypsy Queen is especially good for flower arrangements*
Below and bottom left: lonicera, or honeysuckle, can climb up to 6m (20 ft) over a sunny wall, but shade its roots
Right: a characteristic fall of laburnum, one of the broad-leaved trees

Previously we explained some of the different categories used to describe various members of the plant family. Now we carry on with trees and shrubs – which you may not always think of as plants – and the complex group of bulbs.

Trees

These are usually defined as perennial plants that are woody, with one main stem (trunk), and a mass of branches and stems above. Trees usually grow over 4m (13 ft) tall. They are generally sub-divided into two categories: the broad-leaved kinds which can have a variety of different shaped leaves showing a network of veins – such as the tilia (lime), aesculus (horse chestnut) and laburnum – and the conifers, like taxus (yew) and picea (Christmas tree) which have needle-like or 'scale' leaves.

Trees can take many years to mature. They can also be either hardy, half-hardy or tender, and obviously it is only wise with such a long-term plant to buy a hardy type. Trees and shrubs are often referred to as evergreen (that is, they retain their leaves in winter) or deciduous (that is, they shed their leaves in autumn and produce new ones in the following spring).

Shrubs

Unlike trees, these are woody perennials that branch naturally from the base and have more than one main stem. They can grow as tall as 8m (26 ft) or be only

Below: one of the many shrubs – or bushes – a rhododendron with a profusion of ball-shaped blooms

a few centimetres (1–2 in) high. Like trees, they can be hardy, half-hardy, or tender. Again it is sensible to plant only the hardy kinds outdoors. There are innumerable examples suitable for gardens, such as rhododendron, camellia, syringa (lilac) and buddleia. Shrubs are sometimes called bushes, and this term can also refer to a cluster of shrubs.

Climbers

True climbers are a group of plants that grow upwards naturally and are able to support themselves against an object such as another plant, trellis, wall, string, netting, pergola and so on. They can do this by various means, such as tendrils (short, twisted leafless growths), aerial roots (short stems with little roots), sucker pads (self-adhesive growths), leaf stalks which twist round the support, hooked spines, or by the twining growth of their stems. Examples of some of the different methods are lonicera (honeysuckle), by twining; hedera (ivy), by aerial roots; clematis, by tendrils; parthenocissus (Virginia creeper), by sucker pads; lathyrus (sweet pea), by tendrils; blackberry, by hooked spines; and convolvulus, by twining of the stems.

Above: a pair of popular true climbers from the favourite clematis genus
Right: lilies are among the true bulbs

Climbers may be perennials or annuals, hardy, half-hardy or tender. In addition to the climbers, there are other plants, such as 'climbing' and 'rambling' rosa (rose), quince, ceanothus, some pyracantha (firethorn) and cotoneasters that are basically shrubs but grow in such a way that they can be trained against supports, provided they are given a helping hand by twisting or tying in the shoots to the supports, and in some cases by careful pruning.

Bulbs

Many people when they refer to bulbs also include plant organs which are similar in function (as food stores), but which should strictly be referred to as corms, tubers, or rhizomes. A true bulb is an underground 'bud' that has fleshy or scaly leaves around it, all growing upwards from a basal 'plate'. These are plant food storage leaves. Inside are the rudiments of flower, flower stalk and leaves. When conditions are right, roots grow down into the soil from the basal plate and the rudimentary flowers and leaves grow upwards to give the above-ground parts of the plant. The leaves and roots absorb plant foods during growth and feed these back into the bulb or a 'daughter bulb', before they die back at the end of their season. In this way, they prepare for the next growth period by again forming rudimentary flowers and leaves. Sometimes several bulbils or 'daughter bulbs' are formed around the original parent, and these can be used to increase the plants.

True bulbs include lilium (lily), hyacinth, narcissus (daffodil), tulipa (tulip) and galanthus (snowdrop). All bulbs are easy to grow and have the advantage of rapid growth when conditions are suitable. Some are hardy and can be left in the ground all the year round (tulips and daffodils) whereas others (nerine and vallota) are half-hardy and are best lifted from the ground, dried and stored in cool, frost-free conditions (or well protected with straw outdoors). Yet others are tender and require greenhouse conditions throughout the year, such as amaryllis and lachenalia.

Tubers

Tubers are thickened parts of underground stems or roots which store food and carry buds for leaves and flowers above ground; and roots below. Typical examples of these are dahlias and some begonias. Such plants are usually treated as half-hardy annuals and can be sown from seed. Usually, however, the tubers are stored in cool, dry conditions during the winter months, cut up into sections and started into growth in a cool greenhouse in spring, for planting out when hardened off.

Below: dahlias are classed as tubers and have food-storing, thickened underground stems and roots
Below left: one of the corms, crocus has swollen and solid food-storing underground stem bases
Bottom: lily of the valley, a rhizome with fleshy, root-like food storage organ

Corms

These are fleshy, swollen and solid underground stem bases with scales (outside leaves) that can be round (crocus) or flat (gladiolus). Like bulbs, they are food storage organs and contain embryo flowers and leaves that grow from the upper surface, while roots grow from a 'disc' below. They can be considered annuals because each year a new corm is formed above the old one.

Hardy corms, like crocus, can be left in the ground all year, but half-hardy ones, such as gladiolus, are best dug up, dried and stored carefully each autumn for planting the following spring. Propagation is by the small 'cormlets' also produced, but these may take a year or two before they flower.

Rhizomes

A rhizome is a fleshy underground or creeping, root-like food storage organ from which leaves, stems and flowers grow upwards and roots downwards. It tends to be scaly and look 'jointed'. Typical examples are flag irises, convallaria (lily of the valley) and polygonatum (Solomon's Seal), all hardy plants.

COVERING THE TRELLIS AND PERGOLAS

with climbing roses

Do your boundary walls look bare and uninteresting? Are they high enough to grow all the plants you would like? Do you wish to hide, as we do, an unsightly feature? In our garden where the shed is fully visible from the house, an attractive disguise is required. Here you can see we have made full use of trellis work extending at either side of the shed, as well as the two pergolas leading to the utility end of the garden, providing ideal places to grow climbing and rambling roses.

A trellis will give your boundary walls additional height and you more privacy.

If you are erecting trellis work against the walls, it is always advisable – and a friendly gesture – to inform your immediate neighbours beforehand. Furthermore, make sure the trellis doesn't interfere with their garden designs or cut out what is known as 'reasonable light and air'. (There is no definite ruling as to what height a trellis may reach, but 2·5–3m (8–10 ft) from ground level is generally acceptable.)

Buying the trellis

Although trellis is easy enough to make, it is quicker and generally far preferable to buy it ready-made. It can be bought in various patterns, lengths and heights and, if you are armed with the measurements, it should present no problem to get just what you want, in the form of prefabricated panels. You will also need some timber supporting posts, which should preferably be 5×5cm (2×2 in); add a further 60cm (2 ft) onto the required length, to allow for sinking the posts into the ground.

Before erecting the trellis posts and panels, paint them with a wood preservative that is not harmful to plants. The supporting posts, too, need similar treatment and, as an extra precaution, soak the bottom ends in creosote to a height of 60cm (2 ft) to give added protection against rotting in the ground.

Fixing to the walls

Use the normal type of plastic wall plugs and screws to fix the top, middle and bottom of each main vertical lath of the panel. To prevent contact between the wall and the timber (which could cause rotting) use 100mm (4 in) long fixing screws with a 35mm (1½ in) long plastic tube spacer over the screw shank.

Fixing above the walls

For this type of trellis support posts are necessary, sunk into concrete at 1·80m (6 ft) intervals. First dig a hole 90cm (3 ft) deep, fill the bottom 30cm (12 in) with rubble (hardcore), place the post in position, put more rubble around it and tread it firmly into place.

Make a cement mix, using either a ready-mix type according to manufacturer's instructions, or 1 part cement to 4 parts coarse sand and enough water to make it sufficiently liquid to handle. Shovel this into the rubble-filled hole, and check that the post is vertical with a spirit level. Finally, smooth the cement surface to form a slightly convex top, so that rainwater will fall away from the post. Repeat this for all the posts and allow several days for cement to set.

It is then a simple matter to screw the trellis panels to these upright posts, inserting 100mm (4 in) screws with

Below: how to fix a trellis against, and above, a wall
Right: the Flower Garden pergola
Below right: when extended, a diamond-shaped trellis will not reach its full height
Rigid trellis is available in either wood or plastic-coated wire

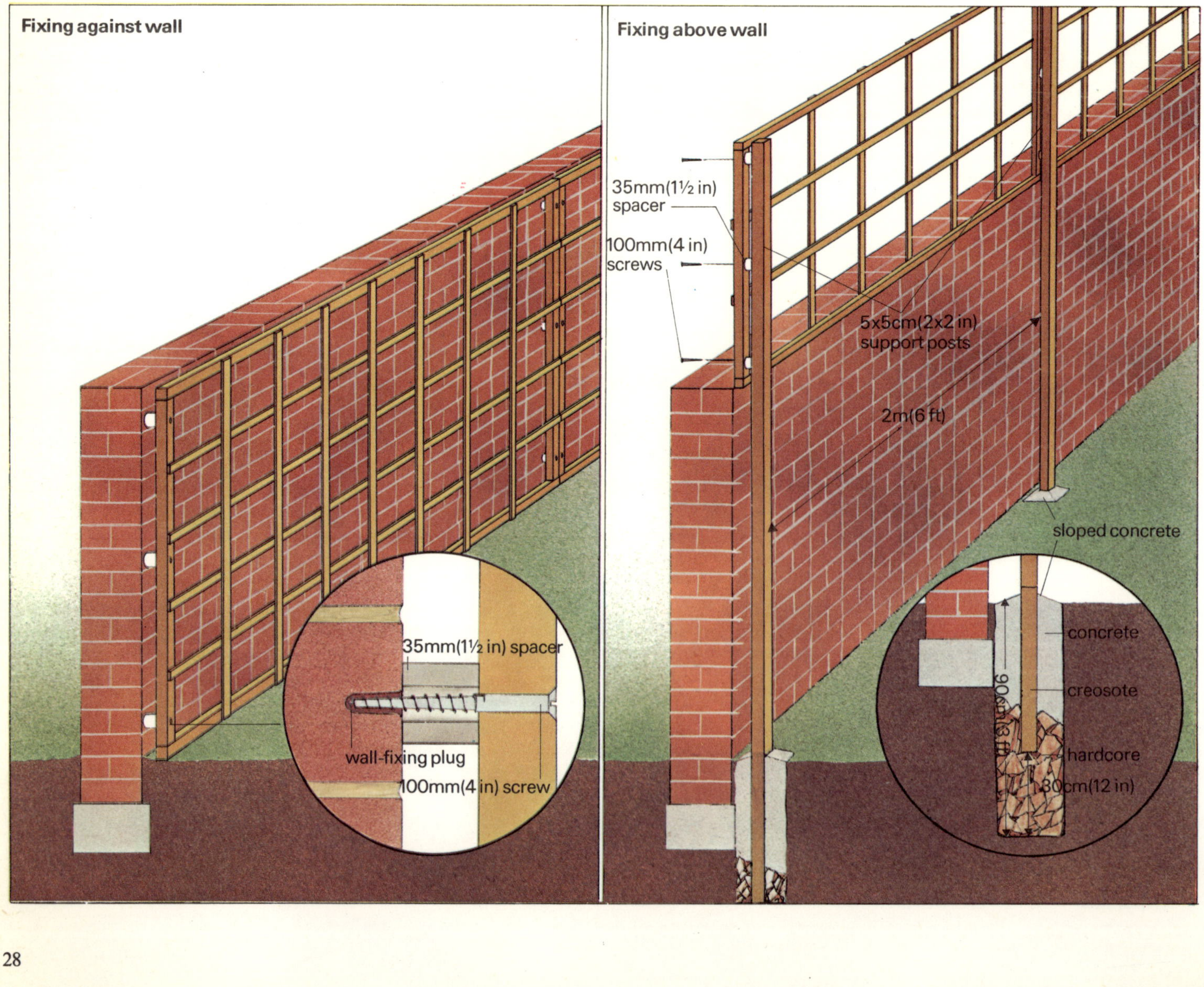

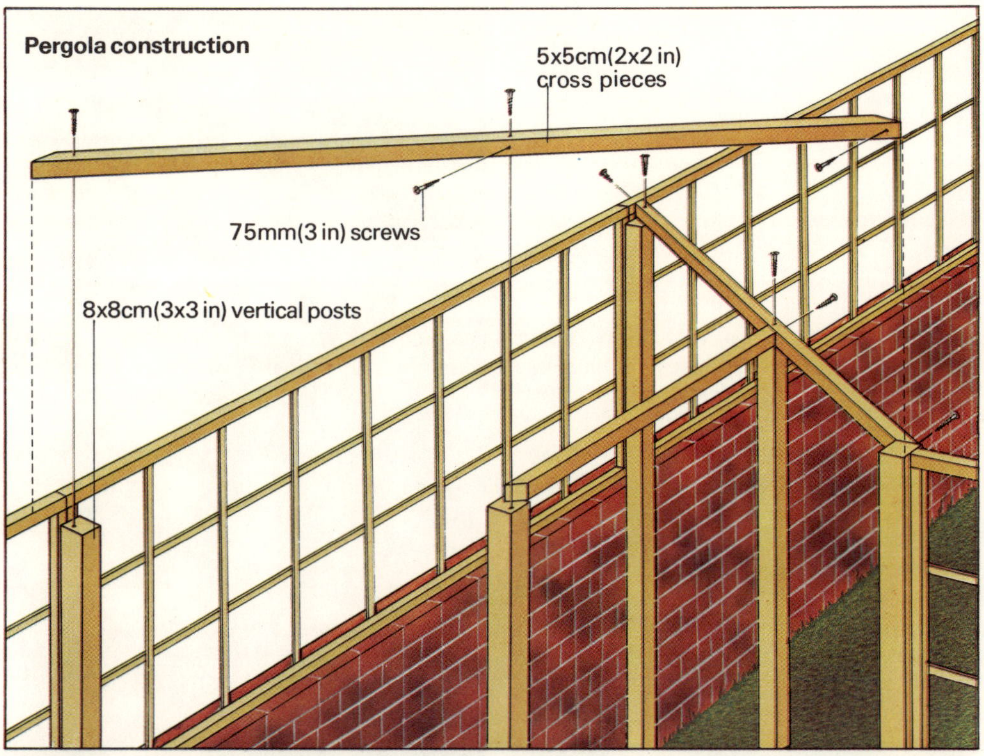

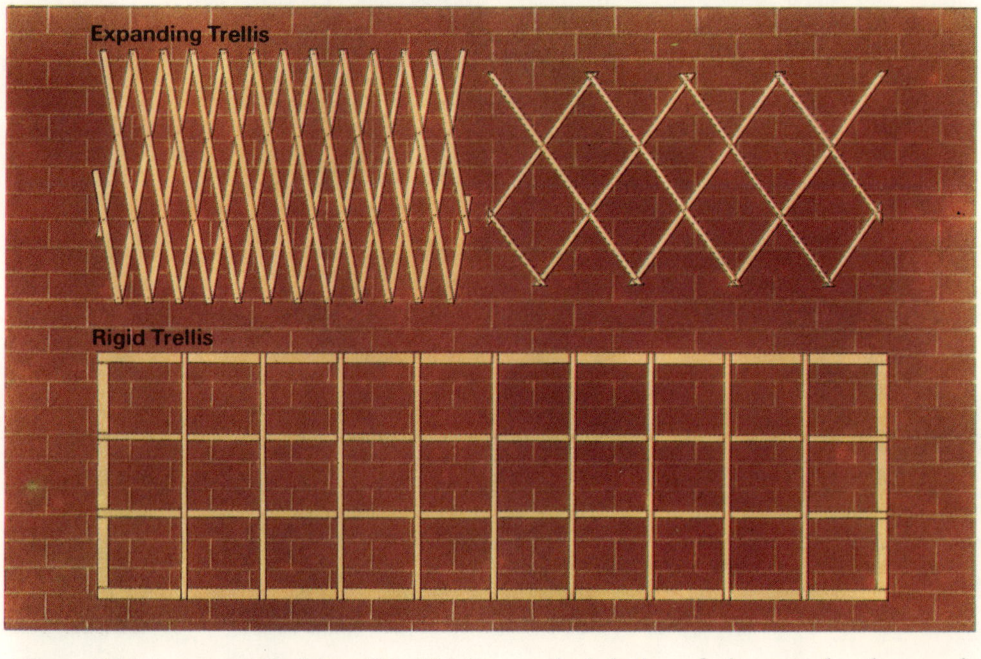

35mm (1½ in) spacers 30–45cm (12–18 in) apart as previously described.

To give the trellis and posts an attractive, finished appearance, convex wood capping pieces on each end post and above the top laths of trellis are effective, as well as useful in discouraging rainwater from accumulating.

Fixing trellis against the shed
This length of trellis in our garden is 3·65m (12 ft) long and so will require three supporting posts and probably two 1·8m square (6 ft square) panels of prefabricated trellis. Erect them as previously described and make sure the vertical laths of the panels abut each other for a clean and tidy finished appearance.

Erecting the pergolas
The vertical 8×8cm (3×3 in) painted poles can be erected in the same way as the trellis posts. Fix the supporting cross pieces by nailing or screwing them into position, as indicated in the construction diagram above. In our garden the pergolas have been designed in triangular form, see above, to hide the utility area behind and to create interesting walk-ways through from one part of the garden to the other.

GENERAL WORK

Mid spring (March)
If any buxus (box) edging plants have become straggly or died away at the base by mid spring, it is time to dig them up. Divide the clusters by pulling them apart and then trim the best portions of each plant – both roots and branches – with secateurs. Replant them 15cm (6 in) apart, treading them in firmly. The newly set-out plants will quickly re-establish themselves and give a much more satisfactory result later in the season than if you had just cut them back with shears.

Hoe carefully between your spring and early summer flowering biennial plants, such as wallflowers, forget-me-not, sweet William, Canterbury bells, and honesty, so as to catch and kill the weeds in an early stage of growth. If antirrhinums are overcrowded, or you have any left from last year that have overwintered outside, a good place to plant them is among the tulip bulbs that are now pushing their noses through the soil. This will give a second splash of colour to the tulip areas once your bulbs have finished flowering.

If you have not yet prepared the planting areas for new trees and shrubs, do so as soon as weather conditions allow – when the temperature is above freezing and the soil not so wet that it sticks to your boots or shoes. Don't forget to dig the area as deep and as wide as possible and add plenty of humus-forming matter, such as well-rotted compost or manure, to the lower soil. You should also prepare supporting stakes for the trees and shrubs and make sure you have suitable ties for holding the two together.

If your garden is relatively warm and sheltered, it is quite possible in mid spring (March) to sow some sweet pea seeds outdoors in a patch of light soil to which sand and peat have been added. Sow them in clusters and transplant them to their flowering positions later on.

If any new plants arrive during a frosty period, when the ground will be hard or very cold, don't attempt to plant the newcomers but keep them wrapped in a cool but frost-free place. For extra protection cover them with straw or sacks. If the cold spell is very prolonged, you may have to uncover the branches to let light and air get to them, but keep the roots covered. Only when the ground has warmed up and is workable should the new plants be set outside. If they are evergreens it pays to give them a protective sheeting of polythene or sacking from north and east winds after planting.

Climbing roses for the flower garden

As the trellis in front of the shed is designed to render it invisible from the house, an evergreen climber is ideal.

Unusual evergreens

Although there are only a few evergreen roses, they are an unusual and attractive choice for this purpose in the garden. From the point of view of flowers, easily the most spectacular is the single yellow Mermaid which blooms from mid summer (June) onwards and although it is only semi evergreen, it does retain some leaves throughout the winter. On the other hand, it is slightly tender and the stems can be killed right down to ground level in very severe weather.

The thickest-leaved evergreen rose for this situation is *R. wichuraiana* which has attractive glossy leaves and heads of bunched smallish flowers. Its greatest attraction, however, is its piercing fragrance – and the fact that it does not start flowering until early autumn (August), when most climbing roses are past their best. It also has a second season of colour when the small red heps (fruit) cover it in late autumn (October). There are many handsome *wichuraiana* hybrids, but none is completely evergreen.

There are two hybrids from the evergreen Mediterranean rose (*R. sempervirens*) which, although only semi evergreen, could be considered for this situation. The first is Adelaide d'Orléans, whose flowers are much the colour of strawberries and cream, with rather more cream than strawberries; they are small and very double, like a Japanese Cherry bloom, and open in mid summer (June). With rather more persistent leaves is Adelaide's sister, Félicité et Perpétué, which has white flowers opening from crimson buds in late summer (July). Once these two have flowered they have finished for the year, but the display is dazzling.

Below: Pink Perpétué flowers in summer and winter. Bottom: semi-evergreen, Mermaid, with large single blooms

Right: Rosette-shaped Dorothy Perkins is prone to mildew. Below: Crimson Shower bears trusses of flowers from late July

For the pergola

Here it is not so important that the roses be evergreen, so there is a much wider choice. You could choose a wild species, such as *R. helenae*; this is a very vigorous plant, so that one at each end of the pergola on opposite sides is quite sufficient. In mid to late summer (June to July) it bears huge heads of pure white flowers; individually these are small but on a well-grown plant they are produced literally by the thousand. In late autumn (October) they are followed by small scarlet heps, which will hang on until after Christmas; so it is a rewarding plant.

Below: Parkdirektor Riggers, almost continuous flowering and disease resistance

R. helenae sometimes takes a year or two to get going satisfactorily, but then it will throw great growths, sometimes up to six metres (20 feet) in a single season. These are extremely brittle when young, so they should not be tied into the pergola until late in the season, when the wood has hardened. They are also very thorny, so gloves are a necessity.

Rambler and pillar roses

If you want something a little less vigorous, there is a lot to be said for the old rambler roses. With these you have to cut out the flowering growths once the flowers are finished and tie in the new growths that will take their place. Crimson Shower comes into flower in late summer (July), will keep going until mid autumn (September) and has crimson flowers. It is much like the old Crimson Rambler, but less susceptible to rose mildew disease. For the same reason, Debutante is preferable to Dorothy Perkins with the same clear pink flowers. If you want blooms out of the ordinary colour range, choose Weilchenblau or Violette, with violet-maroon flowers; both these varieties are thornless.

There are a number of so-called pillar roses which have the attraction of being continuous-flowering, but which seem undecided on whether to be climbers or sprawling bushes. They are attractive, however, and would clothe the supports of the pergola nicely, but are unlikely to reach the crossbars. A particularly pleasant type is Parade, with crimson-pink flowers, that are much the size of the ordinary hybrid tea (HT) bush rose. Others include the rose-pink Pink Cloud, the crimson Parkdirektor Riggers, the orange-scarlet Danse du Feu and the attractive, yellow Golden Showers. All

Left: Danse du Feu blooms continuously from summer to autumn. Below: Golden Showers, good pillar rose, but prone to black spot

these have the advantage of flowering from early summer (May) until autumn, although they do have a tendency to have two main bursts, with a few odd flowers in between.

There are also a number of vigorous climbing sports of HT roses that have the large flowers of their type, but only flower once and tend to make rather gaunt plants. However, they mingle happily with the pillar roses. A favourite is Guinée, with very fragrant flowers that are almost black when they open. New Dawn tends to keep on flowering and has silvery pink blooms, while Climbing Crimson Glory has large crimson flowers.

Finally there are some large-flowered hybrids of *R. wichuraiana*, characterized by glossy leaves and flowers in size between the HT and the ramblers. Of these, one of the best is Albéric Barbier, with yellow flowers that turn to cream and a sweet scent. Emily Gray is an old favourite with buff-coloured flowers, while those of François Juranville are coral pink. Paul Transon has salmon-pink flowers and usually blooms again in the autumn, while May Queen has lilac-pink ones. All these are a blaze of flower at mid summer, but usually that is the full extent of their contribution to the garden, although the glossy, dark green leaves are attractive for long periods. They need little pruning, except to be thinned out when the growths get too crowded. This is most easily done in winter.

All these climbing roses have to be tied in to the pergola, but otherwise they require little attention – except for the ramblers, from which you have to remove the flowering growths once the flowering is over and then tie in their new growths later on.

Some of the interesting varieties described here may be difficult to obtain, but are well worth searching out. Also illustrated are some of the more popular and readily available varieties of climbers.

Right: Schoolgirl and below, Galway Bay, both disease-resistant with frequent flowering
Below left: Albéric Barbier

A LAWN IN SPRING

As our designer points out, a straight edge to a border makes it all wide, or narrow, whereas curves give additional interest by varying the depth and allowing you to make more interesting groupings of plants than would otherwise be possible in a long, narrow site like our Flower Garden.

Deciduous trees, shrubs and roses can be planted in mid spring (March) if the soil is dry and workable and the weather reasonably mild. If the plants you ordered earlier arrive during a bad weather period, either store them in a frostproof place still in their root packaging, or open them up and put them into a temporary trench outdoors. If your planting sites have been previously prepared, all you have to do now is dig a hole large enough to take the roots comfortably without squashing them. Examine any existing trees and shrubs with stakes to check that both are securely in the ground and haven't been moved by winter gales. Look at any tree ties to make sure that they aren't strangling the plants in any way or chafing the stems.

Check your trellis work and pergola timbers. Any rotting timber is best removed, or at least reinforced, and nails and screws should be examined to make sure that they are still firmly in position.

Existing lawns need their first mow in mid spring (March), but the grass should not be cut too low at this time of the year: cutting back to 5cm (2 in) is quite sufficient. To cut the grass cleanly the lawn-mower must have sharp blades.

For this first cut it is always advisable to collect the cuttings in a grass-box or bag while mowing; they can be added to the compost heap or used for mulching (unless a wormkiller has been applied).

After this first cut of the season, any mossy areas should be very apparent. So now is the time to apply a lawn mosskiller at the rate recommended by the makers. As moss is usually a sign of badly drained soil, it is wise to aerate the lawn's mossy patches by sticking in the tines of a fork every 10–15cm (4–6 in), wiggling it backwards and forwards to enlarge the holes slightly and then brushing in a 50/50 mixture of soil and peat to aid drainage. Once the moss has been killed, rake it out and, if necessary, re-seed the area with suitable grass seed.

You can also deal with any worn areas or broken edges now. Cut out worn patches and replace them with pieces of turf cut from areas which are not much used or not visible from the house. To make good the resulting bare patches, fill up the holes with soil, firm it with the feet, level it and sow with grass seed. (See page 100 for further details.)

THE TREES IN YOUR GARDEN

Trees are the most attractive and rewarding features of a garden. They add height and interest, and give a touch of elegance to even the very simplest of plots.

There are two types of trees: evergreen or deciduous; they may be tolerant of acid or alkaline soil. The varied shapes include widespreading, weeping and columnar.

In addition to contributing height and interest to a garden, they can be put to many practical uses, from providing shade or acting as a windbreak to hiding an obstinate eyesore. It is a pity to remove existing trees unless absolutely necessary, as they may have taken years to mature.

Making the right choice

The majority of trees will grow happily in a soil that has an almost neutral pH or is slightly acid. Some, such as birches, trees of heaven (ailanthus), elms and some poplars, have a definite preference for acid soils. Others, for example the decorative members of the apple and cherry genera, maples and crataegus (thorns), prefer some free lime.

Waterlogged or boggy ground suits very few trees, such as weeping willows and alders; dry or shallow soils do not worry many except the moisture-loving ones, provided the lower soil is not composed of solid chalk. (If chalk is a problem dig it out as deeply as possible and replace with good topsoil.)

For the best results with all varieties make sure the soil is deep, friable, well-drained and well-manured. A specific tree may prefer acidity or alkalinity and either can be provided for when preparing the ground for planting. If necessary, top dressings or feeds of special fertilizers can be given each year.

When to plant

It is best to buy and plant trees during the autumn and spring months when the weather is reasonably mild and the soil is not too wet or frozen. Some can be planted in winter if conditions are suitable, but generally trees do not pick up and grow as well in the first season, as their roots are in their most active state during that period.

The Common Laburnum that was already in existence in our Flower Garden

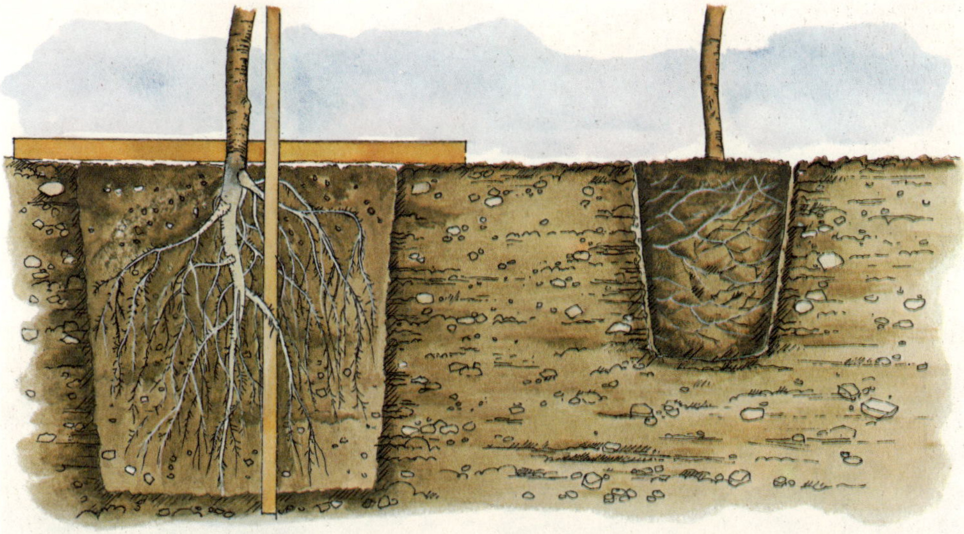

Trees must be planted to the correct depth and their roots well spread out; damaged or broken parts must be removed

Trees for planting in autumn and spring are often in the 'bare-rooted' state. This means there is little or no soil on their roots, or that the roots are in polythene or sacking containing a little loose soil. Bare-rooted trees are ideal for planting during their dormant period of non-active growth but *not* at any other time of year.

'Container-grown trees' – most nurseries and garden centres supply them – have been grown in soil-filled plastic, metal, whalehide or polythene containers from an early age, and their roots are well-established in the soil. The object of container-grown trees is to lengthen the planting season, so that they can be set in the garden at any time of year.

In theory this seems to work quite well, but in practice, after planting during the summer months, you must be especially careful to ensure that the roots get plenty of water during a dry spell and the leaves are sprayed every day for four to six weeks to help overcome any possible transitional shock.

If both bare-rooted and container-grown trees are available, you can plant at virtually any time of year, and have no excuse for a bare area. It also allows for impulse-buying should you see a specific tree you have not been able to obtain previously.

You will have to pay rather more for container-grown trees or plants of any kind, as they are more expensive to raise and transport to retailers.

Considering the many years a tree spends in the ground, it pays to prepare its site thoroughly. Begin by digging out the soil to the depth of a spade or the fork tines, and make a hole 1–1·5m (3–5 ft) in diameter. Then dig over the next layer to the same depth and add to this as much well-rotted manure or compost as you have available. Tread it firm and follow this with a light scuttling of the top 5–7cm (2–3 in) of soil with the fork or a large rake.

During preparation remove any large stones or weeds.

Planting bare-rooted trees
Trees must be planted to the same depth as they were previously growing; this is shown by the soil mark on the stem above the roots. Place the tree in the hole and check the depth by the level of the soil mark. If the hole is too shallow remove more soil; if it is too deep, put back some topsoil and lightly firm it.

Then get a wooden stake, about 4cm (1½ in) square, preferably with a sharpened end, and firmly hammer it into the centre of the hole. It should be long enough to reach as high as the first set of branches.

Put the tree back in the hole, carefully placing the roots around the stake. If there are any broken roots cut off the damaged portions with a sharp knife or secateurs. Make sure all the other roots are spread out.

If you can get someone to hold the tree in position the planting will be easier. If not, tie the tree to the stake. Shovel the topsoil back into the hole so that it gets well round the roots (slightly shaking the tree will help). Return all the soil, firming it from time to time, and make sure the tree remains upright.

Planting container-grown trees
First water the soil in the container and leave it to drain. Then place the tree, in its container, into the prepared hole to ensure the correct depth.

Next remove the container either by slitting the sides or tipping out the soil-ball round the roots. Hold the tree in position, return the topsoil and firm it. A stake of suitable length is again required, but in this case it is advisable to hammer it in *after* planting, taking care not to disturb the soil ball.

Caring for young trees
First tie the trunk of a new tree to its stake. Use one of the proprietary tree ties available or, if that is not possible, a nylon stocking. Don't use coarse string as it may chafe the bark. Fix a tie about 10cm (4 in) above soil level and another at about the same distance from the top of the stake.

After planting, a good watering is advisable and, especially in spring, the plants should be sprayed daily for about a month. A layer of mulch over the whole planting area will help to conserve moisture and provide food for the roots.

Until the trees are established, which could be up to three years after planting, keep the soil area free of weeds and grass that might inhibit healthy growth.

IN OUR FLOWER GARDEN

We 'inherited' two large and mature trees – silver birch (*Betula pendula*) and an Indian horse chestnut (*Aesculus indica*) – at the far end of the garden. They are both deciduous and, mainly because of their size, commonly associated with woodlands or parks. They can, however, look equally right in a garden, provided they are carefully sited (if being newly planted) or incorporated into the landscaping as in this instance – where they form features with underplanting for added interest.

Birches
Silver birch trees are most elegant in form with golden-yellow diamond-shaped leaves in autumn and white peeling bark, which develops as the trees mature, the final height being about 8m (25 ft).

Because of the tracery framework of their branches, silver birches do not cast dense shade, but they are rather shallow-rooting and plants set beneath them should not have roots that penetrate too deeply (hence our choice of azaleas). The only soil they don't like is a chalky one (again, like the azaleas).

There are a number of other fine birch trees. For example, *Betula costata*, with white peeling bark in summer that turns orange in winter; *B. pendula* Tristis, tall and slender with hanging branches; *B. pendula* Youngii, a smaller tree with weeping branches of delicate leaves that reach the ground; and *B. utilis*, with its greyish trunk and russet-brown branches contrasting with each other.

Horse chestnuts

Among the horse chestnuts, *Aesculus indica* is one of the most attractive, with its 'candles' of white, pink and yellow flowers in mid to late summer (June to July), followed by smooth-coated 'conkers' later in the year.

Other horse chestnuts are *A. flava* (sweet buckeye) which has yellow flowers and finely toothed, smallish leaves that colour attractively in autumn; *A. carnea* Briottii with deep rosy red flowers and smooth 'conkers'; and *A. hippocastanum* (common horse chestnut) with its summer 'candles' of white flowers up to 30cm (12 in) high followed by the 'conkers' loved by children. All horse chestnuts grow freely in most soils, except very chalky ones, and they create dense shade beneath, so underplants have to be carefully chosen.

Laburnums

We also inherit a laburnum sited on the south edge of the lawn. There are few smallish, drooping-shaped trees – they grow to about 6m (20 ft) – that are more attractive. They beautify a garden in late spring to mid summer (April to June) by their long, pendulous yellow pea-like

Right: slow-growing Japanese maple, Acer palmatum, *with glorious autumn foliage*
Below left: common horse chestnut, Aesculus hippocastanum, *bears 'candle' blooms and conkers. Below right: spindle* Euonymus europaeus, *has flowers and fruit*

flowers, followed in autumn with brown seed pods and in winter with green twigs.

All parts of the plant are poisonous, particularly the seeds, so obviously care should be taken where there are children.

The most common laburnum is *L. anagyroides* with various forms, such as *L. anagyroides* Aureum, with golden yellow leaves; and *L. a.* Autumnale, which often flowers for a second time in autumn. *L. vossii*, also very popular, is later-flowering than most, has darker glossy green leaves and is more erect in habit.

In our mixed flower border we added three small garden trees: a spindle, miniature maple, and a lilac.

Spindle tree

The spindle is one of the few trees among the Euonymus family of shrubs and is correctly called *Euonymus europaeus.* It grows to about 6m (20 ft), and its inconspicuous yellow-green small flowers are followed by a wealth of clusters of pinkish-red fruits, which open to reveal orange-coloured seeds. In autumn the leaves turn beautiful yellow and red hues. It is one of the easiest of trees to grow in almost any position.

Maples

The small maple, *Acer palmatum*, slowly grows to a height of about 4m (12 ft). We chose it for its attractive lobed leaves, which are pale green in summer and gorgeous orange and red tones in autumn. It is sometimes commonly called the Japanese maple and there are many cultivars of it, all equally attractive and easy to grow, if the soil is not too chalky.

There are several other forms of maples which are mainly much larger trees and more suitable for bigger gardens, or for planting in a far corner for shade or to hide an unpleasant view.

Syringas

Our lilac tree is more correctly called Syringa. The many trees and shrubs in this genus produce a mass of fragrant flowers in early to mid summer (May to June), and remain shapely green-leaved plants from early spring to late autumn (February to October).

Lilacs grow well in all but the most chalky soils, and they give their best in a sunny position. The most common varieties grown in gardens are those of *Syringa vulgaris.* They provide a wide colour range of flowers – from white, pale pink, dark red, mauve, purple, yellow to greenish-tinged – and can be either single or double flowered. There are so many that it is advisable to choose a colour to harmonize with other blooms in the immediate vicinity.

Some good ones are *Syringa vulgaris* Clarke's Giant (lavender-pink); Olivier de Serres (mauvish-pink); Esther Staley (carmine-pink); Charles Joby (purple-red); Mrs. Edward Harding (red); Maud Notcutt (white); and Souvenir d'Alice Harding (alabaster – off-white).

Left: the graceful birch, Betula pendula, *has attractive leaf shapes, such as heart or diamond, as well as some splendid stem colours. Below: the lilac tree,* Syringa vulgaris, *has many varieties which happily mix with other surrounding plants.*

HEATHERS FOR WINTER COLOUR

Winter colour in the garden is often considered a problem, but a never-failing source of coloured leaves and flowers comes from winter heathers. In the design we have made a special corner for them at the end of the south mixed flower border so that not only can they be given the soil conditions and aspect they prefer, but also you then have a delightful area to look at, and flowers to pick, during the so-called 'dead' months of the year. The winter jasmine arching on the trellis behind adds to the overall pleasing picture.

Heather is the common name generally taken to include the true heathers (erica), the heaths (daboecia) and ling (calluna), as each genus is very similar in appearance and requirement. They are rightly popular and with careful selection they provide colour and form throughout the whole year. They are not, however, as widely grown as they might be, for many people seem to think they need the conditions of their native habitat, moorlands. In fact, heathers are among the easiest plants to grow and require little attention. They prefer a sunny position but will thrive in partial shade, though flower colour may not be as good. They are not unduly fussy about soil, provided it is on the peaty, acid side without lime, but even so there are some cultivars and hybrids, for instance *Erica carnea*, *E.* × *darleyensis*, *E. mediterranea*, *E. arborea* and *E. terminalis*, which will grow as happily in soils containing free lime (but not solid chalk) as in acid ground. The ideal pH to aim for is 5.6 to 6.0.

Planting preparation

All the heathers are best planted in late spring to early summer (April to May) or late autumn or early winter (October to November). Even if you have good, suitable soil it still pays dividends to prepare it thoroughly and weed it in advance of planting, by forking in plenty of peat and leaf mould (rotted leaves). If the ground is at all limey, then it is advisable to dig out the soil to the depth of two spade blades and replace it with lime-free topsoil (brought in if necessary) mixed with plenty of peat. The surplus soil can be used elsewhere in the garden or heaped somewhere for future use.

After digging, it pays to allow the soil to settle naturally for a week or so if time allows. If it doesn't, then tread the soil firm and rake it over afterwards.

Planning for heathers

When planted individually among other plants, heathers never look their best, except possibly the tree forms. It is far better to mass them in one place where they can set each other off to best advantage. It is also far easier to take care of their few requirements when they are all together in one spot.

In our garden the heathers have been selected for winter flower and leaf colour throughout the year. They have been massed together in part of the mixed flower border on the south side of the

For a colourful mixed border, choose heathers in white-tinged pale pinks to deep mauves

garden, facing to the west, where they will get the open conditions they like. On the other hand, because it is possible to produce a mass of colour throughout the year, either from flowers or leaves, many people prefer to put them in an 'island' bed – a flowerbed that stands on its own and can be seen all round from a variety of angles. In this case, 'dot' (individual) specimens of other acid soil-loving plants such as dwarf rhododendrons, azaleas and conifers are often added to give even further interest. A heather edge to a border or low hedges along paths are other effective ways to use these plants.

Before buying your plants, it is wise to draw on paper a scale plan of the types and varieties you want. By doing this you can ensure that there are no colour clashes, you get the right plants of the correct heights in the places you want them, and you can work out in advance how many plants of each variety you need. Again, with the exception of the tree heathers, it is more effective visually to put a number of plants of the same type in one clump, and to blend the clumps into one another. In this way you get bold hummocks and mats of flowers and leaves that create a most attractive appearance.

Most heathers are generally best kept to a height of 60cm (24 in) or less, except of course, tree heathers which will grow up to 3m (10 ft) or more. But even the latter can be kept smaller by pruning. It is advisable to purchase small plants that have been raised from cuttings (rather than division), as these grow more quickly and reach maturity sooner. The average distance between each plant should be about 45cm (18 in). This may make them look thin on the ground initially but they will soon grow to intermingle with each other and cover the ground to act as most useful suppressors of annual weeds.

Five cultivars of Erica carnea*: (left to right, top) Springwood White, Pink Spangle; (centre) Winter Beauty, Vivelli; (bottom) Ruby Glow,* E. arborea *Goldtips*

Putting in the plants

From your scale plan, draw out with a stake the areas where each group of heathers is to be planted. Then place the plants, still in their pots if possible, or with a minimum of disturbance to the soil ball if not, on the surface of the 'clump' areas to finalize where each plant is to go. Next plant each heather by digging out a hole of the right size with a trowel (or spade for larger areas) and removing the pots (if plastic), or tearing down one side (if they are peat pots). Make sure the soil level is where it was originally on the plant, and firm it with your fingers (or feet, if a larger plant).

Planting should only take place when the soil is suitably dry and workable, and afterwards the plants should be watered in carefully. During a dry period they may need watering and spraying regularly for a month or so in order to get them well established.

After-care of heathers

The only attention required by heathers after planting should be careful, shallow hoeing to remove the weeds until the plants have spread sufficiently to smother them for you. You must remove dead heads with shears immediately after flowering. (Incidentally, these can be most attractive used in dried flower arrangements.) The tree heathers, especially if they get too big or straggly, should be cut back hard into the old wood some time in late spring (April).

The only other attention that may be required is if your heathers are growing on a soil that is not sufficiently acid for them. In this case they may show their displeasure by poor growth and unusual leaf discoloration. These symptoms are caused by the lack of certain essential plant foods in the soil. To overcome the

Heather garden at the Royal Horticultural Society garden at Wisley, ablaze with Erica × darleyensis *Furzey,* E. arborea, *and* E. mediterranea *W. J. Rockliff*

GENERAL WORK

Late spring (April).

Continue to remove dead heads of spring flowering bulbs regularly.

Finish planting gladiolus corms (as described on page 17) if not already completed in mid spring (March).

Complete the clearing of mixed and other flower borders of leaves and general winter debris.

Pruning of roses (as described on page 18) should be completed immediately if not already done. Also complete pruning of shrubs that have flowered during the winter by cutting out all old, dead, diseased or crossing branches. This includes hedging plants.

If moss and wormkiller treatments were not applied to lawns in mid spring (March), do so now. Repeat the treatments if either appears not to have been fully effective. Mow the lawn as necessary, still keeping the height of cut about 5cm (2 in). Apply a general lawn fertilizer at the rate recommended by the manufacturer.

Tread firm any soil loosened by frost.

problem, apply a special fertilizer containing the necessary nutrients (such as Sequestrene) once or twice a year.

Choice of heathers

The two groups with winter flowers that compliment each other well are *Erica carnea* and *Erica × darleyensis*. The former grow about 15 to 30cm (6–12 in) high and are ideal for planting in front of the latter which grow about 60cm (24 in) tall. Both groups contain cultivars and hybrids and flower through from early winter to late spring (November to April), with the majority being mid-season (January to March). Both are tolerant of a certain amount of lime in the soil and are thus suitable for growing in most gardens and are rightly among the most popular of low-growing shrubs.

In our garden, we have selected four cultivars of *Erica carnea*, namely:

Ruby Glow – rich carmine-red flowers rising from bronze-coloured foliage.

Springwood Pink – rose-pink flowers with dense leaves and branches that trail over the ground and smother weeds.

Springwood White – a fine white-flowered heather with a similar growing habit to Springwood Pink.

Vivellii – flowers the deepest red of all winter heathers and superb dark bronze leaves (which are dark green in summer). Makes a good foil to white-flowered forms.

To give height to this part of the border, we planted at the back two clumps of hybrids of *Erica × darleyensis:*

Arthur Johnson – free-flowering sprays of magenta pink standing up from light green leaves; excellent for cutting. Alba (sometimes called Silberschmelze) – also produces dense sprays of sweetly-scented white flowers for a long period.

There are a number of other varieties of *Erica carnea* and *E. × darleyensis* that flower during the winter months. Among those worthy of note are:

E. carnea Eileen Porter – deep rich carmine and pale pink flowers for a long period.

E. carnea Gracilis, compact plants with rose pink blooms.

December Red, purplish flowers and low spreading growth.

King George (sometimes called Winter Beauty) with bright carmine, brown-tipped flowers.

Of the *Erica × darleyensis* hybrids, outstanding is Darley Dale, which produces pink blooms for a very long period.

SHRUBS AND CLIMBERS

Late spring (April)
If the soil is suitably dry and not sticky plant out unsprouted dahlia tubers in their final positions. Protect them against frost with a 2–3cm (1 in) layer of mulch. Label and stake the varieties; the stakes can later be used for tying in growing plants.

Hoe the planted area, taking care not to damage the roots, and remove as many weeds as possible. Give them a few days to die, then hoe or rake in a general fertilizer, such as Growmore, and put a layer of mulch round all the perennial plants, trees and shrubs.

Eliminate slugs and snails—they can leave a trail of woe at this time of year—by covering plants and surrounding soil with liquid slugkiller or pellets, such as metaldehyde. Repeat as necessary.

Plant out evergreen hedging plants not later than the end of this month. Water them regularly if the weather is dry, and keep hoeing to control weeds.

Shrubs and climbers are ideal for all gardens (including paved areas, as many can be grown in containers), for they supply colour, framework and form all year round. They act as useful low-growing weed-suppressors as well as ornamental screens. They can be an endless source of interest, require little attention and mix well with other plants that may be of only seasonal interest. Here we suggest a suitable selection.

In our Flower Garden we have decided on mainly mixed borders to show how a variety of plants can harmonize together and give greater pleasure than the more old-fashioned borders that tend to be strictly for one type of plant only, such as herbaceous or annuals, which require more upkeep.

Budgeting ahead
One point to bear in mind when planning for mixed borders is that shrubs and climbers are generally more expensive to buy initially than many other types of plants. However, they more than compensate for this over the years. If you don't wish to get involved in too great an outlay when making a new garden, or renovating an existing one, it is advisable to plan for all the shrubs and climbers in advance, so that you know exactly where they are to be positioned, and then buy a few each year until you have completed your original design. The gaps left by the as yet unbought shrubs can be temporarily filled with annuals, bedding plants, bulbs or some cheap herbaceous perennials.

Behind the shed and pergola in our Flower Garden a fine camellia bush grows well on the south wall

Planning ahead

Apart from varying shapes and sizes, shrubs can be evergreen or deciduous and have a variety of features such as variegated or different-coloured leaves, colourful and/or fragrant flowers, decorative bark or aromatic leaves. They can change leaf colours in autumn, produce interesting and colourful fruits, and be suitable for planting in all types of soil, sun or shade.

Always remember to keep down the number of shrubs and climbers in your garden and not plant too many, otherwise they grow into a tangly mess and swamp other plants in the border. The best policy is to put young plants close together and then, when the selected ones are reaching maturity, pull out and discard the remainder; but this is expensive and unnecessary with mixed flower borders.

As with all plantings it is wise to plan the borders on paper beforehand and draw them out on graph paper, as we described on page 15.

List your choice of shrubs and climbers—most good plant catalogues describe them in detail—and alongside each add its ultimate height and diameter, the colouring of leaves, flowers and fruit, their timing, whether evergreen or deciduous, soil preference, sun-or shade-lover, and any other specific requirement.

When and how to plant

As with trees, deciduous shrubs and climbers are best planted in autumn or spring, and evergreens in spring. Both types are available in bare-rooted and container-grown forms, the latter being suitable for planting at more or less any time of year provided the necessary precautions are taken. The preparation for, and the planting of, shrubs and climbers are essentially the same as for trees.

Stakes are not likely to be required except for large specimens, shrubs that have a floppy habit of growth and need some form of control, and those that are to be trained as climbers and will require a form of permanent framework up which to grow. After-care of the newly planted shrubs is also similar to that of trees.

Flower Garden ground plan key

1	azalea	10	erica	19	rhododendron
2	berberis	11	euonymus	20	vinca
3	buddleia	12	garrya	21	clematis
4	buxus	13	hamamelis	22	jasminum
5	camellia	14	hydrangea	23	lonicera
6	ceanothus	15	hypericum	24	polygonum
7	chaenomeles	16	lavendula	25	rosa
8	cotoneaster	17	mahonia		
9	cytisus	18	pyracantha		

IN OUR FLOWER GARDEN

We selected a variety of shrubs for different purposes here and, after the initial planting as shown in the ground plan (page 10), we added shrubs that can be planted almost anywhere in the mixed borders—aucuba, choisya, skimmia and viburnum—and olearia, which likes a sunny position. They are described in alphabetical order.

Aucuba

Really hardy and versatile evergreens that grow to about 1·5m high and spread to 1·5m (5 × 5 ft), in sun or shade, town or country, and any type of soil. *Aucuba japonica*, the common form, has glossy, oval leaves and brilliant scarlet berries on the female plants.

Aucuba japonica Crotonifolia (male) and *A.j.*Variegata (female) are both variegated forms.

Azalea

Here there is a wealth of hybrids from which to choose including some deciduous ones that are 2–3m (6–10 ft) tall, and evergreens 1–1·5m (3–5 ft) tall. In many catalogues these are listed under rhododendron as they belong to the same family and have the same requirements, of which an important one for both types is that the soil should have an acid pH and contain no free lime. If your garden does not have a naturally acid soil you must prepare the ground before planting as you did for heathers (see page 38), that is either providing lime-free topsoil with plenty of peat, or forking in adequate quantities of peat and leaf mould.

As the azaleas in our Flower Garden are growing under the shade of the deciduous silver birch, we have selected a mixture of evergreen cultivars (varieties) to give interest all year round, with the emphasis on different coloured flowers in early summer. A few popular evergreen ones from which to choose are:

Addy Wery	vermilion
Blue Danube	purple-blue
Hinodegiri	bright crimson
Orange Beauty	salmon-orange
Rosebud	pink
Palestrina	ivory
Mother's Day	rose-red

The deciduous forms of azalea, although without the advantage of being

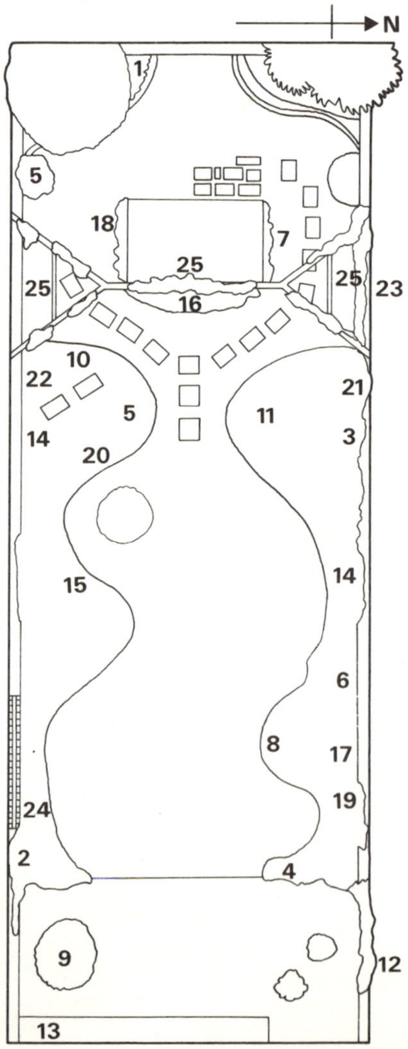

Top left: silver-flowered azalea
Above left: Aucuba japonica *Variegata*
Left: blue berries of Berberis darwinii
Above: sweet-scented Buddleia globosa

evergreen, do have special attractions in that they produce an even wider range of flower colours and are usually fragrant, and the leaves turn to beautiful red tints in autumn. They are, however, rather larger than the evergreens and so require more planting space. Among the best deciduous ones to choose are:

Knap Hill Exbury hybrids	single colours or mixed
Directeur Moerlands	gold and orange
Coccinea Speciosa	orange-red
Aida	peach-pink
Koster's Brilliant Red	orange-red
White Swan	white
Narcissiflorum	pale yellow

Berberis (barberry)
Another family of plants with both deciduous and evergreen forms that can vary enormously in habit from horizontal ground cover growth to dwarf bushes 60cm high, 60cm spread (2 × 2 ft) or medium ones 1·5m high, 1·5m spread (5 × 5 ft). They can be planted as individuals or hedges, are easy to grow in any soil and tolerate shade; the evergreens will thrive in the shade. The flowers in spring and summer are usually yellow or orange, and the autumn fruits are very showy. Many berberis species also produce brilliant leaf tints in autumn and winter; all of them are more or less spiny, so you will need your gloves when clipping back.

In our garden we needed a low-growing form that would help visually to break the edge of the paved area near the house, but would also blend well with both the mixed border and the paving stones. For this purpose we selected *B.candidula*, an evergreen variety.

Berberis candidula Leaves with silvery undersides, yellow flowers and purple oval-shaped berries. Grows only about 45cm (18 in) high, 1–1·5m (4–5 ft) spread.

B. darwinii and *B.stenophylla* Bear their flowers and berries on arching stems and make ideal, unusual hedging plants.

B.verruculosa White undersides to evergreen leaves that colour well in autumn; golden yellow flowers on arching branches followed by rich purple berries. Grows to about 1m high, 1m spread (4 × 4 ft).

Two attractive deciduous types are:

B.thunbergii Brilliant leaf colours and scarlet fruits in autumn; mainly compact bushes.

B.wilsoniae Almost evergreen leaves that turn rich red and orange in autumn, and blend well with the clusters of coral-coloured berries. Smallish in size, tending to form mound-shaped bushes.

Buddleia (butterfly bush)
Quick-growing deciduous shrubs producing panicles (elongated branches) of flowers in late summer and mid autumn. As their common name indicates, they are much loved by butterflies for the sweet fragrance produced by most species. They thrive in any soil, and particularly love sun. For our garden we have chosen the very popular *B.davidii.*

Buddleia davidii Grows quickly anywhere to a medium size and flowers freely even in its second year. There are many varieties of this shrub with flowers colours varying from the usual bluish purple to white, rose, lavender and shades of purple.

B.alternifolia Almost tree-like in form, with fragrant lilac flowers in long, thin sprays. Grows freely, particularly against a warm wall.

B.globosa Virtually evergreen buddleia that produces in early summer sweetly scented flowers, round and orange in colour, on short stems; long tapering leaves that are grey underneath.

B.fallowiana Silvery-leaved with sweet smelling lavender-blue flowers in late summer. Alba is a white-blooming form.

Buxus (box)
Very useful shiny green evergreens that are ideal for hedging, edging borders and paths or, as in our garden, forming a link between the north side mixed flower border and the paved area. They grow anywhere and withstand hard treatment. The larger boxes can be used for hedges or topiary (clipping of trees or hedges to make 'sculpted' designs). For our garden we chose *B.sempervirens.*
Buxus sempervirens Often sold as a low-growing shrub, 60cm high, 60cm spread (2 × 2 ft). Other popular boxes are:
*B.s.*Aurea Variation of *B.sempervirens*, with yellow-edged leaves. This dual coloration does not always make a good contrast to other plants.
B.s.suffruticosa Common edging box normally seen in small formal gardens. Its medium-sized leaves of bright green set off other plants to advantage.

Camellia
These beautiful shiny-leaved evergreen winter- and spring-flowering plants are not nearly as difficult to grow as is frequently thought. They are, in fact, as hardy as the common laurel. However, they do like the same acid, peaty soil conditions as azaleas, rhododendrons and heathers, hence in our garden we have planted them by the azaleas and heathers on the north-facing side, so all these plants can have the same treatment. They like protection from north and east winds and not too much direct winter and early spring sun, which can damage the flowers following a frosty night. An ideal position, if you have it, is a lightly wooded part of the garden that offers frost protection. Camellias grow from 1·5 to 3m (5 to 10 ft) high 1·5m (5 ft) spread.

There is a vast range of camellias from which to choose, many with different flower shapes, and we have selected one of the early-flowering *C.williamsii* hybrids to grow by itself at the far end of the garden, and two of the later *C.japonica* hybrids to complement the heathers at the lower end of the flower border.

Camellia flowers may be in any shade of white, pink, red, peach or multi-coloured and some of the best to select from are:

Camellia williamsii Donation	orchid pink
C.w. J. C. Williams	pale pink
C.w. November Pink	pink
C.japonica Mathotiana	crimson
C.j. Elegans	salmon-rose, splashed white
C.j. Adolphe Audusson	blood-red, yellow centre
C.j. Lady Vansittart	pink and white striped
C.j. Mercury	light red
C.j. Lady Clare	pale pink

Ceanothus
Sometimes called California lilac. The most appealing feature of these evergreen or deciduous shrubs is that they are among the best hardy blue-flowering ones available. They vary in size, and do best in a sunny position where the soil is well-drained and not too chalky. Gloire de Versailles, a popular deciduous type, is the one we have selected for our south-facing wall and we suggest a few others:
Gloire de Versailles, with sky-blue flowers borne on arching branches in late summer or late autumn.
Topaz (deciduous), with deeper blue flowers.
C.thyrsiflorus (evergreen) is one of the hardiest, with bright blue blooms in early summer.
C.thyrsiflorus repens (evergreen), a very attractive weed-suppressor, growing only up to about 1m (3 ft) high, but spreading to 2·5m–3m (8–10 ft).

Far left: well-trimmed Buxus sempervirens
Left: ceanothus Gloire de Versailles
Below left: camellia D. Olga Anderson
Bottom left: Camellia japonica *C. M. Wilson*
Right: chaenomeles bears edible berries
Below: C. japonica *Hearn's Pink Dawn*

Chaenomeles (quince, japonica)
Sometimes called *cydonia.* Very easy deciduous shrubs to grow either in natural form or to train as a climber. They do well in any soil and any position, regularly produce a mass of flowers from mid spring to early summer and tend to produce further blooms intermittently all year round. After saucer-shaped flowers in shades of red, pink, orange or white, they all bear edible quince fruits.

To grow up the north-facing end of our garden shed, we selected the crimson-flowering variety, *Chaenomeles superba* Rowallane. Other varieties worthy of note are:

C.superba	
Knap Hill Scarlet	orange-scarlet
Pink Lady	rose-pink
Crimson and Gold	crimson with gold centres
Boule de Feu	orange-red
C. speciosa	
Moerloosii	pink and white in clusters
Nivalis	pure white
Umbilicata	deep salmon-pink
Rubra Grandiflora	extra large, crimson
Eximea	brick-red

Choisya (Mexican orange blossom)
Choisya ternata, the only species in this small genus of evergreens, is virtually essential for all gardens. As its common name implies, it comes from Mexico and has sweetly fragrant, white flowers of orange blossom; its foliage is also aromatic when crushed. Useful on most soils and in sun or shade, it flowers spasmodically throughout the year, but most profusely in summer. It forms a rounded bush of about 2m (6 ft) spread and can be grown against a wall.

Cotoneaster
A large genus of plants that can be evergreen or deciduous; low-growing creepers, bushes or trees. They survive well in varying soils and positions, and they all produce white or pink-tinged flowers in summer, attractive autumn leaf colours and brilliant fruits. The ground covering plants are excellent weed-smotherers. For our purpose we selected a prostrate-growing evergreen form, such as *C.salicifolius*, for the front of the south-facing mixed border. *C.s* Autumn Fire, has longish, willowy leaves and orange-red berries. Other good examples are:

Cotoneaster dammeri	scarlet berries
C.microphyllus	crimson berries
C. Skogholm	coral-red berries
C.conspicuus	bright red berries carried on arching branches

A popular deciduous form for low-growing or training up walls is *C.horizontalis*, the 'fish bone' cotoneaster (its branches grow herring-bone fashion), whose berries and leaves produce a riot of colour in autumn and look very effective.

Most of the taller-growing varieties are semi-evergreen; *C.lacteus* is one of the popular, though few, fully evergreen forms for hedging or screening, with its fruits lasting well after mid winter. Other good taller types are:

Cotoneaster bullatus	red cherry-like berries
C.divaricatus	superb scarlet in autumn
C.rotundifolius	upright, small-leaved, berries last until late spring
C.franchetii	sage green leaves, scarlet berries

Cytisus (broom)
Varying in size from low-growing plants to small trees, all cytisus have pea-shaped flowers (usually yellow) and most of them like a sandy, rather acid soil and plenty of sun. In general they flower in spring and summer but some produce blooms in early autumn thus providing a long season of colour and interest.

For the planting space in the paved area of our garden we selected *C.purgans*. This dense, almost leafless shrub with fragrant yellow flowers in spring will give colour and fragrance near the house in the early part of the year. It grows to about 1·2m (4 ft) high maximum, and 45cm (18 in) spread. Other pretty low-growing species are:

Cytisus purpureus	lilac-purple flowers in summer
C.×beanii	golden-yellow, early summer

Others of note are the hybrid forms with flowers of yellow, red, white or pink, and species such as:

Cytisus×praecox	very floriferous
C.battandieri	beautiful leaves, pineapple scent
C.nigricans	late summer and early autumn
C.grandiflorus	grey woolly seed pods

Opposite page, far left: Cotoneaster conspicuus *bears bright red berries in autumn. Opposite page, left: glossy-leaved evergreen* Cotoneasta microphyllus
This page, left: dwarf Cytisus × beanii
Above: low-growing Cytisus purpureus, *known as purple broom*
Below left: the common broom, Cytisus scoparius *Canary Bird*
Below: the tall Cytisus battandieri *has unusual pineapple-scented flowers*

The following shrubs and climbers were described earlier on: aucuba, azalea, berberis, buddleia, buxus, camellia, ceanothus, chaenomeles, choisya, cotoneaster and cytisus. On the succeeding pages we conclude the selection we have made for you—from evica to vinca.

Erica (heather and heath)
Provide colour in flower or leaf form all year round, and are easy to grow. We described these in detail on page 40.

Euonymus (spindle)
Mainly evergreen and deciduous shrubs, but *E. europaeus* and its forms make attractive small trees for gardens. Spindles are easily grown and especially useful where the soil is chalky. Special attractions lie in their autumn leaf tints, the colours of the berries on the deciduous forms and the fact that they tend not to grow too large.

In our Flower Garden we wanted a spindle bush that would harmonize with the buddleia behind it and the grey cineraria alongside, and also give colour throughout the year. For this we chose the pretty evergreen *E. fortunei* Silver Queen variegata. Most of the *E. fortunei* forms are very hardy, trailing or climbing evergreens with a variety of uses.
Euonymus fortunei Silver Queen variegata Compact with silver variegations to the leaves and attractive rose tints in winter.
E. japonicus Another hardy type; does well in town, country or by the sea. There are a number of variegated-leaved forms.
E. alatus Superb deciduous spindle with corky bark, feathery leaves in spring turning to rich red in autumn, and purple berries with orange seeds.
E. sachalinensis Handsome shrub that is also highly colourful in autumn.

Garrya
A fascinating and decorative, quick-growing evergreen that we have planted to be trained as a climber against the north wall of our garden (unless you plan to put up a lean-to greenhouse here). It is available in male and female forms; the latter are the more popular for their long-dangling, grey-green silky catkins produced during winter.
Garrya elliptica Most common species; does well in all soils provided they are not heavy and are well-drained. It does not need a sunny site.

Hamamelis (witch hazel)
Produce the most fascinating winter and early spring clusters of flowers that withstand the coldest weather; and they enchant with fragrance and curious strap-like bright yellow and red petals borne on leafless branches. As a genus they are shrubs or small trees, and we have put one against the house wall in the south-east corner, but it can be grown in almost any position. Being deciduous it is a useful plant as it produces hairy, hazel-like leaves during spring which turn golden yellow in autumn, thus giving the plant a second season of attraction. *H. mollis* is the best and most popular of all the witch hazels, other species, such as *H.* × *intermedia*, *H. japonica* and *H. vernalis*, are not so frequently found in catalogues:
Hamamelis mollis Pallida Dark yellow.

Hydrangea
Highly prized plants in many gardens for their prolonged display of flowers during summer and early autumn. All of them like a sunny position, but not where the soil dries out round their roots, so it pays to give them a deep, well-manured site and regularly mulch them every spring. They are all deciduous, but grow in a variety of forms from small to medium-sized bushes, 60cm–2·5m (2–8 ft) high, and some are genuine climbers, such as the one we have growing on the north-facing wall:
Hydrangea petiolaris Climber with flat heads of white flowers.

Hydrangea flower-heads are of three types: large and rounded (known as hortensias or mop-heads); large and flat or dome-shaped (known as lacecaps); and species (with heads of various shapes). These last are easy and reward-

Top: Hamamelis mollis *(witch hazel) flowers throughout winter and spring*
Above: Hydrangea paniculata *flowers through summer and early autumn*
Left: Euonymus alatus *deciduous spindle*

Top: Hypericum calycinum *(St John's wort) in flower, a semi-evergreen plant*
Top right: Hypericum Elstead *in fruit*
Above and above right: Mahonia aquifolium—*its berries are good for jam*

ing shrubs to grow, and we have chosen *H. involucrata* for the south-facing wall:

Hydrangea involucrata Late-flowering dwarf bluish-purple and white blooms.
H. arborescens Grandiflora Greeny-white flowers that turn bronze-brown in winter.
H. villosa Pale blue flowers, grey-green leaves.
H. paniculata Grandiflora Creamy white to pink semi-arching branches of flowers.

As their name implies, lacecaps have flat, lacy flower-heads with pink or blue flowers and among the most popular are: Bluewave, Mariesii, Veitchii and Whitewave.

The hortensias are the hydrangeas most frequently seen as pot-grown specimens in florists' shops, and there are a large number of cultivars, mainly with shades of pink or blue globular flowers. It is an interesting fact that on acid soil blue flowers will appear, whereas on chalky alkaline soil pink blooms will be produced. (This is thought to be due to the 'locking-up' of certain chemicals in different soils which affect the flower coloration.) These hardy hortensias grow to medium-sized shrubs and their dead flower-heads are much sought after for dried flower arrangements.

Hypericum (St John's wort)
Semi-evergreen shrubs. Some are low-growing, and have mat-forming and weed-suppressing growth; others have a delicate, and more branching habit, growing to about 1·2m (4 ft) high. They grow easily in any soil, sun or shade, and have attractive brilliant yellow flowers lasting from mid summer to late autumn. Some, too, have the added advantage of autumn leaf tints or coloured berries. One of the most popular is *H. calycinum* as a spreading plant that keeps weeds under control. It forms a dense mat and the leaves turn a purplish colour in autumn.

For our garden we have chosen a beauty: *Hypericum* Hidcote (*H. patulum* Hidcote). Forms a delightful bush with saucer-shaped golden flowers that blend well with surrounding catmint and iris. Other good species are:

Hypericum elatum	rose-red berries
H. androsaemum	red and black berries, autumn leaf tints
H. × *moseranum* Tricolor	pink, cream and green variegations

Lavandula (lavender)
Much favoured, mainly for their soft grey permanent foliage and delightful fragrance. We have planted a whole border of this in front of the shed trellis so that it makes an attractive spot throughout the year. Lavenders also have a long season, providing their flower spikes from summer to autumn, and they enjoy any well-drained soil and as much sun as possible. They are excellent by the sea and for making dwarf hedges. Forms of *Lavandula spica* are those most commonly grown and in our garden we have a mixture of:

Hidcote	deep purple-blue flowers
Nana Munstead Dwarf	lavender blue
Twickel Purple	purple
Loddon Pink	pinky-blue
Vera	soft blue

Mahonia
Often confused and listed with berberis, but the essential difference is that they have compound leaves (leaves with several lobes) and no prickly spines on the stems. They are all evergreen, grow about 60cm–1m (2–4 ft) high and produce flowers in winter or spring followed by berries which are usually blue-black. They grow in almost any soil, but prefer a well-drained one, and are happy in the shade. We chose *M. japonica* for our garden against the south-facing wall:
Mahonia japonica is similar to *M. bealei* but bearing clusters of two flowers during winter and early spring.

Two of the most popular species are:
M. bealei Scented like lily of the valley.
M. aquifolium Holly-leaved, of bronze colour in spring, purple-red in winter and berries that are excellent for making jam.

Olearia
Attractive and easy to grow when on chalky soil in sunny position, these evergreens (often called daisy bushes) have daisy-like flower-heads usually of a whitish colour, and grow between 1–2m (3–6½ ft) high. They flower from early summer to early autumn and are excellent by the seaside. Our choice is *O.* × *haastii*, one of the hardiest forms:

Olearia × *haastii*. Also good by the sea or in industrial areas. Has delightful fragrant flowers and is ideal in a mixed border.

For olearias with pink, lavender or blue flowers, choose forms of *O. stellulata* Splendens.

Pyracantha (firethorn)
True shrubs but frequently trained as climbers up walls and garden supports so that they are very often listed in the climbing plant section of catalogues. They are the most useful of hardy evergreen, berrying shrubs, growing freely in all positions and soils. They can reach a height of about 4·5m (15 ft), though only half this, particularly if the long shoots are kept cut back, is more customary. Firethorns bear masses of hawthorn-like white flowers in early summer, and clusters of berries in autumn that often last through to spring.

We selected a free-fruiting hybrid, *P.* Watereri, which has dense clusters of bright red berries, to grow against the south side of the garden shed. Other fine varieties are the free-branching:

Pyracantha rogersiana	red berries
P.rogersiana Flava	yellow berries
P.atlantioides Aurea	yellow berries
P. Orange Glow	orange-red berries

One of the most popular, *P. coccinea* Lalandei, has rather broader leaves and bears clusters of orange-red berries throughout autumn and winter.

Rhododendron
One of the largest and most varying groups of shrubs and, as mentioned on page 42, these include azaleas. They both need the same type of acid soil and general treatment. Most are evergreen, they can be prostrate, shrubby or tree-like in habit and usually flower from late spring to late summer. Broadly, they can be classified into hardy or pedigree hybrids and species. We wanted a rhododendron in our garden to go between the mahonia and syringa, but were restricted for space. We therefore selected the hardy hybrid Britannia with its glowing crimson flowers for good contrast and its semi-dwarf habit as it grows only to about 1·2m high and spreads to 1·2m (4 ft × 4 ft). Rhododendrons will be illustrated and described in some of the reference volumes recommended at the back.

Above left: Viburnum betulifolium *with berries that last through into winter*
Far left: Lavandula *Nana Munstead, dwarf fragrant lavender, good for hedges*
Left: Viburnum davidii, *low-growing evergreen with bright berries contrasting well with rich-toned branches*
Below, far left: Olearia × scilloniensis, *profusely flowering, evergreen daisy bush*
Below: Viburnum tomentosum, *whose leaves turn plum-colour in autumn*
Above, and below right: *pyracantha (firethorn) in fruit and flower. This evergreen shrub trains well as a climber*

Skimmia
Small evergreen shrubs with aromatic, long, glossy leaves and fragrant flowers in late spring and early summer. If male and female plants are grown together (as these shrubs bear all male or female flowers on separate plants) then you can expect a profusion of coloured berries on the females in the autumn.
Skimmia japonica Most popular and hardy anywhere and in almost any soil. It is available in a variety of forms and the male Rubella (red buds in winter, white flowers in spring) grown alongside the female Foremanii (brilliant red berries in autumn) make an attractive combination.

Viburnum
Large genus of shrubs in evergreen or deciduous form. Most produce white, often sweetly scented, flowers followed by autumn leaf tints and/or coloured berries. They can be grown in almost any position. The plants grow about 1–3m (3–10 ft) high. As they vary so much in their season of attraction, the easiest way to describe them is to divide them into three groups: winter-flowering. spring/early-summer flowering, and autumn colour:

WINTER-FLOWERING
Viburnum tinus (Laurustinus) Highly sought after, has pink-budded white flowers from late autumn to early spring among evergreen dark glossy leaves, and blue-black berries from late summer.

Another good variety is *V. fragrans* with bronze-coloured young leaves, fragrant winter flowers and scarlet berries.

SPRING- AND EARLY SUMMER-FLOWERING
V. tomentosum Very popular with its large clusters of snow-white flowers and pendant green leaves that turn plum-colour in autumn.
V. × *burkwoodii* (evergreen) Large fragrant white flowers opening from pink buds and leaves that are dark shiny green above with brownish-grey 'felt' beneath.

AUTUMN COLOUR
V. betulifolium One of the best of all the berrying shrubs, producing berries in redcurrant-like form after small white flowers in spring.
V. opulus (guelder rose) White flowers in mid summer followed by autumn leaf colour and translucent berries.
V. davidii (low-growing evergreen) If male and female forms are planted together, the female produces exceptional turquoise-blue berries.

Vinca (periwinkle)
Most popular of low-growing glossy, evergreen shrubs for planting as weed-suppressors, in shady or sunny sites, on banks, or any difficult spot where nothing else wants to grow.
Vinca major These forms flower in early summer; *V. m.* Maculata has yellow-blotched leaves and *V. m.* Variegata creamy-white ones that set off the blue blooms to advantage.

V. minor Its forms are smaller versions of *V. major*, flowering in late spring and early summer and intermittently until autumn, in various shades of blue or white and some with variegated leaves.

CHOICE OF VINE CLIMBERS

Climbing plants are ideal for adding an extra dimension to the back of mixed flower borders or for growing naturally up trellis or other supports, to give additional height, or to act as a screen to partition the garden into interesting sections. Here we have chosen various popular vine climbers for our garden in addition to the shrubs that can be grown as climbers which were listed earlier on.

Clematis

Among the most versatile of climbers. As long as the soil is well-drained and the site sunny, but with a shady root area, clematis rarely fail to give endless pleasure. They support themselves with curling leaf stalks and except for pruning need little attention.

Clematis are a large genus and for easy distinction you can divide them into the species and large-flowering groups. Of the species we suggest the following:

Clematis tangutica Mass of yellow flowers in mid summer, followed by silky old man's beard berries (superior form of those seen in hedgerows).

C. montana (white) and *C. m. rubens* (rose-red) have scented flowers which smother the plant in early summer.

If you want an evergreen clematis, two good species are:

C. armandii White.

C. balearica Pale yellow with bronze fern-shaped leaves.

Of the large-flowered group we suggest the following:

Nelly Moser	pale mauve and carmine
Barbara Dibley	bright violet
Comtesse de Bouchaud	rose pink
Gravetye Beauty	cherry red
Lasurstern	lavender blue
Marie Boisselot	white
The President	purple-claret

Right: Clematis montana, *favoured for its scent. Below:* C. patens *Barbara Dibley Bottom:* Jasminum officinale, *common white jasmine, a fragrant semi-evergreen*

Jasminum (jasmine)
Always popular, especially the winter-flowering one *J. nudiflorum.*
Jasminum nudiflorum Bears yellow trumpet-shaped flowers from early winter to late spring on naked green branches. During the remainder of the year it is clothed with small, shiny green leaves.
J. officinale Common white, summer-flowering jasmine that is sweetly scented and opens from pale pink buds; it has many-lobed leaves.
J. × stephanense Another summer-flowering hybrid that requires plenty of space to show off its sometimes variegated leaves and pale pink flowers followed by glossy black berries.

Lonicera (honeysuckle)
Love to ramble over pergolas, arches or old tree trunks and are best given their freedom rather than trained against walls or other supports. Most flower in summer, but some continue blooming until late autumn; they all grow in almost any soil and aspect but, like clematis, prefer to have their roots in the shade. With the exception of *L. japonica* and its forms (which are evergreen), the remainder are all deciduous, though *L.×purpusii* is winter-flowering.

Among the most popular are the early and late blooming Dutch honeysuckles:
Lonicera periclymenum Scented tube flowers of rose-purple and yellow.
L. tellmanniana Produces 5cm (2 in) long trumpet flowers but no perfume.
L. × americana Spectacular hybrid with large trusses of white to yellow, sweetly fragrant flowers.

Polygonum (Russian vine)
Sometimes known as mile-a-minute vine, this rampant climber grows rapidly in any position and will completely smother a wall or building in one year. The most commonly grown is:
Polygonum baldschuanicum Often confused with *aubertii*, its pale heart-shaped leaves and froth of creamy-pink flowers make a wonderful sight each year from late summer to late autumn.

Rosa (climbing rose)
We described our choice for covering the trellis and pergolas and illustrated some popular varieties on page 30.

Above right: Vinca major *Elegantissima (periwinkle) a good weed-suppressor*
Left: Jasminum nudiflorum, *Chinese winter jasmine, even blooms well in hard winters*
Right: Lonicera sempervirens *(honeysuckle), is better as a rambler than trained climber*

BULBS IN YOUR GARDEN

GENERAL WORK

Late spring (April)

If weather conditions are favourable and the soil is dry enough to work without it sticking to the rake or your boots, make the first outdoor sowings of hardy annual seeds (as described on page 18). Thoroughly prepare the ground for chrysanthemums, add a general fertilizer, such as Growmore, and set the plants in position within two weeks.

Finish planting bare-rooted trees, shrubs and hardy herbaceous plants. Container-grown types can be planted at any time of year provided conditions are suitable and the plants are regularly watered.

Pot-grown clematis can be planted now. The soil level from the pot should be set 2–5cm (1–2 in) below ground level and the roots firmly pressed down. Prune the new plants back to about 30cm (12 in).

Carefully tie in to their supports new shoots of shrubs trained as climbers or those climbers that need assistance. Keep an eye open for greenfly and blackfly and spray as soon as they appear with malathion or a systemic insecticide.

Now is the time to start planning your bulb display for next year. Bulbs in friends' gardens and in public display are still in full bloom and, seeing them in the open air and in natural surroundings (rather than the isolation of the bulb-grower's catalogue), you can more easily decide upon the varieties and colours that you would like to have.

It is at the far end of our Flower Garden that we have decided to make a special feature of bulbs, where they can be seen at their best during spring from the upper windows of the house. The word 'bulb' is, of course, used here rather loosely, as the term is intended to cover also corms and tubers.

The function of the bulb itself (or corm, or tuber) is to be a form of food storage, to help the plants survive not only the long cold winter, but also the hot dry summer that is common in the parts of the world where these plants grow wild. Most bulbs are found naturally in mountainous regions, where they are covered with snow for much of the winter. Directly the snow melts the leaves and flowers appear; and during this period, although they get plenty of water, the soil in which they grow drains quickly.

There are, of course, exceptions to this. The various members of the narcissus family often grow in alpine water meadows, and there are one or two bulbs that have no objection to quite marshy conditions, such as the spring and summer snowflake, *Leucojum vernum* and *L. aestivum* and the big summer-flowering Peruvian squill (*Scilla peruviana*).

Where to plant

Generally, however, it is safe to assume that bulbs do best where the soil is reasonably light and well-drained. In practice, they will thrive in most gardens. And since bulbs will have made most, if not all, of their growth by early summer (mid May), they will be perfectly happy under deciduous trees and shrubs, where they can get enough light for their growth before the leaves have developed too much. They should not be planted beneath evergreens, however, as they will not get enough light to produce food to store for the coming year.

How to plant

There are a lot of old gardeners' tales about the correct planting depth for bulbs: one of the favourites is that the top of the bulb should be the same distance from the surface as the length of the bulb. But in the wild, bulbs are almost always considerably deeper than this, and you can safely say that the tops of small bulbs should be at least 10cm (4 in) below the surface, while larger bulbs should be 15cm (6 in) below. If they are less deep there is always a risk that hoeing or some other operation will bring them to the surface. Small bulbs can be planted close together, say 5–8cm (2–3 in) apart, but the larger ones should have 15–20cm (6–8 in) between them.

Most spring bulbs should be put in the ground as soon after early autumn (August) as you can obtain them, and they will start making roots within a month. Narcissus, in fact, are scarcely ever without roots and must inevitably receive a slight check if they have been lifted and dried off, although it may be barely noticeable.

The main exception to this generalization is the tulips, which can well be left until early winter (November) before planting.

Soil or sand?

If your soil is very damp and heavy there is probably some advantage in planting your bulbs on a layer of sharp sand, which drains fast and will prevent water from lodging immediately around the basal plate of the bulb, the part most susceptible to fungus rot. This makes con-

Above: the scented Iris reticulata *Harmony has prominent gold markings*
Left: Galanthus miralis *(snowdrops), one of the earliest flowers of the year*
Below: crocus, easy-to-grow and free-flowering for several years; this genus likes a light rich soil and can be grown in sun or shade, in beds, borders or lawns

siderably more work: it is fine if you are only planting 10 or 12 bulbs, but quite another matter if you are planting hundreds. Nevertheless, it is certainly worth doing with expensive bulbs.

It is of even greater importance to make sure that the base of the bulb is in contact with the soil (or the sand). With rather large bulbs it is only too easy to take out a trowel full of soil and put your bulb in so that it lodges halfway down the hole with its base suspended in air. When the roots emerge they are unable to find any nourishment, and they may well perish. There is enough nourishment stored in the bulb to produce leaves and possibly even a flower, but the bulb cannot renew itself and will eventually die. Seeing that plants get off to a good start is one of the main secrets of success in gardening.

Dividing the clumps

If your bulbs are doing well they will, in the course of five or six years, form clumps. These will eventually get so crowded that flower production suffers. When this happens you must lift the clumps and divide them up. The best time to do this is in the early summer, when you see the leaves just starting to yellow. The bulbs should be good and plump by then and the new corms should have been formed. Some bulbs, most notably snowdrops, never seem to become overcrowded and there is no need to lift and divide them unless you wish to increase the area of these bulbs. To help you plan your 'calendar of bulbs' for the early spring we suggest a selection of winter aconite, snowdrops, iris, crocus, narcissus and tulips.

Winter aconite

The first to appear is usually the winter aconite *Eranthis hyemalis*. This has a tuber from which springs a little ruff of leaves, in the centre of which is a yellow flower not unlike a buttercup. The plant grows wild in woodland and does best in a shady position. If it is happy it spreads quite extensively and will also seed itself, but it is not happy everywhere. It seems to like the sort of woodland soil that has plenty of leaf mould and if you have either a very sandy or a very clayey soil you may well find that it does not persist for more than two or three years. *E.* × *tubergenii* is a hybrid between the ordinary winter aconite and the larger species from western Asia, *E. cilicica.* It has larger flowers which, however, never set seed, and is somewhat more expensive.

Snowdrop

After the winter aconite come the snowdrops. There are many species of these, all looking rather similar and chiefly distinguished by the way their leaves emerge from the ground. The one most widely grown is *Galanthus nivalis*, that is available with either single or double flowers. We are always told that snowdrops should be moved when they are still in active growth. This is fine if you are moving them from one bed to another, or if you can get some from your friends, but firms only sell the dried-off bulbs and when you are buying new snowdrops you will have to make do with these. They seem to grow adequately, although the display the first spring after planting may not be quite as good as you would expect. However, do not lose heart, it will almost certainly be much more satisfactory the following year.

Among other species, *Galanthus elwesii* is supposed to be a much larger-flowered snowdrop, but the large flowers are seldom maintained for long in cultivation and after a few years you can only distinguish *G. elwesii* from the ordinary snowdrop by its broad glaucous leaves. If you can obtain *G. caucasicus*, particularly in its double form, you will find that it flowers earlier than *G. nivalis*, usually in late winter (January), and has the added advantage of increasing faster.

Iris

We come now to the dwarf bulbous iris, of which three are worth having. The most spectacular is *Iris histrioides* Major. This produces blue flowers up to 10cm (4 in) across, which usually open in late winter (mid January) and, although they look very exotic, are completely unmoved by the worst that the winter can unleash. They are often frozen and covered with snow without showing any ill effects. They are not, alas, cheap, but they persist and increase, although not very rapidly.

Then there is the charming little yellow *I. danfordiae*. In most gardens, after flowering, it splits up into several smaller bulbs which take a long time to flower again, so frequently they have to be replaced each year. It is said that if the bulbs are planted very deeply, at least 23cm (9 in), they are less liable to split up.

The commonest of the early iris is *I. reticulata*, which flowers usually in early spring (February). It has rather narrow violet flowers (although purple or blue in some forms) with an exquisite violet scent. Provided they have well-drained soil all these bulbous iris are very easy to grow. An infection to be watched out for is the dreaded fungus disease known as ink-spot, which causes the bulbs to rot. There is no simple cure for this, if indeed there is any. It has been suggested that if the bulbs are lifted, dried off completely and then soaked for two hours in a very weak solution of formaldehyde (one part in 300), they can be protected, but this only applies to healthy bulbs, not to infected ones.

Crocus

Perhaps of all the spring bulbs the crocus is the favourite, and here we have an enormous choice. For many of us the first sign of spring is the Dutch yellow crocus. This is a sterile form of the eastern Mediterranean *Crocus aureus*, which has been known in gardens for nearly 300 years. Since it never sets seed it increases rapidly by producing extra corms, and soon makes large clumps. The true *C. aureus* flowers slightly earlier and has rather richer coloured flowers, as well as increasing by seed.

However, if you want a crocus that increases by seed the best is *C. tomasinianus*, a very slender plant with grassy leaves and a thin flower, which is nearly invisible until the sun opens the lavender petals. There are also some darker purple varieties, such as Taplow Ruby, Barr's Purple and Whitewell Purple. *C. tomasinianus* increases at a prodigious rate, both from extra corms and from self-sown seedlings, which may flower the second year after germinating. Very similar, but with a larger flower, is *C. dalmaticus*.

C. chrysanthus has a large number of forms, all characterized by bunches of rather globular flowers, mainly in varying shades of yellow, but including some very good blues, which unfortunately are usually very slow to increase, while the yellow and cream forms are vigorous.

The Cloth of Gold crocus, *C. susianus*, is prodigal with its rather small yellow flowers which have dark brown stripes on their outside. A very attractive crocus is *C. etruscus*, that is usually only obtainable in the form known as Zwanenburg and that flowers in early spring (late February). The flowers are quite large and a very fine shade of lavender-mauve. Another very popular crocus is the deep mauve *C. sieberi*. Finally there are the huge Dutch hybrids, that flower in mid spring (March) but some people find rather gross. Best of these is the showy silver-lavender Vanguard.

Narcissus

Daffodils (with a trumpet centre) and narcissus (with flatter, cup centre) all belong to the genus *Narcissus* and they all like ample water when they are growing. They are exquisite in flower, but they have very long leaves, which persist until mid summer (June) and tend to look unsightly. They are probably best placed between shrubs, where their leaves will not be so noticeable. Whatever you do, do not cut the leaves off or plait them into dainty bundles, as that will wreck your chances of good flowers in the next season. You must just make up your mind that when you grow narcissus, you must put up with these disadvantages.

Above: Blue Parrot, another variety of tulip, characterized by fringed petals
Far left, above and below: two daffodil varieties – Penrose and White Lion
Left: Apeldoorn, a Darwin hybrid type of tulip that is good for display

Tulip

Most tulips come rather late, but the water-lily tulip, *Tulipa kaufmanniana*, is usually in flower by mid to late spring (March–April) thus linking early and late spring displays. Many tulips tend to deteriorate after a year or so, but *kaufmanniana* is fairly reliable, although rather slow to increase. The wild plant has a flower that is long and pointed, cream outside, with a broad crimson stripe down each petal, and ivory inside. The flower opens nearly flat in sunlight. It has now been hybridized, producing blooms in deep yellow, pinks and even scarlets.

HERBACEOUS PLANTS

in the flower garden

Our gardens would look rather sad places without the herbaceous plants that flower, most particularly in the late summer (from mid July onwards), when there are few flowering shrubs left and we must depend on perennials and roses for colour in the garden.

All annuals and biennials are strictly speaking herbaceous – all the word means is that the stems are of only annual duration and die down each autumn, so that in that sense even bulbs are herbaceous – but the term is usually used of herbaceous perennials. Perennials are plants that go on growing for many seasons, increasing in dimensions as they do so. They are normally planted either in the autumn or in the early spring, although there are one or two exceptions.

When to plant

Ideally autumn is the best time to plant, if you do so early enough. This enables the plants to root into the fresh soil before winter comes, so that they will be in a good condition to grow away as soon as the days lengthen and the air warms up. Plants that are transplanted in the spring have to start to grow away at once, so that if the spring is exceptionally cold or exceptionally dry their initial growth can be checked quite considerably. However there are one or two plants which seem to make very little growth after being transplanted in the autumn, with the result that they often die during the first winter and for these spring planting is obviously better. The most well-known of these is that large scabious, *Scabiosa caucasica*, one of the best herbaceous plants to grow for cutting.

When to transplant

There are a number of plants that really loathe any root disturbance, either because they have long tap roots, which may cause the death of the plant if they are damaged, or for less recognizable reasons. There seems no obvious reason why hellebores should dislike being moved, but they certainly do and may sulk for a year or so after they are transplanted. We find the same thing with paeonies, but this may be because they have such a vast amount of tubers underground that it is almost impossible

to move a good-sized plant without seriously damaging the root system. Plants with long tap roots, such as lupins or oriental poppies, should only be moved as young plants and once planted should be left.

In any case it is always best to start off with small plants, whether they be seedlings or divisions from other plants. Such plants usually arrive with their roots more or less undamaged and soon grow on to make vigorous specimens.

Caring for herbaceous plants

You can find herbaceous plants to fit any soil or situation, but the majority will be perfectly happy in a soil that is reasonably deep and not inclined to water-logging. Most like full sunlight, although it is possible to grow bog plants and shade-lovers where conditions allow.

After a time some herbaceous plants may become very large, in which case they should be lifted and divided up. Some plants get their roots so interlocked that it is by no means easy to divide them; the answer is to get two garden forks and insert them back to back in the clump and then lever them apart. The centre of the clump is probably impoverished, due to the fact that it will have exhausted the soil where it was originally planted; also the centre tends to get overgrown by the stronger outside parts which are in fresh soil; so when clumps are split up the centre is usually discarded and the plantlets on the outside are preserved.

There are many hundreds of herbaceous perennials to choose from, so for our Flower Garden we have selected a number of plants which are easy to grow and which will establish themselves in the border quickly.

Hellebore

Helleborus niger (the Christmas rose) is the earliest-flowering of our selection. It grows on the edge of woodlands in the wild, so a position giving dappled shade is ideal. Almost all the hellebores are somewhat greedy plants, so the soil cannot be too rich. The white flowers will emerge from the ground at any time from early winter to early spring (November–February) and the new leaves start to emerge at the same time. Later the leaves are going to be quite large, so a position among or just in front of shrubs should prove very suitable. Some Christmas roses have the unfortunate habit of producing only very short stems, so that the flowers easily become splashed with mud in bad weather. If you are ordering plants by mail there is not much you can do about this; but if you go to a nursery, pick out the long-stemmed plants.

Otherwise you might prefer to grow one of the hybrids of *H. orientalis* (the Lenten rose). These all have long-stemmed flowers, which usually do not open before early spring (February). There are a few whites among them, but most are some shade of pink or greenish-pink, while a few are a very deep maroon. They require the same treatment as the Christmas rose, but have very much larger leaves, which take up a lot of room later in the season. There are also a number of hellebores with green flowers.

Hellebores may be transplanted in the autumn (September), and the earlier the

better. The old leaves of the Lenten rose often persist while the flowers are opening, but the plants seem to come to no harm if you cut these off before the flowers open: the leaves begin to look rather tattered by that time. This is not a problem with the Christmas rose.

Alyssum

Our next plant is *Alyssum saxatile*, which flowers in late spring (April). Strictly speaking it is not herbaceous at all, but a small shrub, which carries its grey leaves throughout the winter and makes the border interesting during the dreary season. In the spring it covers itself with golden, sweet-smelling flowers. It likes full sun and has no objection to rather poor soil. After about four years it gets somewhat leggy, but it is very easily propagated by cuttings or by seed.

Senecio cineraria

The grey-leaved cineraria (which you might otherwise know as *Cineraria maritima*) is a good example of the sort of

Top: Helleborus niger, *the Christmas rose*
Above: double dianthus. Pink Diane
Above left: delicate Scabiosa caucasica *is best planted in the spring*
Left: the leaves of Alyssum saxatile *give winter interest, the flowers appear in late spring. Right:* Hosta albo-marginata, *the plantain lily, thrives in shade*

plants that are grown for their foliage colour rather than for their flowers. Such plants are very valuable since they remain attractive for more than six months; this is more than can be said for most flowering plants, which seldom carry their flowers longer than three weeks and often considerably less. The grey (or, in the variety White Diamond, the silvery-white) leaves are very attractive, and they gain much of their appeal from their contrast with more usual green leaves. Don't try to overdo this effect, because unfortunately the cineraria bears rather crude yellow daisy-like flowers which are not very appealing.

Most grey or silver-leaved plants will not survive in soils that retain too much wet and our grey cineraria is also liable to perish during particularly severe winters. Fortunately cuttings root very easily, so it is always a good idea to root a few in late summer (July) and keep them in pots under cover during the winter, in case disaster strikes. In any case, the plants become rather gaunt after a few years and are best replaced.

Hosta
Another plant with unusual foliage but also with quite attractive lily-like flowers, is the plantain lily, a species of hosta (sometimes known as funkia). This vanishes completely during the winter and the new shoots can often be wrecked by slugs, so it is as well to mark their positions and put down bait in late spring (April) when young leaves are emerging.

The leaves vary in size and in colour and some are variegated with ivory, but they are all handsome plants, which get more effective as they get larger. There is really no need to split up their clumps at any time, as they can go on getting larger and larger without any ill effects. In summer (June–July) they send up spikes of lily-like flowers, usually about 5cm (2 in) long, trumpet-shaped and white or mauve in colour. These plants thrive in dense or partial shade.

Dianthus (pinks)
These plants also have pretty grey leaves, but they are grown mainly for the sake of their small, fragrant, carnation-like flowers. They prefer a limey soil and, if you have the sort of soil that will grow rhododendrons, you will probably have to add some lime before you plant your dianthus. These again are evergreen and look interesting during the winter, but they very soon become gaunt and need frequent replacing. This is done by means of cuttings, usually known as pipings, which are ready in late summer or early autumn (July and August).

Above: peach-leafed Campanula persicifolia *Telham Beauty is easy to grow*

Dianthus are not particularly showy flowers, but their heady scent makes them worth all the trouble. They look attractive massed together or along the front of a border. The flowers are usually white, pink or crimson, and popular varieties are Mrs Simkins, Red Clove, and the newer Imperial Pink.

Campanula
Two species of these nice trouble-free plants are generally grown in borders. One is the peach-leafed *Campanula persicifolia*, which grows about 45cm (18 in) high and has flat blue or white flowers in mid summer (June). These are only slightly bell-shaped and reach about 5cm (2 in) across. The other is the tall *C. lactiflora*, which can grow to 1·2m (4 ft) and has a huge head of small mauve, rather spidery flowers in late summer

(July). Although the individual flowers are only about 2–3cm (1 in) across, they are borne in large numbers and a plant in full flower is a wonderful sight. There are shorter forms of *C. lactiflora* and also some pinky-purple ones.

Agapanthus (African lily)
An attractive plant flowering in late summer (July and August). The plants to obtain are called Headbourne hybrids and are all hardy, whereas the larger *A. africanus* generally requires wintering under cover. The Headbourne hybrids have quite small strap-shaped green leaves, but throw up stems to 75cm (2½ ft), bearing at their tops heads of blue trumpet-shaped, lily-like flowers about 5cm (2 in) long. They like as warm a position as you can give them and full sunlight, but they are very tolerant about soil, so long as it is not waterlogged.

Chrysanthemum
For late autumn (October) we have chrysanthemums. The cut flower types, *C. maximum*, are not the most beautiful plants and are best raised each year from cuttings, but the Korean chrysanthemums are excellent for the border. These bear daisy-like flowers in the greatest profusion, usually some shade of red in colour, and are completely trouble-free. The little pompon chrysanthemums add needed colour in autumn (early October) and are now available in various pastel shades which are preferable to the rather dull colours which they used to be. The ordinary chrysanthemum can be grown as a border plant, if the flowers are not disbudded, but it is less attractive than either the Korean or the pompon types.

Japanese anemone (wind flower)
The Japanese anemone, in pinky-purple or in white, is a marvellous plant, being completely trouble-free and increasing with ease, and always flowering well in mid to late autumn (September–October). It does not really like being moved, so it is best left undisturbed as long as possible.

Pyrethrum
Botanically derived from *Chrysanthemum roseum*, these are invaluable for their single white, pink or carmine daisy-like flowers on long stems in early and mid summer (May–June). They like a sunny position and deep well-drained soil.

Lupins
Excellent companions for the pyrethrums are *Lupinus* (lupins) which like the same conditions and produce their spires of pea-like flowers above decorative leaves about the same time. They are available in a wide range of colours of white, pink, yellow, red and lavender-blue, and are often bi-coloured. The Russell hybrids are a good strain but there are many varieties from which to choose. If you remove the old flower-heads as they fade, you will encourage a second season of blooming.

Top: pompon chrysanthemum London Gazette, give welcome autumn colour
Above: mixed lupins, including Harlequins, give a good massed colour effect

Oriental poppy
A third perennial to plant with the two foregoing is *Papaver orientalis* (the Oriental poppy), which also likes the sun and flowers at about the same time. It is available in pink, white, scarlet or crimson flower shades. Incidentally, it likes water if there is a drought period immediately prior to its flowering season in early to mid summer (May–June).

Thyme
This, the first of our two dwarf plants, is the creeping *Thymus serphyllum*, which makes a mat of aromatic foliage covered with crimson or purple flowers in mid summer (late June). These are also fragrant. Thyme spreads rapidly and the plants should be at least 30cm (12 in) apart to avoid congestion.

Sempervivum (houseleek)
Looking like a little cactus with rosettes of fleshy leaves, which are often attractively coloured, this dwarf plant has rather odd looking daisy-like pink flowers on 10cm (4 in) stems. The houseleek produces numerous offshoots each year, so do not place new plants too closely together. The cobweb houseleek has its leaves covered with cobwebby grey hair.

Above: pyrethrum chrysanthemum with daisy-like flowers in early and mid summer

Nepeta (catmint)
A spreading plant, catmint has feathery masses of small, grey-green fragrant leaves, with lavender-coloured feathery flower spikes in summer and autumn (June–September).

These last three plants like rather gravelly soil and it is worthwhile incorporating some gravel if the soil is rather slow-draining.

THE EDIBLE GARDEN

THE EDIBLE GARDEN

In this section of the book we put the case for 'growing your own'. Some people don't see the point of growing vegetables as it's so convenient to buy from the shop around the corner. Why bother to grow your own when it is all there on the shelves for the little effort it takes to put your hand in your purse?

Growing vegetables is worthwhile, not only for reasons of economy, but for many other reasons, too. Let's take economy first. All you need in order to produce 'good stuff' as we gardeners call it, is fertile soil, seed, a few trees and bushes and a little know-how. To make your soil fertile is a matter of adding the right things to it, the cost of seeds, bushes and fruit trees is not so prohibitive, and we will provide the know-how in this book. The cost of your home-grown vegetables and fruit could be a fraction of what you pay in the shops.

Perhaps even more important is the point that only by growing your own can you enjoy the unique, superb flavour of fresh produce compared with the bought variety. Remember that when a vegetable is cut, picked or uprooted it has literally been killed and the longer it remains around between supplier and shop before you buy it, the more impaired is its flavour and goodness. This applies particularly to leafy vegetables such as cabbages, lettuces and sprouting broccoli and rhubarb.

With your own edible garden you have control over how things are grown and, most important, you can decide for yourself whether they are to be treated with chemical pesticides or with pest deterrents which are of organic or natural origin and probably safer to use. You can also pick your vegetables or fruits just before you need them.

You are free to select which variety of a particular vegetable you would like to grow to suit your personal preferences. All too often the varieties grown commercially are chosen for their cropping abilities (that is, the weight-per-plant produced) and their grading and packing qualities, rather than for their flavour. A certain variety of, say, tomato – that fruit

1

2

3

A selection from the many fruits, vegetables and herbs that you will be harvesting, young and fresh, from your garden while following our programme.
1 *raspberries;* **2** *chives in flower;* **3** *runner beans;* **4** *carrots;* **5** *onions;* **6** *capsicum (peppers);* **7** *courgettes*

generally referred to as a vegetable – may be widely grown by market gardeners because it crops heavily and consistently and bears fruit of a good and even shape. If you have eaten no other tomato you accept that its flavour is adequate. But once you start to grow your own varieties, you soon realize that what you previously considered acceptable may be only second best.

You will soon find that growing for the table is enormously therapeutic. Digging the soil on a cold winter's day is both bracing and physically relaxing—once a natural rhythm has been established. The gleaming clods of freshly-turned earth seem to beckon spring, by which time a few sharp frosts will have crumbled them to a workable 'tilth'—the gardener's term for the depth of soil affected by cultivation. Then, when the sun begins to warm through to the shirt on your back it is time to set seed to soil.

Each seed planted brings visions of the best-ever crops that will emerge from the virgin soil. Up come the seedlings, to be thinned, weeded, cajoled and cared for until the produce, fresh and full of flavour, is proudly presented to the pot! It is all immensely satisfying and fulfils the inherent urge to provide for your family—reasons enough why everyone should acquire a vegetable patch, or 'edible garden' as we call it.

4

5

6

7

There's no reason why outdoor space planned for the cultivation of food should not be decorative to the eye as well as productive for the kitchen. Following similar principles to the Flower Garden, our Edible Garden (shown on the following pages) sets new horizons for the gardener with food for the table in mind.

We chose the term 'edible' rather than 'vegetable' for this garden because it includes fruit and herbs as well as vegetables and our design is a far cry from the old-fashioned kitchen garden with its straight path down the middle of the growing area leading from back door to greenhouse. There is nothing wrong with the traditional plan; it is utilitarian and fully functional, but it is hardly attractive.

Basic ground plan

Why not have something different? Our ground plan (overleaf) shows how to get away from the 'straight-back-and-sides' formula to a far more interesting layout, where you can introduce all kinds and permutations of features that will bring colour and variety to the scene, and maintain a reasonable balance between the aspects of leisure, pleasure and the growing of edible plants.

Like everything else, a garden needs pre-planning if it is to provide for all the family requirements. To start with, our path breaks away from the straight line, curving its way to the end of the garden. Purists may criticize it on the grounds that it will take longer for you to travel its length, but who minds spending a few seconds longer on the journey when there is so much more to catch the eye *en route*?

Patio for outdoor living

Immediately outside the back door is a paved patio area with a shoe-scraper pointedly positioned by the doorstep. This should be enough to prevent the thoughtless gardener—or visitor—from bringing the garden into the house on the soles of his shoes. The patio is easily kept clean and provides an area for sitting out and enjoying alfresco meals when the weather invites outdoor living. Nor is it necessary for the patio to be entirely unproductive, as boxes and tubs can be arranged around it in which you can grow a variety of herbs and even fruit, if you wish, such as strawberries.

Green-belted plot

Beyond the patio is the 'food plot', the main growing area, encircled by the grass path. We chose grass because it is pleasant to look at, easily maintained by occasional mowing and springy to walk on. If you prefer, you could extend the paving stones to run all around the plot. This path is wide enough to allow ample room for pushing the wheelbarrow along or taking any other loads that may need conveying from one place to another.

The food plot itself is irregularly-shaped but the variable lengths of the rows at the top (west) end present no problems, and having a path all around makes it easy to weed and tend the various crops. You never have to walk the full length of the rows with the attendant danger of trampling on growing plants.

A pergola for climbing beans

On the north, or right-hand, side of the plot we have included a pergola to relieve an otherwise flat area. It is an interesting and pleasant feature in its own right and it can be used to support a variety of climbing plants. A rose or two would clothe it with perfumed colour all summer long, while a clematis would ramble happily all over it. But you can't eat roses or clematis, so plant runner beans at its base instead. The vines (stems) will grow up the supports, they will look pretty in flower and when the pods are ready you can gather them by the fistful on your way back from trips to the greenhouse or compost heap.

Border space for extras

The pergola pathway is quite wide so you could include a narrow border bed against the wall which is an ideal spot for a seedbed. Or you could plant extra clumps of radish, or even a bank of rhubarb—that space-consuming and permanent resident of its allotted area. Planting rhubarb in this narrow border would solve both problems nicely, for it won't be able to encroach on other crops and, except when you need a few sticks for the pie, a rhubarb fool or a jam-making session, you could forget about it.

Beds for fruit and herbs

Beyond the plot is a sweep of currant bushes, giving a planting of four blackcurrants and one redcurrant. In front of the bushes lies a narrow border, which you can edge with low-growing herbs like parsley, chives, thyme and marjoram.

Behind the currants, by the left-hand (south) boundary fence, stands a standard apple tree next to a bed of soft fruits which includes strawberries and raspberries. This bed is protected by a cage to keep off the birds. The cage need not be an elaborate or permanent structure. Four corner poles with additional supports between them and nylon mesh netting stretched over the whole will prevent the most persistent birds from stealing the fruit. If you feel so inclined, you could make this structure more decorative.

Espalier-trained fruit trees

You will notice that we have tried to make full use of every bit of available space. Even the boundary walls support their quota of plants. Espalier-trained pear and peach trees need little space yet reward the gardener with abundant fruit. All they ask in return is timely pruning and adequate feeding.

Greenhouses and garden frames

There is always the question of whether or not to invest in a greenhouse. Even a modest structure is an expensive item, but a properly-managed and fully-productive greenhouse will pay for itself in two or three years. In it you can grow upwards of 25kg (50lb) of tomatoes every year, a cucumber plant, winter lettuce, pot plants and a host of other good things.

If you have a greenhouse, you can garden all the year round, come rain, snow or shine. All owners, no matter what the size of their greenhouse, yearn

This unusual design for our colourful Edible Garden is enough to tempt any gardener from a beginner to an experienced enthusiast. It is quite easy to carry the plan through with the help of our instructions

for something still bigger. Once you've got one it opens up an entirely new world of gardening. You begin with easy things, progress to the more ambitious, and end up growing exotic specimens and proudly showing them off to your envious neighbours. The best attitude is to think big, buy big and grow plenty.

Key to the ground plan (below) identifies the various features included in our Edible Garden, which takes up an area of 22 by 7·5 metres (72 by 25 feet)

Key to ground plan

1 cooking apple **2** compost
3 espaliered pear tree **4** paved area
5 Kentish cob **6** greenhouse
7 espaliered peach tree **8** nasturtium
9 paving stones set in grass
10 runner beans climbing on pergola
11 herb rock garden **12** tub **13** terrace
14 bay tree **15** hanging basket
16 grass **17** damson **18** food plot
19 water tap (hidden) **20** eating apple
21 herbs **22** seed bed
23 rosemary bush **24** garden seat
25 currant bushes
26 raspberries and strawberries
27 fruit cage

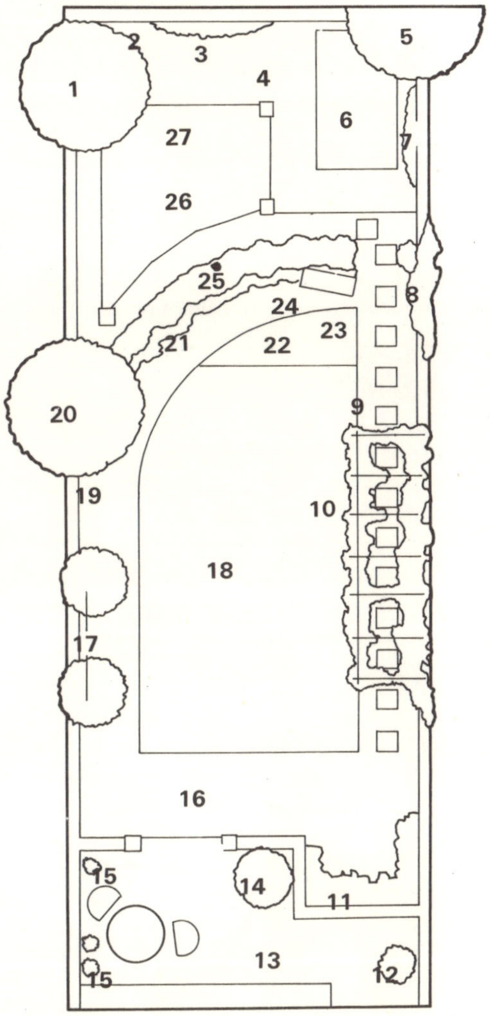

Once you have a greenhouse, then a garden frame is almost a must. If you haven't got one, you won't have anywhere to harden off (adapt from hot to cool conditions) the tender plants raised in the all-embracing warmth of the greenhouse before you plant them out. In fact it may be a good idea to *start* with the garden frame. If your funds won't yet run to a greenhouse, then you should build your own frame or buy one ready-made. At the very least you will be able to start seeds off in it weeks before you could do so outdoors, and in the summer it will come in handy for growing less hardy crops, such as ridge cucumbers, melons or courgettes.

Statutory compost heap

The remaining area is to a degree flexible. The only thing it must have is a compost heap. These are often thought of as obnoxious mounds that attract flies and offend the neighbours. Properly tended compost heaps do neither and we will be advising you on how to go about maintaining one. They are the natural way to dispose of garden and kitchen waste whilst at the same time producing high-grade soil-conditioning and feeding material at little or no cost.

The average family and garden create a large amount of organic waste which will provide virtually free, natural plant food. So a compost heap you must have.

Optional play area

From now on your choice is determined by family and finance. If you have small children it would be in the common interest to provide them with a sandpit and a portable paddling pool. They love sand and water and as soon as they come to realize that a specific area, however small, is exclusively theirs, it will be much easier to discourage them from jumping up and down on your prized vegetables.

Getting it all together

So this is what our new-style Edible Garden is all about. It is a pleasure to look at, and in return for a reasonable amount of attention it will do much to keep your plates filled and your appetites satisfied from one year's end to the next.

This introduction sets the scene for you, explaining how the various elements of our Edible Garden fit together. As the weeks go by, we will be trying to give you all the help and advice we can as we take you through the various stages from planning to end-product in greater detail. And our useful weekly instructions will help to keep you on the path to successful growing . . . and good eating.

The new cucumber variety called Pepinex is recommended because it needs very little attention

GROWING UNDER GLASS
in the edible garden

We will now start you off in early spring growing tomatoes and cucumbers in the propagator, and tending the greenhouse vine. As the weeks go by we will be advising you on the continuing care of your growing plants.
To have a greenhouse widens the horizons of any fruit and vegetable gardening enthusiast. You can enjoy your garden all year round and keep the kitchen supplied at the same time.

Most greenhouse owners find that having their greenhouse heated just enough to provide full frost protection – with a few degrees spare to be on the safe side – is quite sufficient. This will be ample for growing tomatoes, cucumbers, peppers and aubergines under glass, as well as providing pot plants for the house. In other words, you need sufficient heating to keep out frost, plus enough extra capacity to get seeds germinating and plants growing early in the year.

The Edible Garden greenhouse is just such a 'cool' greenhouse. From mid autumn to mid winter (September to December) it needs frost protection and nothing more. But after that the situation changes. The keen gardener will want to sow seeds of onions, tomatoes and other early crops, and they need a constant minimum temperature of 10–13°C (50–55°F). So you have a problem. In theory your heating equipment must be capable of giving this temperature range, yet it is required only for two or three months of the year. This means that from late winter to mid spring (January to March) you will be spending precious money just to germinate seeds and keep them growing steadily.

The way round this costly problem is to use a small propagator for sowing seeds that need a high temperature in order to germinate. Keep it in a convenient place in your home and you need not wire the greenhouse for electricity.

Heating by paraffin
You will need a heating appliance in the greenhouse that is capable of maintaining a constant minimum temperature of 7°C (45°F). Bearing the need for economy in mind, but without wishing to sacrifice earliness or quality, a paraffin heater will be perfectly satisfactory. The heater itself is comparatively inexpensive; it requires no fitting or wiring and, compared with other fuels, paraffin running costs are fairly low. Admittedly most models have no thermostatic controls, but it is no trouble to turn the smokeless flame up or down as the occasion (or the weather) demands. The most important point is that the maximum heat output should be sufficient to give the necessary minimum temperature for the cubic capacity of your greenhouse when outside temperatures are several degrees below freezing.

You will find that one paraffin lamp provides adequate light to work by in the greenhouse, during those dark evenings before the onset of summer.

Choice of staging
In this greenhouse the staging runs down the right-hand (north) side, leaving a soil bed area opposite for growing tomatoes, cucumbers and other plants. The staging is vitally important. If it is properly constructed it can affect the quality of

A SIMPLE PROPAGATOR
There are several different kinds of propagator on the market, some heated some not. The heated ones are inexpensive to run, and they do give you the opportunity of starting your sowings really early. The one we use will give you years of faithful service. It consists of a plastic trough into which protrudes a brass lamp-holder, fitted with an earthing terminal and a 25W lamp bulb. A standard seed tray fits neatly on the top and the whole thing is covered with a polythene shroud.

To operate it is simplicity itself. A couple of centimetres (1 in) of water provides humidity for eight or so cube-shaped peat pots of seed compost in the seed tray. Into each pot sow the chosen seeds, water them, put the 'shroud' in position and switch on. The 25W lamp generates enough heat under the shroud for the seeds to germinate, maintaining an even temperature of around 15°C (60°F) for a minimal daily running cost. For starting off tomatoes and cucumbers in a propagator before transplanting them to the greenhouse.

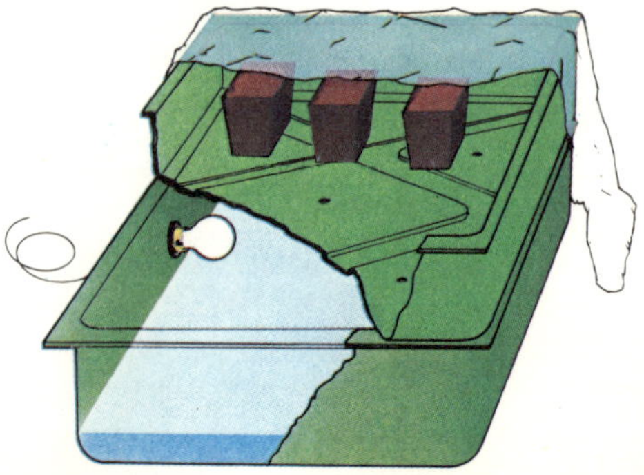

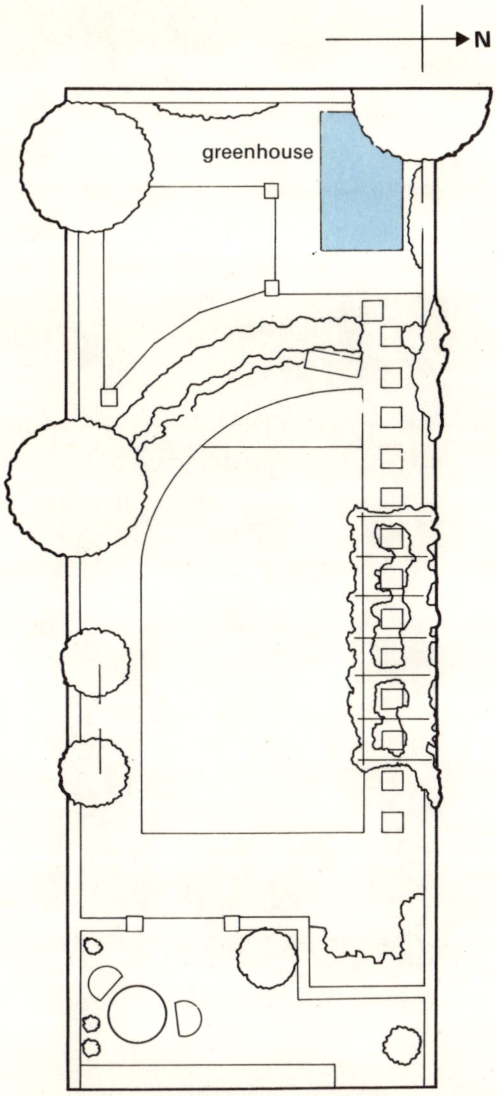

your plants to advantage and save you a lot of time and trouble.

Here the staging is made up from sheets of corrugated iron, supported by stout stakes driven into the ground and covered with a 5cm (2 in) layer of sphagnum peat, kept in place by turning up the side-edges of the corrugated iron by an equivalent amount. (Asbestos sheeting would do as well as corrugated iron – or any other material that would hold the basal aggregate in place.) This form of unbroken staging does not go right up to the glass; a space 2.5 cm (1 in) wide allows warm air to rise and circulate.

This staging may not look very smart but the plants will love it. If the peat is kept constantly moist, the plant roots grow right down into it. They also appreciate the moist, warm air that rises from the peat and circulates up, through and around their leaves. And as long as you keep the peat moist, you will have far less pot-watering to do.

A concrete path

Although not essential, a path will prevent you slithering about on hard, slimy soil and it creates a hygienic division between the greenhouse bed and its surroundings. Concrete makes the easiest and cleanest path.

Air in the greenhouse

All greenhouses have to be ventilated. Correct ventilation spells the difference between success and failure, as plants can suffer just as much from overheating as from intense cold.

The greenhouse here is fitted with automatic vent-openers that cost nothing to operate. They work on the fundamental principle that metals and liquids expand and contract in direct relation to temperature. The higher the temperature inside the wider the vents open, and within limits you can adjust them to close fully at whatever temperature you prefer. It makes life very easy as you don't have to dash out to open or close the vents every time the sun blazes forth or the sky clouds over.

Fighting off the sun

Some good blinds of a pale green polythene, fitted to the inside ridge of the greenhouse, are easy to pull down on hot, cloudless days when plants need protection from the rays of the sun.

Finally, don't forget to equip the greenhouse with a thermometer – the kind that records both maximum and minimum temperatures.

Tending the vine

About this time, in early spring, the Black Hamburg vine, which has been in the greenhouse now for several years, needs some attention. Tie the rods (stems) into place on the training wires and water regularly to keep the soil moist. Daily spraying is helpful as well. Those of you thinking of planting a vine should choose a one-year-old plant and set it in position in late summer or early autumn. The first year of growth should not be allowed to fruit, but thereafter it should produce a crop each autumn.

Starting the tomatoes

Carters Fruit tomatoes are the best for transplanting later to the greenhouse. In order to start them off you will need your packet of seeds, some John Innes seed sowing compost to put them in and a few cube-shaped Jiffy Pots. These pots are made of compressed peat and last for one season only. Afterwards you can add them to the compost heap.

Fill each pot with seed compost to within 2–3 cm (1 in) or so of the rim, firm it gently and sow a few tomato seeds on the surface. Then cover the seeds with a little more compost – just enough to hide them – and gently firm again. Water them by standing the pots in a bowl with 2–3 cm (1 in) of water in the bottom. The pots absorb the water which passes into the compost until, after a few hours, it is thoroughly and evenly soaked. Put the pots in the propagator and in about ten days you will see the tiny seedlings pushing through in search of the light.

When the seedlings are large enough, you can continue growing your tomato plants by the ring culture method.

Sowing cucumbers under glass

With summer salads in mind your next sowing in the propagator is cucumbers, choosing a comparatively new variety called Pepinex. Of the older varieties, Conqueror and Telegraph both give good crops in cool greenhouses. Pepinex, however, has one great advantage over the older varieties in that it bears almost all female flowers. As these are the ones that produce the cucumbers (the male flowers have to be removed immediately they appear), it means that Pepinex needs less attention than many other varieties and crops more heavily.

You will only need to produce one seedling, for a single, well-grown plant should yield anything from 20 to 50 crisp, juicy cucumbers, which is ample for the average family. Therefore sow only two seeds, 13 mm ($\frac{1}{2}$ in) apart, in a peat pot. If both come up, take the weaker out, leaving the stronger to grow.

A useful tip when sowing is to push the seeds on edge into the compost. As cucumber seeds are comparatively large and flattish, sowing them on edge reduces the risk of rotting before germination.

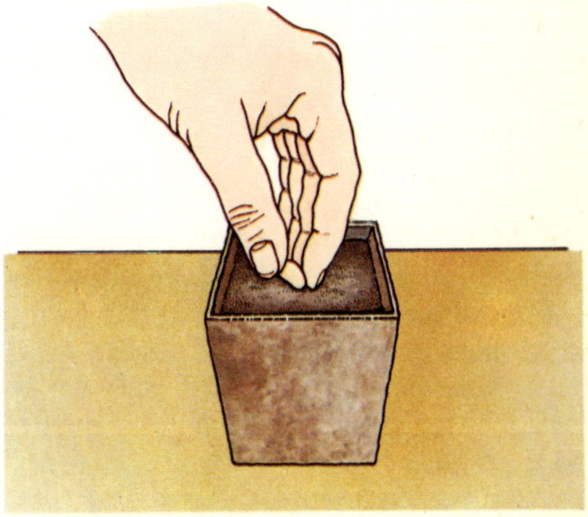

The cucumber seed is pushed, on edge, into the seed compost and then watered, using a fine rose on the watering can

DIGGING THE FOOD PLOT

'Single digging' means digging the soil to one spade's depth (one 'spit'); double digging is done to a depth of two spits. The latter was widely practised in private gardens of old, where it was commonly – and more colourfully – called 'bastard trenching'.
If you are unfortunate enough to acquire a garden on a heavy clay soil with poor drainage, then a few years of double digging will help to improve both the soil fertility and the drainage. Otherwise, as we shall see, single digging is all you need to do.

The object of single digging (which from now on we shall refer to simply as digging) is to turn over the top 20–30cm (9–12 in) of soil; the lower levels are then exposed and aerated. At the same time annual weeds, such as groundsel and chickweed, are turned in and buried so that they will provide valuable humus. Perennial weeds with long tap-roots (like docks and dandelions) will re-emerge if they are buried, so they should be pulled out, left on the path to die, and then placed in the middle of the compost heap. That way every scrap of organic fertilizer that nature provides free is put back into the soil.

Tools for the job
The basic equipment for digging consists of a few layers of warm clothes, stout footwear and a good, strong spade or fork. What you wear on your feet is important. The tendency nowadays is to wear wellingtons but a robust pair of boots or shoes is perhaps preferable.

Wellingtons are heavy, tend to chaff the ankles and are inclined to 'sweat', but gardening boots have thick soles made of some composite material that stands a good deal of rough treatment.

When it comes to the choice of implement you can opt for a spade or a fork. Both are available with two kinds of handle – T-grip and D-grip. We prefer the D-handle because all four fingers of the hand are placed inside the D giving a stronger grip and better leverage.

Whichever you choose it is better to pay a little extra and buy a good-quality tool. A good spade or fork is a sound investment that, properly used and cared

*Four steps to successful single digging: **1** marking the spit; **2** placing the spade at the correct digging angle; **3** turning the soil over into the first trench; **4** turning soil from third trench into second one after filling it with manure*

for, will last a lifetime. Half- or fully-polished blade or prongs slip more easily into the soil and earth is less inclined to cling to them.

For spring digging you can use either a spade or a fork. If you have a light or sandy soil, or a good loam, a spade will do a better job; but on a very heavy clay, which has lain undisturbed over the winter a fork will make digging easier and the end result will be just as good. So select whichever tool best suits you and your soil.

It is advisable to dig your vegetable plot at least a week or two before you are ready to sow or plant as the soil should have time to settle before you start.

And so to work

For many people the thought of digging is a very off-putting idea. They regard it as a back-breaking slog that must be avoided if possible. But this need not be the case if the job is approached in the right frame of mind. So relax, enjoy it and remember that it takes you out into the open air and that it is a marvellous muscle-toner. Don't set yourself impossible goals and stop before you get exhausted.

First of all dig out a trench one spit deep and about 3–3·5m (10–12 ft) long at one end of the plot. Don't make the trench any longer; it is far better for your morale to finish digging a short strip than to half-finish a longer one. Put the soil from the trench into a wheelbarrow and push it to the other end of the plot (where it will be used to fill in the final trench).

Go back to the start of the row and work your way down the second trench, turning the soil over into the first one. Continue in this manner until you have finished the strip. A word of advice – don't try to speed the job up by digging great slices out of the soil. It is much easier, and a lot less tiring, to handle chunks no wider than 15cm (6 in) – at least until you have established a relaxed rhythm. Carry on digging down to the end, fill in the last trench, have a rest and then start on the second strip. Do it this way and you will be surprised how quickly the work gets done.

The newly-turned earth is now an uneven surface of gleaming clods of soil. Leave it like this until the day you are ready to sow and plant, to give it a chance to dry out and settle. Then all you need do on a dry day is shuffle and tramp all over it to break down the lumps before raking it to a fine tilth.

Fertilizers and manures

If you are to get a good, healthy crop fertilizers are absolutely essential. Assuming that none were used in the previous autumn I suggest that a top dressing of general fertilizer, such as Growmore or Fish, blood and bone, or one of the proprietary, concentrated animal manures should be spread over the soil at 70–145g per sq m (2–4 oz per sq yd) before you start digging. Digging the plot puts the fertilizer down into the soil where the plant roots will reach and benefit from it in due course.

We also suggest that you keep some of the fertilizer you use and put a little of it, say about 35g per sq m (1 oz per sq yd) over the whole plot just before you start sowing and planting. This will give the germinating seedlings a boost until their roots reach the main feed below.

Organics and inorganics

Incidentally, fertilizers are basically of two different types – organic and inorganic. Organic ones are those from natural origins of dead or waste plant or animal materials which have been specially processed to render them ideal fertilizers for plant use. Fish, blood and bone is a typical example of one of these. Inorganic fertilizers are of purely chemical origin and contain essential plant foods in readily available form, such as Growmore. Make sure the nitrogen (N), phosphate (P), and potash (K) content is clearly stated on the pack.

When and where to lime

Now we come to the question of whether or not to lime – and if so, when? Some plants are lime-haters and should never have lime on, or anywhere near, them: priceless rhododendrons, azaleas and other flowering shrubs, for instance. In the vegetable plot, however, lime, used carefully, is extremely beneficial. Being alkaline, lime corrects the over-acidity that repeated doses of fertilizer tend to create and also breaks down heavy clay. But it has other advantages as well.

Its main chemical element is calcium which is essential to the healthy growth of many vegetables, especially peas and beans and all members of the cabbage family – the brassicas. Furthermore, its presence in the soil seems to discourage some of the deadly pests and diseases that attack vegetables.

It is often said that the average vegetable garden should be limed once every three years to keep the soil sweet. On the other hand some vegetables react adversely to freshly-limed soil, and unless you keep careful records there is a danger of forgetting whether the three-year period is up.

Potatoes are a prime example of vegetables that do not need lime and, indeed, are adversely affected by it. In newly-limed soil their tender, parchment-thin skins are damaged, resulting in scab-like lesions. These superficial injuries mar the appearance of the tubers and, to a degree, greatly reduce their keeping qualities.

The crop rotation system

A good solution to the liming problem is to suggest that you link your liming to a simple crop rotation programme. Under this system, when the vegetable plot is in full production, roughly one-third of the total area will be occupied by brassicas – summer cabbages, brussels sprouts, cauliflowers and so on. The brassicas are grown in their own special section, with a second section devoted to root crops such as carrots, turnips, beetroot and swedes and a third to peas, beans, onions and salad crops.

The crop rotation system entails switching these sections around so that no one group of crops occupies the same ground more than once every three years. So liming only the 'cabbage patch' every year becomes equivalent to liming the whole plot once every three years.

The brassica section is chosen because lime is especially beneficial to cabbages and similar crops. It encourages their growth and discourages slugs from nibbling at the stems of the young plants. It also appears to act as a deterrent to club root disease, for my limed patch has never been troubled by this scourge of the cabbage family.

Incidentally, lime should not be mixed with manures or fertilizers, so dig it into the soil at least two months before an application of fertilizer, or alternatively one month later.

Warming the earth

Before leaving the vegetable plot try to get down a row or two of cloches. The type used are made of translucent plastic. This is because you may have big feet, for before the invention of the plastic cloche the glass ones – which are expensive to replace – were often smashed. Both rows will be placed on the bare, unsown earth and left there for a week or two – depending on the weather. The reason for this is to warm up the soil ready to receive sowings of early peas, lettuce and radish later on in the year.

IN THE GREENHOUSE

Early to mid spring is an awkward time in the greenhouse. The weather can vary from very warm to icy cold and deciding how much ventilation is required can be a problem. Mostly it is a question of common sense, bearing in mind that too much ventilation is preferable to too little.

The ideal conditions for most greenhouse plants involve the free circulation of warm, moist air and as steady a temperature as possible. A hot, humid atmosphere with little or no ventilation are the conditions that invite fungus disease. On cold nights the greenhouse is closed down completely, but during the day the top ventilator should be opened an inch or so on cold, dull days, and more if the sun is out for long stretches.

Diseases in the greenhouse

Similar do's and don't's apply to the seedlings which are coming through in the propagator. Newly-emerged seedlings are tender and vulnerable to attack by a fungus disease called 'damping-off'. The disease makes its onslaught at soil level, infecting the soft stems of the seedlings. The first visible signs of attack are dead and dying seedlings. If this happens the best plan is to throw the whole batch away and start again.

To prevent attack sow thinly to avoid overcrowding, take the cover off the propagator on warm days and do not over-water. As a further precaution put the prescribed quantity of Cheshunt Compound (fungicide) in the water before watering the seed trays or peat pots.

Greenhouse pests

Insect pests are not usually troublesome under glass so early in the year, but watch out for them just the same. Woodlice can be an unexpected hazard. To deal with them soak the soil under the greenhouse staging with a disinfectant such as Jeyes Fluid, and dust around any possible entry holes and cracks with a strong insecticide.

Pricking out the tomatoes

If the tomato seedlings have germinated take them out of the propagator and get ready to transplant them. If the second pair of leaves is just unfurling, then they are ready to be transferred singly into peat pots containing potting compost. The difference between seed and potting composts is that the latter is quite a bit stronger. It has a higher concentration of plant food, enough to keep the young plant growing strongly until it is ready for its final planting.

Always handle a seedling by its rounded cotyledons or seed leaves. Second pair will be the first 'true' leaves

You will notice that the second and subsequent leaves that form are of a different shape from the first pair, which are the cotyledon or seed leaves. The latter's function is to start the plant life and their usefulness is finished once the true leaves take over.

Tending the cucumber

Next take a look at the cucumber pots. If there are two seedlings, take out the weaker one and firm the compost back around the roots of the remaining seedling. Leave it undisturbed in its original pot of seed compost but give it a weekly feed of a good soluble fertilizer, such as Phostrogen, to supplement the rapidly diminishing plant food in the compost.

Both tomato and cucumber seedlings should then be put near the glass, where they will get maximum light. Always remember that seedlings raised in insufficient natural light grow long and lanky and will never make good plants, nor yield their full potential.

SPRAYING AND SOWING

in the edible garden

Things are moving in the fruit garden. The sap is rising in the apple and pear trees and the eggs of the aphides, laid last summer and dormant all winter, are beginning to hatch under the influence of the warming sun. Soon they will be swarming in their thousands over the unfurling leaves, sucking the sap and restricting growth. They will reproduce at an alarming rate . . . unless you take action now.

If you have many fruit trees, then a large-capacity garden spray may save much time. This model has a shoulder strap and a lance cradle, leaving both hands free for climbing. Wear protective clothing for all spraying work and thoroughly wash yourself and your equipment after the job is finished

To check the spread of aphides, start spraying with an insecticide such as BHC or malathion as soon as you see the leaf buds opening. Use the mixture according to the manufacturer's instructions, preferably on calm days so that the spray does not carry too far or blow back into your face. When you have finished wash yourself and your equipment thoroughly.

The strawberry bed

The next job is to clean up the strawberry bed. Cut and compost all dead leaves and any runners that you may have missed last time. Next, weed thoroughly between the rows and plants and follow up with a dressing of sulphate of potash which improves the quality of the fruits and strengthens the plants. (Feeds containing too much nitrogen will induce soft growth which will then be prone to disease and frost damage.)

An excellent way of nurturing strawberries is to provide them with a special polythene 'undersheet'. Use lengths of 150 gauge black polythene and lay them over the whole bed. Where a plant lies beneath the polythene, cut a cross-shaped hole big enough for the plant to pass through. Repeat this procedure all the way down the rows until all the plants are poking through holes and the polythene is neatly tucked in all round them.

You now have a surface layer which will conserve moisture, stop weeds, prevent the fruit from being splashed with wet soil and give protection from slugs.

The food plot

In the vegetable patch, work depends on the weather. If the days are dry, and the soil nice and crumbly, get it ready now for sowing and planting. Rake it over until the surface is as fine as sand, removing stones, twigs and weeds as you go. Finish off with a top dressing of general fertilizer (applied according to manufacturer's instructions), and you are ready to start sowing, providing conditions are right.

If the soil feels warm to the touch, if the birds are in full voice and if weeds are beginning to push through, the worst of winter is past and the time for spring sowing has arrived.

Our first sowings are of peas and broad beans. These are large seeds and are sown, not in drills (grooves in the earth) like the fine seeds of lettuce and carrots, but in shallow trenches.

Tools for sowing

You will need some basic equipment: a rake, a garden line, packets of seeds and, for later sowings, a swan-necked hoe.

The garden line you can easily make yourself. All you need are two fairly stout pieces of wood, 30cm (12 in) long and about 3cm (1¼ in) in diameter. Through the end of each wooden stake drill a hole wide enough to take a length of strong nylon cord. Knot each end so that it will not pass back through the hole. The length of cord you require depends upon the length of your longest row, plus an extra 3m (10 ft) or so to allow for winding round the pegs and for moving the line, end by end, from one row to the next.

Aligning the rows by the sun

Before you start note which direction is north–south because that is the way in which your rows should run. This is to give each side of the rows an equal ration of sunshine as the sun travels from east to west crossing over them in its path. All crops grow better this way. If the rows run east to west, the north side of the rows will be in permanent shade and the crop on that side will be sparse and slow to mature.

Marking out the trench

When you have decided on the lie of the land, push one end of the garden line into the ground where your row will start. Take the other peg to the far end of the row, push it 15cm (6 in) into the ground and rotate it until the line has been pulled as tight as a violin string. Then push the peg right in.

Sowing peas and broad beans

Peas and beans are sown in rows 45–60cm (18–24 in) apart. The same distance will be left between them and any rows of other, smaller vegetables that are planted on either side of them. Following the line and using a spade, dig a shallow, flat-bottomed trench about 25cm (9 in) wide and 3–5 cm (1–2 in) deep. Move the line on to its next position and sow the newly-made trench.

Broad beans Here we have a tall variety, Rentpayer, for one row, and a dwarf variety, The Midget, for the second. Place the seeds in 15cm (6 in) apart along one side of the trench and the same distance apart along the other side but with the seeds alternating from side to side. Pop in a few extra at the ends of the rows for filling in gaps later.

After sowing cover the seeds with not more than 3cm (1¼ in) of soil and hammer it down with the back of a rake to firm the seeds in. Finally, label the rows carefully with the date of planting and the crop sown.

Peas For this time of year we have chosen Kelvedon Wonder and Early Bird, both early varieties, which will be ready for picking 15–20 days earlier than the main-crop sowings.

Place the peas in their trench so that there is 5–8cm (2–3 in) between each seed, but otherwise get as many seeds in as possible (plus a few extra at the end of each row). Many gardeners are not so painstaking, they scatter the peas thinly in the trench or just throw them in – and sometimes get good crops. But you will probably get more reliable results from placing them carefully. After sowing, cover and firm as for broad beans.

Discouraging mice Before sowing peas bear in mind that mice are very fond of them. They wait a few days until the pea seeds are swollen, soft and tender, then they descend on the row and may leave you with nothing but an empty trench.

Traps baited with cheese may catch some of them, but a far better method is to soak the seeds for an hour or two in a paste made of red lead and paraffin and then sow them immediately.

Alternatively, if you have a holly tree in the garden collect the fallen leaves and strew them in the trench, with the peas, before closing it. The mice have long, soft noses and the holly leaves have hard, prickly points; bits of gorse in the trench will have the same effect.

IN THE PROPAGATOR

As there is now some room in the propagator it is time to make a few more sowings.

Cauliflowers and summer cabbage Start off a few cauliflowers (we suggest the variety Early Snowball) for cutting weeks earlier than those from outdoor sowings. Cauliflowers have a habit of all coming ready at once, and the only way to avoid a glut is to sow several small batches of seeds at different times.

In another pot start some Golden Acre summer cabbage for cutting when shop prices are sky-high.

Leeks for the autumn With an eye to the future, I also intend sowing leeks for autumn and winter use. We have chosen Marble Pillar for its fine flavour and good length of white stem. I am also going to try a few plants of the brand new Catalina variety which has a thicker stem and consequently should give a higher yield. Sow the seeds thinly in trays or pots of seed compost and prick them out when they are about 2–3cm (1 in) high.

SPRING SOWING
in the edible garden

Sweet peppers (capsicums) and celery are expensive to buy but easy to cultivate. In this section we start both these popular vegetables into growth, explaining the benefits of successional sowing and planting onions and shallots before going on to potatoes and strawberries.

It is often asked what is the difference between the red and the green varieties of peppers. The answer is that both red and green fruits appear on the same plant: green when young, turning red as they age. Pick them when they are young and green to encourage further cropping.

The variety we have chosen is Canapé, which matures early and has a sweet, mild flavour. Sow the seeds in the propagator in trays or pots of seed compost; pots are best as you can move them outside in early mid summer (early June) when the weather becomes warm.

Celery for salads

Being a half-hardy plant, celery should be sown in the propagator now for planting out in early and mid summer (May and June). As the Edible Garden is not very large we have chosen Golden Self-Blanching which can be planted fairly close together and needs neither earthing up nor blanching collars to produce fine, tender stems. It has a good, nutty flavour and grows easily. Sow the seeds thinly in trays or pots of seed compost in the propagator.

Midsummer lettuce

A few lettuce sown now will be ready for planting out under cloches in about two months' time, and ready for cutting in mid summer when they are scarce and expensive. Sow very thinly in a tray of seed compost. With a little patience you can space them out 5cm (2 in) apart, thereby avoiding having to prick out; lettuce prefer not to be disturbed. If they show any sign of slow growth, before you are ready to plant them out give them a liquid feed and they will respond rapidly. We can thoroughly recommend the varieties All The Year Round, Buttercrunch and the recent Ilo which stands better in hot, dry weather than almost any other variety known.

Successional sowing

Do not rush to sow outdoors as over the years you will find you get better crops from seeds sown in a warm, hospitable soil.

Before starting our main sowings we should explain the concept of successional sowing, as it plays an important part in avoiding gluts yet giving a steady supply of any particular vegetable.

The usual mistake is to sow too long a row, so that at harvesting time there are many more plants than you can use. With vegetables such as lettuce and radish the answer is to sow a short, or part, row about 1.25–1.75m (4–6 ft) long. When the seedlings of the first row are showing above the soil, sow another short row; continue in this manner right through until midsummer for a fresh and steady supply. You can also enjoy different varieties by alternating, for example, a row of butterhead lettuce with a row of cos.

Another way of sowing for succession is by making use of the varying maturing times of different varieties of one vegetable. Early potatoes, for instance, are planted from two to four weeks earlier than maincrop varieties; together the two types will provide you with potatoes from midsummer through to planting time the following year.

Peas can be controlled in the same way. Early peas are followed by the second-early and maincrop varieties so that the rows are ready for picking one after the other. The seemingly odd thing about peas is that for a late sowing you choose an early variety. This is because a pea is

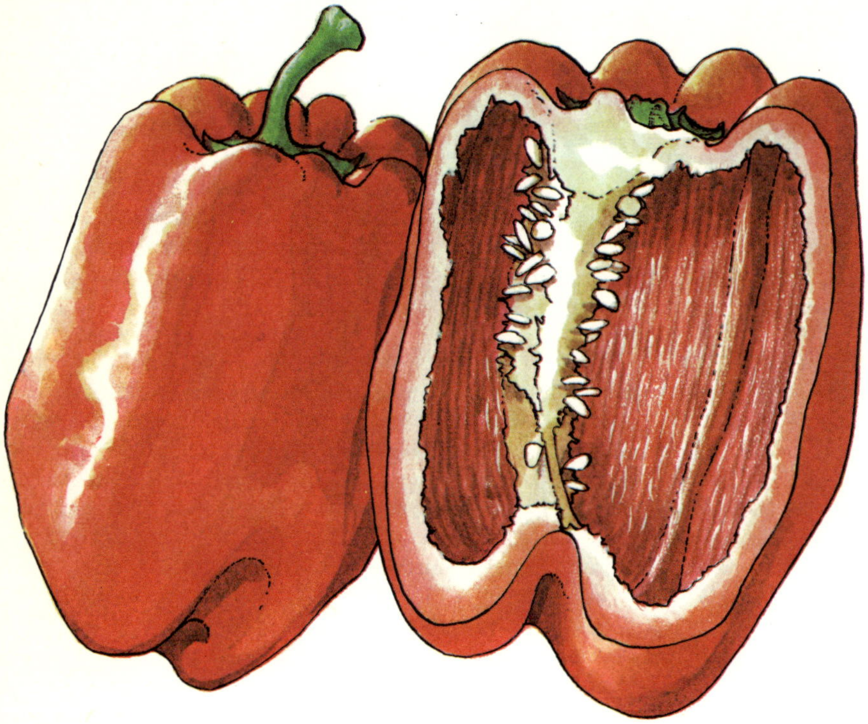

Canapé (F.1 hybrid) is a mild-flavoured and early-maturing sweet pepper that crops heavily. It is hardy enough to be grown outdoors in a sheltered position

classed as early if it matures and 'pods up' quickly; and in order to get a usable crop from a mid summer sowing, the variety that matures earliest is best.

Onions from sets

Providing there is no frost in the soil and it is dry enough, I want to start planting the onion rows.

Nowadays onion 'sets' have almost completely superseded seeds. Buy small sets rather than big ones; they seem to produce better onions.

We have chosen Stuttgarter Giant, which grows into a good-sized onion, and Sturon, which yields fine crops of globe-shaped bulbs.

Buy your sets as soon as you see them in the shops. If you leave it too long they become soft bulbs with pale yellow necks that have been forced into growth by the surrounding high temperature.

Once you have bought them, open the bags or cartons and spread them out in a cool, frost-free room or shed. Look them over and throw out any that show signs of mould.

Digging the onion bed

The first essential is a really rich and fertile soil. So dig a trench, about 30cm (12 in) deep and spread a 15cm (6 in) layer of well-rotted compost in it. On top of this sprinkle a few handfuls of bonemeal and then turn the soil from the next trench over on top of it. Wear tight-fitting rubber gloves when handling bonemeal; it may well be imported stock which has not been sufficiently heat-sterilized to kill infectious diseases.

Raking and top dressing

Before planting, break down the surface lumps by stamping all over them. Then rake to a fine tilth, removing stones at the same time. Finally, add a top dressing of Fish, blood and bone fertilizer at 70g per sq m (2 oz per sq yd).

Planting the sets

Onion sets have two main advantages over seeds: they don't need thinning and, because they have a head start, they are not so prone to the troubles that can beset young seedlings.

But sets have an annoying habit of popping out of the ground. Birds are usually blamed for this – but they neither eat onions nor use them to line their nests. Our observations led us to conclude that birds may pull out one or two, just for the fun of it, but the main culprits are incorrect planting and over-ambitious worms.

Sets often have a long tail of outer skin which, after planting, gets wet and soft and trails along the ground. The nocturnal worm takes it to be ideal nesting material and tries to pull it down into its burrow. Out comes the set, to be left lying uselessly on its side once the worm realizes its mistake. So cut off the tail before planting.

By incorrect planting we refer to the practice of pushing the sets into the soil rather than placing them on the ground and then piling soil around them. If you push a set in, a hard pad of soil forms underneath the base of the bulbs and the emerging roots have difficulty in getting through it. The result is that the roots push the set out of the ground as they exert pressure on the compacted soil.

The correct way to plant is to draw out a shallow drill 13mm ($\frac{1}{2}$ in) deep. Mark out the row with a line (as explained for the broad bean trench on page 74). Then put the blade of a swan-necked hoe against it at an angle of 45 degrees with its pointed corner just below soil surface. With both feet on the line to prevent it from 'bellying out', walk slowly backwards along the line. The drill should be reasonably straight and of even depth. Place the sets in it 15–25cm (6–8 in) apart and surround each one with a little soil to keep it upright and in place.

Planting shallots

You can plant shallots from early spring to mid summer (February to June). Plant as for onion sets, but leave more space between rows and bulbs; place them 30cm (12 in) apart. This is because the shallot splits and yields several young bulbs, each of which grows as big as its parent.

IN THE GREENHOUSE

All that the tomato and cucumber seedlings need to keep them growing is plenty of light, warmth and enough water. Keep the compost in the pots moist rather than wet as too much water invites fungus diseases. Place the pots as near to the glass as possible to give the plants all the available daylight. If the glass is dirty, or has become coated with green algal growth, then the amount of light admitted is greatly reduced. So wash the glass regularly with hot, soapy water, but be sure to move the plants well out of the way before you start cleaning.

There is no need to feed the seedlings yet. Potting composts contain enough nutrients to nourish the plants for six to eight weeks, by which time they will have been moved on into larger pots.

This week's sowing is onions for planting out in early summer. Both Ailsa Craig and Showmaster will give you excellent yields, or try the F.1 hybrid Superba which crops very early.

In a good spring, the soil temperature is high enough to germinate the seeds and the lengthening days ensure that the seedlings have enough daylight to meet their needs. Day length is almost as important as temperature in determining how well plants grow. Experiments indicate that seedlings growing in insufficient light suffer appreciable growth checks from which they seldom fully recover, and if they are vegetables their cropping potential is diminished.

It is, of course, pointless to sow in a cold soil. Unless the minimum germination temperature has been reached the seeds will just lie dormant until they rot. So if the soil feels cold to the touch leave the seeds in their packets. The same applies to wet soil. If conditions are right it should crumble easily under foot and rake to a fine tilth without the teeth of the rake becoming clogged with soil.

But remember that you are the only one who can assess the situation in your garden and decide whether or not to make a start. Choosing the right day can make all the difference between a good and a mediocre crop, but this is something you can learn by experience.

Arran Pilot – excellent on light soils

Early potatoes

The first things to go in are the early seed potatoes. Potatoes are listed in three categories: earlies, second earlies and maincrops. The earlies grow quickest and mature first. They are not for lifting and storing, but are intended for immediate eating – as 'new potatoes' – generally from late summer to early autumn (July to August).

One favourite variety is Ulster Chieftain, which crops heavily in a medium loam and is ready earlier than most other varieties. For light soils choose Arran Pilot, whereas Home Guard will do well on a heavy soil.

Now to buying the 'seed' – which is a misnomer. A seed potato is in fact a small tuber (swollen root) from the previous year's crop. You must be sure to buy certified stock. This means that the tubers have been grown by a specialist grower and are free of virus diseases.

For the Edible Garden plot, 3kg (7 lb) of 'seed' should be enough. Examine each tuber to make sure it is healthy and not too soft. If there are shoots already sprouting from the 'eyes' rub off the weak ones with your thumbs, leaving just three or four of the strongest. Some varieties have more eyes than others, and if you leave all the shoots on you will find, at harvesting time, only a small clutch of new potatoes the size of mothballs. Three to four shoots on a tuber will yield, on average, between 15 and 20 good-sized potatoes per root.

If you want a good crop, then a certain amount of planning and soil preparation is necessary. Potatoes dislike shade and stony soils and do not yield well in dry soils because they must have water to swell the tubers. Nor does ground which has been recently limed suit them: they

Early Nantes is a good variety for pulling young

may grow reasonably well in it, but their skins will be covered in scabs. However, although these are ugly, they are only skin deep and do not affect the eating qualities of the potato.

Mark out with your garden line, and dig, a trench about 15cm (6 in) deep and 30cm (12 in) wide and place the seed potatoes in it 25cm (9 in) apart. Then dust the soil on each side of the trench with Growmore or Fish, blood and bone fertilizer at around 30–45g per m (1–1½ oz per yd) of row. Put the soil back over the potatoes and firm with the back of the spade. Remember to leave 60cm (24 in) between rows to give the growing plants plenty of room to develop and so that their large leaves will not interfere with the growth of adjoining crops.

Finally, a word of warning: if your garden is infested with small, black, subterranean slugs you will have to take precautionary measures. These common soil pests will destroy your crop. So after you have placed the seed potatoes in their shallow trenches, give them a good soaking with a disinfectant such as Jeyes Fluid, diluted to the recommended strength (as maker's instructions), before putting the soil back over them.

Growing healthy carrots

The next sowing is carrots and the choice of variety depends on your soil. On deep, light soils the varieties with long, tapering roots, like St Valery, give good yields. In most soils, however, the cylindrical roots with rounded ends are more reliable, and make good eating. Try the old favourites Chantenay Red Cored or Nantes Tip Top (both first-class croppers) or the newer F.1 hybrid variety Pioneer. This is very similar to Nantes Tip Top, but being an F.1 hybrid it exhibits all the characteristics of its kind (see box note).

The greatest problem in growing carrots is carrot fly. This is a destructive and widespread pest and, unless controlled, it can ruin a crop. The fly lays its eggs in early summer (May) on or near the surface of the soil in the vicinity of the young carrots. When the eggs hatch the maggots (or larvae) bore their way into the young roots until they are cracked and riddled with holes. Above soil level you will notice carrot fly attack by reddening and yellowing of the leaves which wilt in the sun. If this happens, pull up the roots and burn them.

However, there are various ways of preventing carrot fly from getting a hold. Sprinkle a special insecticide, such as bromophos, into the seed drill immediately after sowing which, it is claimed, will not taint the carrots and is harmless.

If you are apprehensive about using chemical pesticides on food crops, wait until the carrot fly has finished laying its eggs in early summer (May) and then sow immediately afterwards. By using a quick-growing variety, such as Pioneer, you will get a good crop of clean, delicious carrots for lifting in the autumn.

Another way is to fool the fly into believing that you have no carrots in your garden. It is attracted to the young plants by the smell of their leaves, so the plan is to introduce something with a stronger smell into the carrot patch. Either put down a few tin lids or saucers containing creosote or paraffin, or soak thick twine in either fluid and hang it above the rows during the danger period.

There is one further tip for producing good carrots. Never sow the seeds on ground that has been treated with fresh animal manure. If you do the roots will be forked and contorted; sow in soil which was manured the previous year, or which has only received an even dressing of compound fertilizer more recently.

Don't let all these precautions put you off growing this delicious vegetable. Carrots straight from the garden are sweeter and have a better flavour than any others, so they are worth a little extra trouble.

Summer cabbage and cauliflower

After the carrots come the summer cabbages. Here again there is a choice between F.1 hybrids and ordinary varieties. Taking the hybrids first, we can recommend Stonehead with solid, round heads or Hispi which yields large, pointed heads. Of the ordinary kinds I like Golden Acre with round heads as tight as drums and not too big. The cut heads average about 1kg (2¼ lb) in weight on a good soil, which is quite enough for a family of four. And being smaller, they can be grown closer together so that you get more cabbages per row.

If you like a large cabbage grow Winningstadt. In a fertile soil this can grow to be really enormous with a pointed, rock-hard head.

Many gardeners sow their summer cabbages in seedbeds and transplant the seedlings into the plot some weeks later. This really seems a waste of time and the plants suffer unnecessary root disturbance. The plants will grow, and mature, quicker if the seeds are sown in their final growing place. Sowing *in situ* also reduces the risk of cabbage root fly attack, which is more prevalent in transplanted seedlings.

F.1 HYBRID

An F.1 hybrid is the first generation offspring, resulting from crossing two good varieties. It possesses all the best features of both parents, coupled with a hybrid vigour peculiar to all first-generation crosses. This gives it a built-in resistance to diseases and earlier maturity, and results in a heavier and more uniform crop than is normally obtained from ordinary varieties.

Seeds of F.1 hybrids are always considerably more expensive than others, but in terms of total crop yield and increased disease resistance they are well worth the extra cost.

Early Snowball – ready for summer cutting

IN THE PROPAGATOR

If the summer cauliflower and summer cabbage seedlings have made four leaves, take them out of the propagator and prick them out into 8cm (3 in) peat pots containing potting compost – as you did for the tomato seedlings on page 72.

For the smaller-headed types sow the seeds very thinly 6mm ($\frac{1}{4}$ in) deep in shallow drills 25–30cm (9–12 in) apart. For the larger kinds space the drills 30–45cm (12–18 in) apart. Sow very thinly and when the seedlings have grown four leaves thin them to the same distances apart as the space between the drills.

Summer cauliflower is one crop which must have a moist, rich soil before it will yield good, large white curds (flower-heads). In a poor soil, where the roots have to search for food and water, it may grow reasonably well but the curds will be mere buttons and hardly worth cutting. For the average garden, the variety All the Year Round is a reliable cropper, or Early Snowball which hearts up a little sooner. Sow as for summer cabbage, in rows 45cm (18 in) apart.

Successional sowings
Make several sowings of spring onions, radish, lettuce and summer spinach between now and the end of summer to ensure a fresh and constant supply.

The spring onion (choose White Lisbon) is one of the few vegetables whose seeds are sown fairly thickly and the seedlings left unthinned. This produces a mini-forest of succulent plants for pulling when they are still young and tender – about 15cm (6 in) tall. You can sow short rows from now until early autumn (August).

Next sow a part row of Lettuce Minetto, and a 'clutch' of Cherry Belle radish seeds in between the ends of the onion rows (or in any odd corner).

Another tasty vegetable for successional sowing from now until late summer (July) is summer spinach and here we recommend Longstanding Round. Sow thinly in drills 25cm (9 in) apart and thin the seedlings to about 15cm (6 in) apart later on. It is one of the easiest of crops to grow providing, like cauliflowers, it is given plenty of water during dry spells. If left short of moisture at the roots the plants run to seed quickly and the leaves become bitter.

Container-grown strawberries
Those of you who haven't got a strawberry bed are going to regret the omission when summer comes.

It is too late to plant bare-root plants; these must be left until mid to late autumn (September to October) but container-grown plants can be planted right now. These are plants grown from runners rooted into pots the previous summer. In the pots they have made good fibrous root systems that need not be disturbed when transferring them. Simply place two fingers around the neck of the plant, turn the pot upside down and give it a gentle tap with a trowel, and the whole thing will slide out with an unbroken ball of soil.

Golden Acre – fine quality and flavour

Plant strawberries in well-fed soil

With the trowel, make a hole big enough to take the rootball with room to spare, put it in and gently firm the soil back round it. When you have finished the top of the rootball should be level with the surrounding soil. Finish off by giving each plant half a handful of general fertilizer and a good watering.

Whether planting a single row or a bed of strawberries remember that the plants will live there for at least three years. Therefore plant them in the richest, best-fed soil in the garden and give them plenty of room to grow into large, bushy plants. Leave a good 60cm (24 in) between rows and 45cm (18 in) between individual plants. Pot-grown plants, planted in the spring, will not yield heavily the first year, but you can expect a few pickings of juicy berries in late summer and a good crop the following year.

Herbs for the herb bed
So far we've paid little attention to the herb rock garden. For planting this week buy 100g (4 oz) of garlic. The bulb is composed of several bulblets, or cloves, clustered around a central, dry stem.

To get at them, remove the outer parchment-like skin and separate the cloves with finger and thumb. Plant the cloves 25cm (9 in) apart, and about 2–3cm (1 in) deep, in rows approximately 30cm (12 in) apart.

Perennial herbs, like sage and thyme, can be sown outdoors now, but you'll find germination more certain if you sow seeds in pots or trays of seed compost in the propagator. Sown very thinly, the seedlings need not be transplanted until they are big enough to be transferred straight into the herb bed.

THE SEEDBED

Once the major spring sowings have been made, the next jobs are weeding and preparing the seedbed, which will provide you with vegetables later in the year, when the first crops are exhausted. Here we show you how to prepare the soil and recommend the best varieties to grow in it.

The purpose of your seedbed is to activate seeds into life, so it must be sited where it will receive all the available sunshine, and its soil must be the richest and finest in the whole garden. The reasons for having a seedbed are two-fold. First, it is the area in the Edible Garden where seeds have the best chance of germinating quickly and successfully. And second, it acts as a kind of plant bank where reserve stocks are kept until they are needed.

The seedbed need not occupy a very large area. The rows may be no more than 90cm (3 ft) long and 15cm (6 in) apart and, as you are unlikely to be growing more than 10 items at a time, it need not be wider than about 1·5m (5 ft).

A well-formed brussels sprout plant should have tight, hard 'buttons'. Gather from the base upwards

Preparing the seedbed

How you prepared the soil is vitally important. Seeds need warmth, moisture and air to induce them out of dormancy into life. The sooner they burst their seed coats and form their first small roots and shoots, the faster and stronger they will grow, the better plants they will make, and the heavier the crops they will yield.

Therefore the soil in the seedbed must be fertile. It must also be fine and friable so that the seeds are in close contact with the soil particles and in an environment that rapidly warms up in the sun. So dig it deep and dig in as much well-rotted manure or garden compost as you can lay your hands on.

Then tread the bed (to firm the soil) and rake over the surface repeatedly until the top 2–5cm (1–2 in) is as fine as granulated sugar. Top it with a general fertilizer (such as Fish, blood and bone, or Fish meal) at 70g per sq m (2 oz per sq yd), and leave it to work its own way in.

This is the ideal, which you can readily achieve in gardens blessed with sandy soils or light loams. But you will not find it so easy on heavy clay, which is cold and cloying – the worst possible soil for seed germination. For a heavy clay garden you must prepare a contrived surface.

First dig the soil over thoroughly, add organic matter, then rake it down till the surface is as fine as you can make it. Spread a layer of garden peat 5cm (2 in) thick over the entire surface and sow in the seeds. Peat warms up quickly so the seeds will germinate rapidly, and the roots will soon penetrate into the soil beneath – where the food is.

At the end of the season, when you have finished with the seedbed, fork in the peat. Over the years it will darken and break up the clay into a rich loam.

If you are using this surface-peat method you must water it copiously until the seedlings are well established.

How and what to sow

The vegetables you sow in the seedbed will be those that are used as 'follow-ons' when the others have been harvested. These are, in the main, vegetables which mature later in the year and are harvested in the late autumn and winter. They are often the most useful crops of all, as they are ready when fresh vegetables are at a premium. They also make use of the ground vacated by earlier crops, such as early peas, broad beans and potatoes.

Vegetables you can sow between mid-spring and early summer (March to late May) are leeks, brussels sprouts, winter cabbage, purple sprouting broccoli, red cabbage and winter cauliflower. With the exception of leeks, they are all members of the cabbage family.

You may be tempted to buy these as ready-grown plants from market stalls and garden centres, or to accept spare plants from kindly neighbours. But by 'importing' plants you run the terrible risk of introducing disease to your previously 'clean' garden, because the soil around the plants' roots may contain spores of the virulent club root disease, which is lethal to the cabbage family. Avoid this dreadful possibility by growing your own plants from seeds – at a fraction of the cost of buying plants.

The sowing procedure is no different from sowing directly into the food plot. In other words sow shallowly, only 6 mm ($\frac{1}{4}$ in) deep, and thinly, then firm the soil back over the seeds.

As each row is sown, label it, not with empty seed packets, but with a metal or plastic tag that will not fade or blow away. If you forget to label you will find, later on, that you can't tell one row of seedlings from another. This will cause problems at planting-out time.

IN THE GREENHOUSE

Dwarf French beans can now be sown in the greenhouse for an early crop in mid summer (June). Flair and Tendergreen are excellent early (stringless) varieties. The most reliable method is to grow the plants in pots.

Use fairly large pots, 25–30cm (10–12 in) in diameter. Put a layer of well-rotted manure or compost, 5cm (2 in) deep, in the bottom and cover it with good, rich soil to within 8cm (3 in) of the rim. On top of this sow six seeds on end and cover them with 2–3cm (1 in) of soil. Sowing them on end reduces the risk of the seeds rotting and seems to hasten germination.

Until the seeds germinate water them carefully and sparingly – just enough to keep the soil moist.

If the celery and pepper seedlings have made four leaves, and if the leek seedlings are about 2–3cm (1 in) high, prick them out singly into 8cm (3 in) peat pots filled with potting compost.

Remember to keep all the growing seedlings watered; the bigger they get the more water they lose through their leaves, and the more they need to replace the loss.

If you look at the soil in the seed trays or pots you may notice a green growth on the surface. This is an alga which in itself is not harmful, but it is inclined to create over-acidity and to slow down growth by excluding air from the seedling roots. With an old kitchen fork gently break up the soil surface.

Finally a few more herbs: hyssop, sweet marjoram, rosemary and winter savory can all be sown in the propagator now for planting out later.

Seedbed varieties

Brussels sprouts Peer Gynt, an early variety ready for picking from late autumn (October) onwards. Fasolt New matures much later, cropping from mid winter to spring (December to February).

Red cabbage Blood Red for shredding and pickling in the autumn (August to October). One well-grown plant will provide enough for 1kg (2 lb) of pickle.

Winter cabbage Christmas Drumhead, a solid head on short plants, ready for cutting from early to late winter (November to January). January King, a good-flavoured roundhead that stands all winter. Ormskirk Late (savoy) has a large crinkly-leaved heart that is at its best from mid winter to mid spring (December to March).

Winter cauliflower Snow's Winter White for late winter and early spring (January and February) cropping. St George, which curds up for mid to late spring (March to April) eating.

Sprouting broccoli Early Purple Sprouting yields a prolific crop of succulent shoots in mid and late spring (March and April) when fresh green vegetables are still scarce.

One of the most rewarding of all vegetables – the more you cut it the more shoots you get – is Green Sprouting (or Calabrese), a delicious vegetable that deserves greater popularity. The central heads are ready in summer and, after cutting, are followed by a plentiful crop of tender shoots which should be peeled before cooking.

Leek Musselburgh has long, thick stems; Marble Pillar, earlier, with long, slender stems of excellent quality. Leeks are hardy enough to be left in the ground all winter (November to March), and remain in top condition right through to mid spring.

Weeding the food plot

In the food plot the bare soil is beginning to disappear – the weeds are on the march. Work your way along the rows of vegetable seedlings pulling out the small weeds before they get established and begin to use up the food intended for the vegetables. It is always easier to remove a young weed than to uproot a big one; also the vegetable seedlings suffer much less root disturbance.

This done, carefully hoe between the rows with a push (or Dutch) hoe. This tool enables you to work walking backwards so that you don't tread over the ground already hoed. Choose a dry, sunny day for the job and leave the uprooted weeds lying on the surface to wither and die and return some goodness to the soil.

Mulching the raspberries

Before the weather starts getting really warm lay a mulch of well-rotted organic material along the ground between the rows of raspberry canes, taking care not to break any new shoots that are just emerging. Put down a layer 8–10cm (3–4 in) deep along each side of the rows. This will feed the plants as they grow, prevent loss of moisture, keep the roots cool in hot weather and protect them from late, hard frosts.

For top-class leeks, sow in a well-prepared seedbed

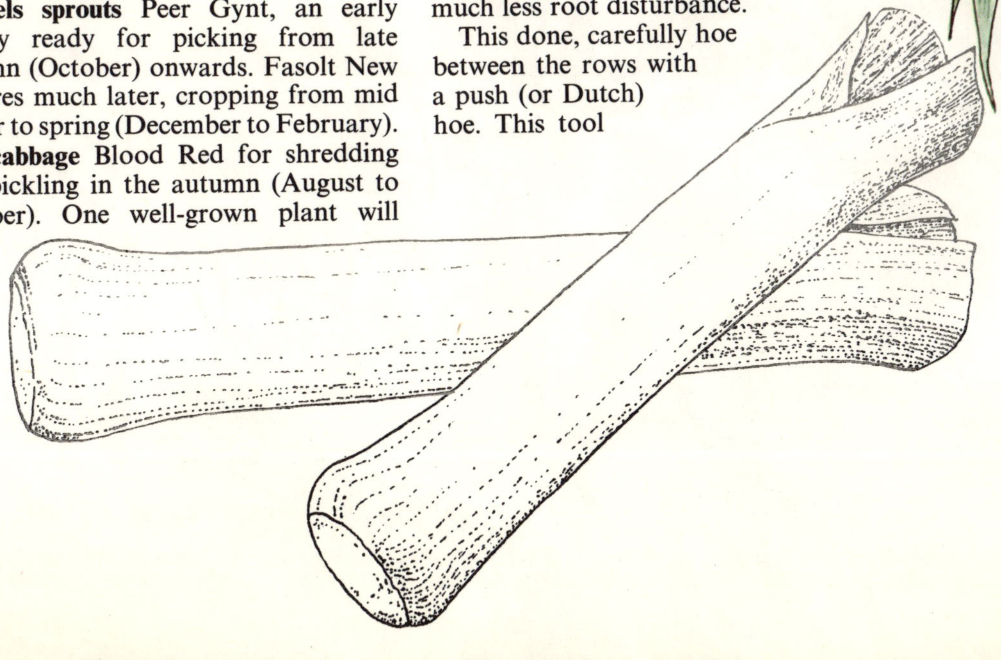

WEEDING AND SPRAYING
in the edible garden

During the last few weeks of spring when the weeds are shooting up amongst the vegetables, manual or chemical weeding becomes an essential weekly task. Here we show you how to stake broad beans, protect early potatoes, tie in raspberries and thin out young vegetable plants

Broadly speaking the chemical weedkillers that are used in the Edible Garden can be divided into those that kill through the leaves and those that kill through the roots. Both types are equally effective but their efficiency and usefulness depend on their being used in the right places, at the right times and at the correct strength.

One which we will *not* be using in the Edible Garden is sodium chlorate – even though it is one of the oldest and most popular of weedkillers. It is an efficient destroyer of plant life, but it does have serious disadvantages. It is fully soluble in water and, when applied to a given area, will spread sideways, endangering other nearby plants. It remains potent in the ground for a considerable time until it is eventually washed out of the soil by rain.

On heavy soils its enduring toxicity makes it unsafe to plant anything for up to a year and even on light, sandy soils the ground must be left fallow for three months or more. So do not use it on the vegetable plot or on the ground around it.

Weedkillers containing simazine are also total root-entering killers but, unlike sodium chlorate, they are not soluble and merely go into suspension when added to water. This means that they do not spread and their destructiveness is confined to the zone of application. You can, therefore, apply them to paths without fear of their toxicity spreading into the food-growing areas.

Then there are the weedkillers containing a chemical called paraquat that revolutionized gardening when it was first introduced. Paraquat kills through the leaves by destroying their internal cell structure and rendering them incapable of sustaining life. It has no effect whatsoever on the soil and is rendered harmless on contact with it. This means that paraquat will only kill what it touches and therefore its application can be accurately controlled. You can use it safely to kill weeds between rows of vegetables providing it does not come into contact with the vegetable leaves.

Unfortunately paraquat can be lethal to humans as well as to plants and you must treat it with great caution. Always wear rubber gloves and wash your face and hands thoroughly when the job is done. Wash the can out, several times, to make sure that all chemical residues are dispersed. You should keep a special watering can for all chemical weedkillers

Dock, thistle, bindweed, deadnettle, speedwell and dandelion – just a few of the weeds that menace your garden

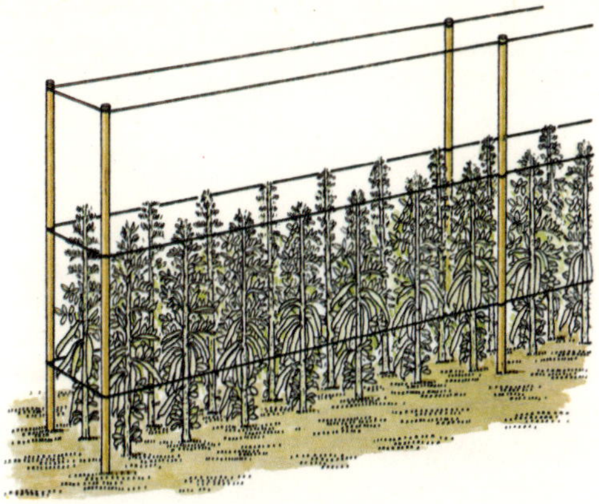

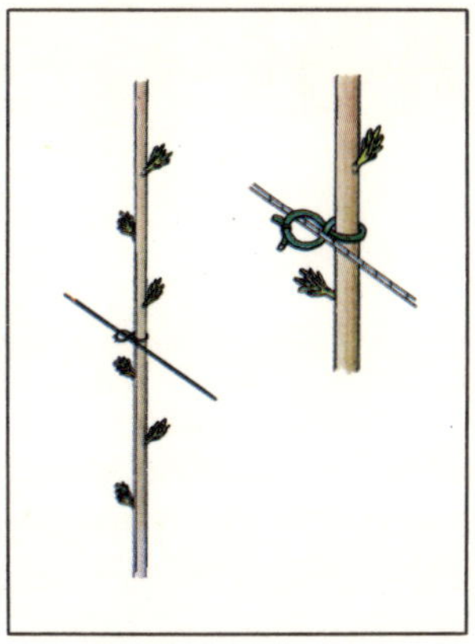

Far left: erect the tall cane support-structure for your broad beans early on as the plants grow very rapidly and soon become top-heavy; once they have fallen over it is not an easy job to get them to stand upright again
Left: raspberries also need supporting. Tie stems in loosely to the wire supports so they can grow without hindrance
Below: useful bees, as well as harmful pests, are affected by insecticides, so spray your apple trees while the flowers are still in bud, and well before bees start pollinating the blossoms

so that you cannot, through error or carelessness, harm your plants with contaminated liquid.

Thinning the seedlings
Some seedlings, such as spring onions, don't need thinning. Also, leave carrots unthinned so as not to loosen the soil around them; loose earth makes it very easy for the larvae of carrot fly to bore their way down to the roots. However, the bulbing onions and summer cabbage sown *in situ* need thinning, to give the selected plants plenty of room to grow and develop from an early age.

Thin to the correct distances apart as soon as the seedlings are big enough to handle easily. You can pull out a small-rooted seedling – before it develops a ramifying (spreading) root system and becomes deep-seated – without disturbing its neighbours. Early thinning also causes less growth check. Help to stabilize and protect the transplanted seedlings by drawing a little soil around with a hoe.

Tending and staking broad beans
The double row of broad beans is also growing well, except for one or two gaps where seeds failed to germinate. Fill the gaps with plants taken from the ends of the rows – where you sowed those extra seeds. Starting a few centimetres away from each plant, dig deep down under them and then lift them gently to avoid breaking the roots. Tease them carefully apart and plant them firmly in the gaps. They will not be much disturbed by the move and will soon catch up.

Broad beans are rapid growers; the tall-growing varieties will need supporting to prevent them being blown over. Use 1.2m or 1.5m (4 ft or 5 ft) long canes and, starting at one end of the row, stick them in at 1.8m (6 ft) intervals on each side. Then run lengths of strong twine from end to end, tying it to each stake. Three lengths of twine should be enough – at 30, 90 and 150cm (1, 3 and 5 ft) above the ground. This structure will provide enough support for the plants at all stages of growth. If your garden is very exposed you may need to criss-cross some twine over the plants for added protection; they will grow up through it.

Protecting the potatoes
Being a half-hardy plant the potato is unable to withstand the least touch of frost, so you must protect the young plants if frost threatens. You won't find the common method of covering the emerging leaves with soil is necessary. The plant has to push its way out again instead of using its leaves to manufacture the food that should be going to the roots to form and swell the young potatoes.

A much simpler way is to take a few sheets of newspaper and throw one over each plant (anchored with a stone) if there is frost in the air. Your garden may look untidy but your potatoes will be protected. But if you miss the weather forecast, or the skies clear in the early morning and frost descends unexpectedly, all is not lost. Get up early and turn the hose on the plants before the sun strikes the leaves. If the sun gets there first the leaves will turn yellow, then brown and finally black. Even so, don't lift the row. Leave it and new growth will emerge from the stems beneath the soil. You will only get about half a crop, and it will take much longer to mature, but at least it will not be a complete loss.

Tying in raspberry canes
In the fruit cage the new raspberry canes will need tying in to their wire supports. Plant ties of paper-covered wire are convenient and inexpensive but you can do the job just as quickly with a ball of garden twine and a sharp knife. Put the ball in your pocket to leave your hands free to hold the loose end of the twine and the knife. Tie in the stems loosely, with the twine forming a figure-of-eight between the stems and the wire. This allows room for the plants to grow without being constricted (see illustration above).

Spraying the apple trees
A number of insect pests which attack apple trees from time to time are at their most vulnerable in late spring. An insecticide spray of BHC or malathion at the tree's 'pink bud' stage will effectively control aphides and capsid bug. If you spray before the flowers open they will not be damaged and there will be no danger of accidentally killing bees while they are 'working' the blossoms.

Remember, as with all garden chemicals, to protect your eyes and skin, and wash yourself and all equipment thoroughly after the job is finished. As an added precaution keep pets away from the area under the trees for a few days.

Spraying with BHC or malathion is not sufficient to conquer woolly aphid, otherwise known as American blight. The fine spray will not penetrate through to the lower layers of the white growth – like cotton wool – that sometimes clothes the branches. The best treatment is to paint the infected parts with a paint brush dipped in tar oil.

IN THE GREENHOUSE
If the onion seedlings are about 2-3cm (1 in or so) high, then prick them out singly into 8cm (3 in) peat pots. In a few weeks time you will be hardening them off, prior to planting them out.

HARDENING OFF
in the edible garden

Mid spring (March) has given place to late spring (April) bringing a greener hue to the Edible Garden. Here we prepare to harden off the greenhouse seedlings outdoors and plant maincrop potatoes.
In the greenhouse the tomatoes are ready for planting out, and a few more sowings in the propagator complete the jobs for the week.

Over the next few weeks (early to late April, depending on how mild an area you live in) the lettuce, cauliflower and cabbage seedlings that were sown earlier under glass must be hardened off before you plant them out.

'Hardening off' means giving the plants an acclimatization period before transferring them from the greenhouse to the open ground. Until now the seedlings have been completely protected from the natural elements; they have never encountered wind or low temperatures. To move them from the still, warm air of the greenhouse to the vegetable plot in one move will, at best, give them a rude shock and, at worst, kill them.

Gradually introduce them to the outdoor world by giving them a few days in an intermediate environment.

Using a frame

If you have a garden frame, put the trays and pots of plants into it for about ten days before planting out. The 'light' can be taken off altogether during the day if the weather is warm, sunny and not too windy, but if it is cold and blustery, leave the light on. Prop it open with a block of wood, or a brick, so as to leave a space 15cm (6 in) wide. For the first four or five nights close the light down completely. Later on it can be left open a few centimetres depending on how cold the weather happens to be. Should you strike a patch of hard frost at the outset of hardening off give the plants added protection by throwing a sack or two (or a sheet of heavy gauge polythene) over the frame at night. After hardening off for about 10 to 14 days, the plants will be sturdy enough to withstand outdoor life.

Hardening off under cloches

Glass or plastic cloches are invaluable for hardening off. Place the trays or pots in a straight line on the vegetable patch and put a row of cloches over them. After closing the ends of the row with appropriate end-pieces, leave them for a week. Then remove the cloches and transplant the vegetables into the prepared ground. Cover them again with cloches and seal both ends of the rows. Placing the end-pieces in position is very important: without them the rows of cloches become miniature wind tunnels, creating highly unsuitable conditions for tender plants.

Cloches that are only being used for hardening off can be removed after seven to ten days for use elsewhere. If you want to bring the crop on (force it to maturity days or even weeks earlier than normal) leave the cloches in position until the growing plants need more headroom. With 'tender' plants—such as outdoor cucumbers or runner beans—leave the cloches over them until you are sure that all danger of frost is past.

These are only a few of the uses to which cloches can be put. For those of you who are gardening on a tight budget, a few pounds spent on cloches will provide you with inexpensive heat-retaining, plant-protecting equipment.

Hardening off in the open

If you don't own a frame or cloches you can harden off the plants by taking the trays and pots out of the greenhouse every morning and placing them in a warm, sheltered part of the garden. An ideal place would be at the foot of a south- or west-facing wall, fence or hedge—somewhere where they will catch the sun. At night, take them back into the greenhouse and repeat the out-and-in procedure until you feel they have toughened up enough to stay out overnight. Then leave them outdoors for four or five days and nights and your plants will be sufficiently robust to face the open-air life.

Maincrop potatoes

Out in the vegetable plot it is about time to plant the maincrop potatoes. Use the same method as for the earlies (see Week 6) but plant the sets or 'seeds' 30–40cm (12–15 in) apart and feed them more generously. Before replacing the soil, cover them with 8–10cm (3–4 in) of rotted manure or compost and sprinkle over a general compound fertilizer, such as Growmore, at around 60g per m run (2 oz per yd) of row. The more you feed potatoes, the heavier the crop will be.

If, by any chance, you run out of 'seed' before you get to the end of the last row, cut the largest in half with a knife, dust the cut ends with lime and plant the two halves. In fact, if the seed potatoes are on the large side when you go to purchase them, buy less, treat them all this way and save money; the crop will be just as good.

Selecting potato varieties

There are many excellent varieties of maincrop potatoes to choose from. The best course is to try several until you find

We have put a cold frame in the Edible Garden in a warm sunny spot, conveniently near the greenhouse (see ground plan below). It is made of timber which retains warmth longer than other materials—an important factor when hardening off seedlings

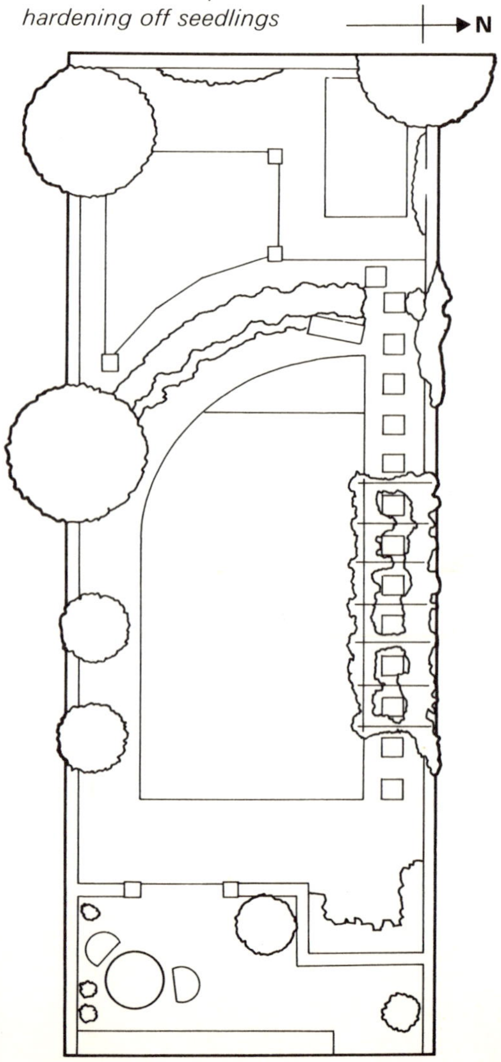

Ring-culture tomatoes growing in the greenhouse. The fruit-laden trusses are supported by tying in to bamboo canes

one that suits your soil and your palate.

King Edward is a heavy cropper in fertile, medium to heavy soils, while Arran Banner does well on light soils. Majestic crops heavily and Pentland Crown stores well. Then there is Golden Wonder—perhaps the finest-flavoured of all potatoes.

Tomatoes for outdoors

A few seeds sown now in the propagator will provide you with tomato plants for planting outside by mid summer (June) when, barring freak weather conditions, frost should be over. Given a reasonably good summer and a sunny, sheltered spot in the garden, each plant will yield several pounds of ripe fruit. Any green fruit left at the end of the season makes a delicious green tomato chutney.

If you don't have a vegetable plot you can still grow tomatoes, in a variety of containers, and put them on patios, terraces or anywhere that the plants will get plenty of sun and shelter from strong winds.

Varieties for outdoors

All tomato varieties can be grown out of doors but not all give good crops. However, a number of varieties have been specially bred for outdoor cultivation. They are somewhat hardier than the accepted greenhouse varieties and, in consequence, they grow better and give a higher yield.

We have tried most of them and have seen nearly all of them growing in seedsmen's trial grounds. We consider one of the best for form, flavour and fulfilment is the F.1 hybrid Gemini. It also matures and ripens some 10 to 20 days earlier than any other.

Gemini is a tall plant and needs a stout cane to keep it upright. If you prefer a shorter variety that doesn't require staking, sow either Amateur or the more recent Sleaford Abundance. Both are bushy, stocky plants that grow only about 30cm (12 in) or so high and are ideal for exposed sites. Of the two, Sleaford Abundance has the advantage of heavier and earlier cropping. The fruits are medium sized, beautifully red and round and have a sweet, tangy flavour.

To avoid root disturbance and growth check later on, sow two seeds per 8cm (3 in) peat or plastic pot in J.I. No 1 or an equivalent soilless compost. If both seedlings emerge, remove one and let the other grow on. Put the pots where they will receive plenty of light.

IN THE GREENHOUSE

It is time to start preparations for planting the tomatoes in their fruiting positions in the greenhouse.

Ring-culture tomatoes

Our recommendation is that you use the ring-culture method for your tomatoes. It entails a certain amount of initial preparation, but once this is done you will be rewarded by season after season of top quality fruit. The fundamental requirement of successful tomato culture is to grow the plant roots in a sterile medium – peat or aggregate – in a polythene-lined trench. Remember, if you use aggregate as the medium, to begin by removing the soil to a depth of 23cm (9 in) at one end of the greenhouse bed, rising to a depth of 15cm (6 in) at the other end. This slight slope provides gradual drainage. If you are using horticultural peat instead of aggregate, a 10–15cm (4–6 in) layer is sufficient. It needs replacing every three to five years, but it is light and easy to handle and comes in very useful later as top dressing.

Place your bottomless rings 60cm (24 in) apart on the base material, fill them with J.I. No 3 to within 2–3cm (1 in) of their rims, soak them with water and leave them for a week before planting the tomatoes.

There are two reasons why you should not plant immediately. First, it gives the compost time to settle. Secondly, it gives it time to warm up and reach the same temperature as the compost in which the tomatoes are already growing in their small pots. If you plant them as soon as the rings are filled, the plant roots find themselves in a growing medium which is several degrees colder than they are accustomed to. The result is a severe growth check at a critical time, and a subsequent detrimental effect on the earliness and cropping ability of the lower trusses.

Planting in soil

You can plant the tomatoes—60cm (24 in) apart—straight into the greenhouse soil bed. The trouble with this method, however, is that after two or three years the soil becomes 'sick', having accumulated toxic elements that are unfavourable to the crop. You will then have to replace the top 30cm (12 in) of the greenhouse soil bed with fresh sterilized soil.

LATE SPRING SOWING
in the edible garden

As the soil gradually warms up and the days lengthen, there is more sowing to be done in the Edible Garden. Here we deal with putting in the maincrop of dwarf French beans as well as parsnips and parsley, and starting off runner beans on a sunny windowsill.

You have already sown a few dwarf French beans in the greenhouse for an early crop; now it is time to sow the main crop outdoors.

Take out a shallow drill 2–5cm (1–2 in) deep and the width of a spade and sow the seeds in it 15cm (6 in) apart, alternately, along each side. Before you put the soil back over the seeds give it a light dusting with Fish, blood and bone. After covering the seeds firm the soil down with the back of the spade. Finally, make some shallow holes at the ends of the row and drop in a few extra seeds to provide reserve seedlings should any of the drill sowings fail.

In mild parts of the country the seeds should germinate normally, unless it turns very cold for a long period. Elsewhere you ought to cover the row with cloches to hasten, and increase, the probability of good germination. Because of its dwarf, bushy growth that rarely exceeds 30–40cm (12–15 in) in height, this is one crop that can stay under cloches until beginning to flower. As the plants get bigger, ventilate them on hot, sunny days by removing the cloche end-pieces.

Dwarf French bean varieties

There are not many varieties of dwarf French bean and those in general cultivation are all good. One fine variety is Tendergreen which has round, fleshy, juicy, stringless pods. Another good choice is Earligreen which, as its name suggests, matures earlier than many others. For something a little different try a golden yellow variety – Kinghorn Wax; its pods are round and waxy and have a superb flavour.

Dwarf French beans are easy to grow and, because they are bushy and compact, are ideal for the small garden. Regular picking of the pods encourages them to keep on cropping. Pick them when they are young, slim and tender. The variety Earligreen (shown left), as its name suggests, is an early cropper

How to grow haricots

Another type of dwarf French bean is the haricot which you can either eat fresh and green or leave to mature on the plant and then pick for storing as dried beans. A good variety is Carters Granda. Sow the seeds as you would the ordinary dwarf French beans.

Leave any unpicked pods on the plant until they turn brown. Towards the end of the season lift the whole plant out of the soil and hang it, upside down, in an airy shed or garage to dry off completely.

IN THE GREENHOUSE

Plant out the cucumber and provide the greenhouse with some kind of shading. In the propagator, start a few early runner beans.

Runner beans

A sowing of runner beans in the propagator now will extend the cropping period by several weeks, and the pods will start forming much earlier.

Runner beans are half-hardy plants; except in mild areas, therefore, you cannot sow them outdoors until well into early summer (the middle of May) at the earliest. This means that they do not begin to yield well until early autumn (August) and only have a short harvest before cold nights and first frosts of autumn finish them off.

But you can lengthen the cropping season by sowing the seeds in warmth some four weeks earlier than you would normally sow outdoors.

Sow the seeds singly, on their ends, and 2–3cm (1 in) deep in 8cm (3 in) pots of seed compost. Until the seedlings break through the surface, keep the compost barely moist; overwatering it (until it is soggy) often rots the seeds before they start to grow.

Germination takes about 10–14 days – sometimes a little longer, depending on room temperature.

Varieties of runner bean

If you like a long-podded bean we

When quite dry shell the pods and store the seeds in bottles, tins or boxes for use as required.

Parsnip cultivation

One popular vegetable which we haven't yet started to grow is the parsnip. It used to be thought that the earlier they were sown the better; but recent experience has proved otherwise.

Parsnips are an easy crop to cultivate, but they are prone to the disfiguring disease known as canker. The best way of avoiding canker is to sow now or even later, rather than in mid spring (March), and to give the rows a light dusting of lime after sowing. There are also one or two canker-resistant varieties now available. One of these is Avonresister, but unfortunately it is a shy seeder (produces little seed) and you may have difficulty buying it. If you can't obtain it, choose instead a long-rooted variety (such as Hollow Crown Improved) and sow from now until early summer (mid May), adding a little lime to help ward off canker.

To sow, take out shallow drills 6mm (¼ in) deep and about 30cm (12 in) apart and sprinkle the seeds in fairly thickly. When the seedlings are large enough to handle easily, thin them out to about 15cm (6 in) apart and draw a little soil around them to prevent them falling over. They require no further attention other than weeding, and are ready for the table in the autumn. Don't lift them until the ground has had a touch or two of frost as only then do they acquire their full flavour and sweetness.

Sowing a patch of parsley

Sow your parsley in a short row or as a clump in the herb bed. It also thrives in tubs and window boxes – or even in an old bucket outside the back door.

For some reason parsley sowing is surrounded by superstition. Some gardeners claim the seeds will only germinate if they are sown when the moon is full, whilst others maintain they only grow if sown on Good Friday. All these mistaken beliefs stem from the fact that the seeds have very hard skins and it takes a lot of moisture, and often considerable time, before they can begin to swell and germinate. Soaking the seeds in water for 48 hours before sowing helps, but then they stick to each other and it becomes extremely difficult to sow them evenly. A method that we've used successfully for many years is to sow thinly in a drill 6mm (¼ in) deep and then pour a kettle of boiling water over the seeds before covering them with soil. The hot water softens the seed coat and germination is asssured, although it may take anything from three to six weeks before you see any visible signs of growth.

Windowsill runner beans

Runner beans can be started in warmth several weeks before outdoor sowings can be made. The seeds will germinate if the pots are placed on a sunny windowsill, providing it does not get bitterly cold at night. For sowing details see below.

suggest the aptly-named variety As Long As Your Arm or the exhibitor's favourite Yardstick. If your preference is for shorter, fatter pods that hang in thick clusters then Cookham Dene, Streamline and Scarlet Emperor are all good choices. If you have previously experienced difficulty in getting the flowers to set pods (a characteristic failing of runner beans, especially in dry and sunny summers) try sowing the variety Fry. Its reliability may be partly due to the fact that its flowers are self-pollinating and therefore not dependent on passing insects for cross pollination. It may also be that its white flowers do not tempt sparrows and other birds to peck at them as the red-flowered varieties seem to do. But whatever the reason, it crops well and regularly, has a good flavour and the pods are stringless and freeze well.

If you can't obtain this variety locally you will find it in most seedsmen's catalogues.

Preparing cucumber ring

Cucumber plants grow quickly and your seedling will now be large enough to plant in its final position.

Cucumbers are odd things. Their requirements are at first sight contradictory. On the one hand they like plenty of water around their roots at all times; on the other hand they must have free open drainage. They are also the greediest of all greenhouse crops – you can't overfeed them.

The problem is how to provide them with adequate water without their roots standing in a permanent bath of it. There are several ways of growing them, but most of them are so complicated as to be hardly worthwhile for the cultivation of one solitary cucumber plant.

The method we consider best is the one used for growing ring-culture tomatoes – in bottomless rings so that they enjoy free drainage, plenty of food and ample water as required.

Half-fill a ring with J.I. No 2 mixed half-and-half with cow dung. If you can't obtain cow dung then rotted garden compost is just as good. Water the ring thoroughly and leave it to stand for a week, as you did for the tomatoes on page 85.

When you come to plant the cucumber you should place the ring in the corner of the greenhouse farthest away from the door because cucumbers hate draughts.

Planting the tomatoes

If you are using the ring-culture method for your greenhouse tomatoes you can now plant them into their well-soaked rings. Put one plant in each ring, then give them a good watering to settle them in. In future only water the base material, never the compost. This encourages the plants to send their roots down into the peat or aggregate.

Beans in pots

A couple of weeks ago you sowed some dwarf French beans in large pots in the greenhouse for an early harvest. The plants should now be through the soil. As they grow, top up the soil in the pots till it comes to within 13mm (½ in) of the rim.

Shading the greenhouse

Too much direct sunlight beating down on plants under glass is not good for them. Unless your greenhouse is fitted with shading blinds, which can be raised or lowered according to the weather, light shading of the glass panes is advisable.

For this you can either use a weak whitewash (made by mixing a little lime in water) or, preferably, use the proprietary roof-shading paint which you can get from any good garden centre or shop. Don't lay it on too thickly or you will cut out valuable light. The object is to reduce the intensity of direct sunlight to an acceptable level, without detracting from the growth of the plants.

If you don't want to paint the outside of the glass, another way (which we learnt from fellow gardeners) is to hang sheets of newspaper over the bar of a plastic-covered or wire coat-hanger. Suspend the hangers from the roof outside. They can easily be moved to provide shade as and when it is needed.

TASKS FOR LATE SPRING
in the edible garden

Spring is now far advanced. In step with the season we show you the best ways of supporting peas, earthing up the early potatoes, hardening off the onions and planting out some of the vegetables that are fully hardened off.

Your row of early peas should now be well through the soil. Take a close look at them, they may require some attention. Young pea seedlings are susceptible to damage by the pea weevil. This insect pest chews neat, semi-circular holes out of the leaf edges and can reduce the total leaf area by as much as a half or more. The smaller the leaf area the less food the plants are able to manufacture for themselves, and in consequence the smaller the crop will be. At the first sign of damage, dust the plants with derris in the early morning when the insects are most active. You will probably have noticed, here and there, some thin, wispy growths that look like small, irregularly-coiled springs. These are the tendrils by which the plants attach themselves to whatever support is available. If no prop is provided they cling to each other in the mistaken belief that they can give adequate mutual support. But come a gust of wind, and the weight of filled pods will easily topple them over. Then they will cease flowering and podding long before they should.

Supporting with twigs

In the 'old days' when, even for town dwellers, the countryside was only a short journey away, every gardener would take his knife or bill-hook to the hedgerows and cut bundles of hazel twigs. If you live in or near the country you can still avail yourself of a free supply of these excellent pea-supports, provided you get the local farmer's permission. Stick them in, at 30–45cm (12–18 in) intervals, along each side of the rows, and the peas will find their own way up them. At the end of the season, when you strip the rows and put the yellowing stems and leaves on the compost heap, the twigs will make fine kindling wood—if you still have an open fireplace and are able to burn wood.

Supporting with netting

If you can't get twigs then a simple net structure is the answer, using either wire or nylon netting, both of which will give several years of faithful service. Wire netting is initially the most expensive but its greater rigidity and stability makes it a worthwhile investment for re-use in the future.

When you buy, bear in mind that the total length you require is double the length of the longest row that you are ever likely to grow. You can always fold any surplus wire round the end of the last supporting post, but you can't stretch it out if you have bought too little.

You must also decide whether you will always be content to grow dwarf varieties, which do not exceed 60–75cm (2–2½ ft) in height, or whether you may want to try a row of tall 1·5–2m (5–6 ft) peas, as this will affect the height of the netting. For dwarf varieties buy 8cm (3 in) mesh wire-netting 1m (3 ft) wide and whatever length you need. For tall peas the netting will need to be 2m (6½ ft) wide.

The pea flower, heralding a good harvest

Erecting the netting

When putting up the support structure ask a friend or neighbour to help you. Wire netting, particularly when fresh from a new coil, tends to spring back just as you are ready to put the retaining cane in. This can damage your temper, your person and your young pea seedlings, which may be bruised or even decapitated in the struggle.

Begin by fixing two stout canes or posts about 30cm (12 in) apart at each end of the row, driven well into the ground, so that they can take the weight of the row in full pod without collapsing. Next, staple or tie the end of the coil to one of the end

1 *Cabbage seedling ready to transplant*
2 *Transplanting to final growing position*
3 *Thinning out for use as spring greens*
4 *Earthing-up with a swan-necked hoe*

posts and unwind about 2–2·5m (6–8 ft) of wire down one side of the row. Get your friend to hold the coil while you thread a cane through the mesh from top to bottom and into the soil about 15cm (6 in) away from the pea plant. Carry on down the row, stopping at intervals of 2–5m (6–8 ft) to insert a stabilizing cane. When you reach the end of the row loop the coil around the two end stakes and tie it to both, then proceed up the other side of the row in similar fashion, and finally tie or staple the end of the coil to the last stake.

This two-sided support structure traps the plants inside and compels them to climb up one side or the other. When the row has finished cropping it is a simple matter to part the plants from the wire and roll it up—still attached to the first stake—until it is needed again. You can use strong nylon or polythene plastic netting instead of wire.

In some gardens you will find a single length of netting used in preference to the double-enclosed system. Certainly one length is cheaper than two and easier to erect, but it does not provide as strong a support and several of the plants will grow away from, rather than on to, it.

When the structure is securely fixed, give the soil at the base of the plants a light dusting of lime, which peas like. It also helps to prevent the condition known as root rot, revealed as yellowing of the leaves and stems just above ground level.

Hardening off onions

The onions sown earlier in the greenhouse will, by now, be some 15cm (6 in) tall, and are ready for hardening off (prior to planting out in a week or so) in the cold frame or under cloches. Remember that if you don't own either you can harden them off by putting them out in a sunny place during the day.

Ideally the onion bed should be thoroughly dug and well manured in the autumn. But our plot, prepared in early spring, is nearly ready. All it needs now is a raking over to remove surface stones, followed by a hoeing to annihilate the carpet of small weeds that pop up all over the bare earth.

Summer cabbages and cauliflowers

The cabbages and cauliflowers that have been hardening off can be planted out now. They should be spaced 45cm (18 in) apart with an equal distance between rows. Make holes in the soil with a dibber and plant the vegetables up to their lowest leaves. Firm round each plant carefully, then water them well in.

Planting out lettuce

It is time to plant out any lettuce still hardening off and also to transplant the seedlings from the outdoor sowings. Lettuce do not take kindly to moving. Their roots are small and fibrous and their leaves are comparatively large and delicate. They lose a vast amount of moisture through their leaves, and after transplanting are inclined to become limp and floppy, because the rate of water flow from the roots to leaves has been interrupted and impaired. Unless you can somehow minimize water loss and this incipient wilt, the seedlings will experience a severe growth check. This will frequently result in the plants running to seed before they have made usable hearts.

Bushy twigs, gathered from hedgerows and woods, make excellent supports for peas. Stick one in beside each plant

One way of reducing the risk is to make sure that you always transplant from a wet soil or compost, even if this means watering an hour or so before tackling the job. Furthermore, try to transplant in the later afternoon or evening of a still, cloudy day when water loss from the leaves is at its lowest ebb. After transplanting, give plenty of water every evening at sundown unless it is raining.

Lift the seedlings out of their trays or beds with care. Never pull them out or you will snap the main root system. Put a trowel well under them, prise them up in groups and tease them gently apart, keeping their roots intact with as much soil as possible still clinging to them, and replant them straight away. After they are in, draw a little soil around each one to prevent them from swaying back and forth in the wind and loosening their roots in the soil. Lastly, if your garden is populated with slugs they will make straight for your transplanted lettuce, so put down some slug pellets.

Successional sowings
Sow some more lettuce for a steady supply throughout the summer. Sow a short, part-row, thinly and shallowly and water afterwards if the soil is dry. Put in a pinch of radish seed anywhere vacant, and a row of spring onions.

Above: pea tendrils twining round netting
Below and below right: earthing up potatoes protects the tubers from being exposed to light and turning green

Earthing up early potatoes
The next job is to give the early potatoes their first earthing. Loosen the soil on each side of the rows with a rake and pull some of it right up to, and around, the emerging stems and leaves. By earthing you protect the plants against buffeting winds and ensure that no young tubers are exposed on the soil surface. Potatoes that are uncovered turn green and, if cooked and eaten, can cause stomach upsets. You also kill any weeds growing between the rows when you earth up.

Keeping up the weeding
Watch those weeds; forget about them and they will get the upper hand. Hoe between the rows once a week to get rid of them when they are no more than seedlings. If you leave them to flower and seed you will have hundreds of weeds flourishing where previously there were only a few.

But hoe with care, for some of the earlier-sown vegetables are growing quite big and many have lateral roots running just below the soil surface. You can, for instance, severely damage the roots of onions and lettuce if you take the hoe right up to the plants. So hoe lightly down the centre of the space between rows and hand-weed the rest.

IN THE GREENHOUSE

Tending the dwarf French beans and tomato seedlings and planting out the cucumber into its ring and the peppers into their final pots are this week's jobs.

Planting out the cucumber
The time has come to place the cucumber in its ring and the ring on the peat or aggregate bed in a corner of the greenhouse well away from the door. Drench the ring with water daily. The excess will drain away into the soil, aggregate or peat below. As the plant grows, top up the ring with a similar mixture (J.I. No 2 mixed half-and-half with cow dung or well-rotted garden compost) until it comes to within 2–3cm (1 in) of the rim.

Dwarf French beans
Dwarf French bean plants tend to get top heavy as they get bigger, so stick a few bushy, branching twigs into the pots to provide a little support. Start feeding the plants once a fortnight.

Tomato seedlings
If the tomatoes (sown in warmth two weeks ago for planting outdoors later) have germinated, take them out of the propagator. If two seedlings have emerged in any of the pots, take one out and leave the other. Put the pots in the greenhouse, making sure they are in full light, till planting out time.

Potting up peppers
If the peppers are now about 15–25cm (6–9 in) tall then they are ready for their final planting. Plant them singly into 20–25cm (8–10 in) pots of potting compost. By putting them in pots you will be able to move them outside in mid summer (June). They will grow perfectly well in the open if you put the pots against a warm, south-facing wall that will protect them from cold winds.

Put a 90cm (3 ft) cane in each pot to support the plants, water regularly and give them a liquid feed every fortnight from mid summer (June) onwards.

FEEDING AND WATERING
in the edible garden

Spring has turned to early summer in the Edible Garden. Feeding and watering the vegetables in the food plot are the main concerns at this time of the year.
Other jobs include pollinating the greenhouse tomatoes, caring for crops under cloches and runner beans indoors, and planting out the onions.

From now until late summer (July) growth will be at its maximum. For the next ten weeks or so the long hours of daylight and the sun's warmth generate frantic activity within the cell structure of plants. Once mid summer has been reached, and the days begin to shorten again, most of our vegetables, with the exception of those that will mature in winter or next spring, slow down and begin ripening.

Food and water

Take full advantage of the period of optimum growth by giving the plants everything they require. First and foremost they need water. Just as you need a free circulation of blood to provide all parts of your body with food and oxygen, so plants need a plentiful supply of water to transport the essential elements that support their life. Do remember that your plants can only use the plant foods in the soil if they are dissolved in water.

Furthermore a high concentration of inorganic fertilizers in a dry soil can kill, rather than feed, them. The less water there is, the more concentrated the fertilizer solution becomes until it may reach a point where, instead of flowing into the roots it draws liquid out of them and the plants die of dehydration (or, at best, suffer a severe check).

Hoses and sprinklers

During long, dry spells, therefore, give the plants plenty of water. Providing there are no water restrictions in force in your area, use a hosepipe in preference to a watering can. There is nothing worse than giving a parched plant a few drops of water when it needs a good soaking. If the soil is already dry it will itself absorb a considerable volume of water, just to moisten its surface. If you merely fill a watering can full and wave it over your vegetables you will wet the leaves and no more. It is tempting to make one can do for a whole row, regardless of its length. Plodding back and forth from tap to plot is time-consuming and tiring; this is why a hosepipe (where permitted) is the answer.

Another invaluable piece of watering equipment is an oscillating sprinkler – an attachment which fits on the end of the hose. Depending on the model, and on how you regulate it, it can give your garden a thorough soaking over an area of some 225 sq m (2,500 sq ft). Attach the free end of the hose to the tap, turn it on and leave it to do the watering for you.

Soluble plant foods

Once the soil is saturated, right down to the deepest roots, start giving the vegetables a booster feed. All crops will give a higher yield if they are given a little extra plant food during their period of rapid growth. The best, and easiest, way of doing this is to use soluble feeds. These are available either as concentrated liquids in bottles or as powders which dissolve readily in water. Of the two the powdered forms are the cheapest, needing only about one teaspoonful to 10 lit (2 gal) of water to give a nutritional solution of the required strength.

The advantages of using a soluble feed are twofold. First, the liquid that falls on the wet soil quickly finds its way down to the roots and is rapidly absorbed into the stems and leaves. Secondly, the liquid that falls on the leaves is taken in through the minute leaf pores, or stomata, and the nutrients become immediately available to the plant. This is called 'foliar feeding' and it is the quickest way there is of getting plants to respond to applied fertilizers.

These liquid feeds must only be regarded as boosters or bonuses. Your main plant feeding programme still entails the proper application of organic

IN THE GREENHOUSE

In order to produce a bumper tomato crop you must make sure that the flowers have set (been pollinated).

Pollinating greenhouse tomatoes

The tomatoes are showing, or are about to show, the first flowers on the bottom trusses. 'Truss' is the term used to describe the cluster of flowers borne on the stem which emerges from the axil of one of the lower leaves. The first truss, the lowest to form on the stem, is always the problem one. Its flowers are almost always reluctant to set.

Before the flower can perform its proper function of developing into a fruit, ripe pollen must drop on to a receptive stigma (the top part of the female flower organ). The pollen then works its way down into the ovary and fertilizes it. Not only must the pollen be ripe, but the conditions for its transference from an anther (the part of the male flower that contains pollen) to a stigma must be favourable. Pollen travels best in warm, humid conditions and worst when the air in the greenhouse is dry and cold. The bottom truss, being low down and near ground level, is sited in the coldest part of the greenhouse because warm air rises and is replaced by colder air. Therefore, in order to get as many of the flowers as possible to set, they need some help. One way is to damp down the path and surrounding ground level area every morning to create a moist atmosphere. At the same time the top ventilator should be opened to keep the atmosphere moving and buoyant. Next, give each plant a few gentle taps to dislodge the pollen and get it airborne.

You may find that you get a better set if you place a sheet of white polythene over the ground beneath the plants to reflect light and warmth upwards onto the trusses. As a last

(continued overleaf)

Damp down greenhouse path; humid air helps tomatoes to pollinate

manures to the soil before planting. These represent the staple diet of the plants; the liquid feeds are supplements applied to give increased yields under intensive cultivation.

Provide your crops with adequate water and ample food, from now until late summer (July) and they will be less liable to run prematurely to seed, and will be bigger, better and tastier as a result.

Caring for cloche crops

Crops under cloches also need water. Being permanently under cover they don't even get the full benefit of natural rainfall. There are one or two self-watering cloches which don't have to be removed in order to water the plants underneath them, but the majority have to be lifted before, and replaced after, watering.

On the other hand the soil under the cloches does not lose water quite as quickly as the soil outside. Much of it condenses on the inside of the glass or plastic and is returned to the soil. So look at the soil under your cloches at regular intervals and weed or water the soil.

Now that the days and nights are warmer you can remove the cloches altogether from most vegetables providing there are no frost warnings. And crops like lettuce, radish and spring onions taste better if they are not forced too much. An early start for seed germination and subsequent weather protection is one thing, but forcing does detract from quality. Lettuce left too long under cloches have a tendency to be limp, loose-hearted and a little leathery. Use the cloches to bring them on by all means, but give them the open air when they are half grown; they will form tighter hearts and have a better flavour. The only crops that still need protection are those that are liable to damage by frost, such as dwarf French beans.

Hardening off leeks

Harden off the leeks for a week or so in a cold frame or under cloches, or introduce them gradually to the elements by putting them outside in a warm spot on sunny days, bringing them in again at night.

Planting out onions

Onions can be awkward vegetables to plant out because they are top heavy at this stage. Their roots consist of no more than one or two white threads attached to the base of a pair of long, lanky, upright leaves. If you try to plant them with their roots just below soil level, they refuse to stand up and are easily dislodged by wind and rain.

Overcome this problem by drawing out a shallow drill 13mm (½ in) deep with hoe and line. Place the seedlings in it, 15–20cm (6–8 in) apart, with 23cm (9 in) between the drills. With your fingers pull a little soil over the roots, and firm gently, then heap some more soil around each plantlet to keep it firm and upright. Finally soak the whole bed with water to give them every opportunity to re-root quickly.

Windowsill runner beans

If the first leaves have appeared, increase watering and keep the plants near to the window for maximum light.

Pigeon-scaring

Are your vegetables being pecked to tatters by pigeons? If so paint some empty bottles or cans a bright red, push a few 1·2m (4 ft) canes into the ground between the rows and stick the inverted bottles or cans on top of them. It will keep the pigeons away for a year at least, although they may eventually get used to them.

Above: white polythene reflects light
Below: tap flowers to help setting

resort you can always obtain a proprietary tomato setting agent which you apply to the flowers to encourage them to set and form fruit.

To feed soilbed tomatoes pour liquid feed into pots sunk in soil

The higher trusses usually set without trouble providing you damp down regularly and follow a consistent feeding programme to keep the plants growing steadily and strongly.

Feeding greenhouse tomatoes

Begin feeding as soon as the first flower opens on the bottom truss. If you are growing your plants by the ring-culture system, feed into the rings once a week using a liquid fertilizer.

There are, on the market, a variety of branded liquid feeds which are especially formulated to encourage tomato plants to grow and produce fine fruit; all do the job cleanly, efficiently and with the minimum fuss and bother.

If you are growing tomatoes in the greenhouse soil bed, apply the liquid fertilizer once a fortnight all over the bed. In this case the soluble feed supplements the fertilizer forked in before planting. The disadvantage of liquid-feeding the whole bed is that it is impossible to give each plant a controlled amount. It also tends to create over-acidity unless the soil is removed and replaced every year. One way of overcoming the problem is to sink 10cm (4 in) pots, up to their rims, into the soil 30–40cm (12–15 in) away from the base of each plant. Once every two to three weeks fill the pots with a standard liquid feed solution which will gradually percolate through to the roots of the adjacent plants. This method achieves a reasonable control of acidity and means that you don't have to apply fertilizer to the entire bed, so it is less wasteful.

Runner beans

If the seeds have germinated, take the pots out of the propagator and follow the advice given in the section on windowsill runner beans (see above).

SOME BASIC PRINCIPLES
in the edible garden

In conclusion, we raise a few general points to be borne in mind by the conscientious gardener. Crop rotation, for instance, will help to eliminate pests and diseases that carry over from season to season, ensuring a healthy, fertile soil that is a pre-condition of a good crop. The flavour of a freshly-picked vegetable can rarely be matched by that of those bought in a shop.

In this, the Edible Garden section of the book, we have tried to convey some of the intense pleasure and satisfaction to be derived from growing your own vegetables. It must be emphasized that the practice of 'growing one's own' is not difficult or demanding. Success is assured provided a few basic principles are recognized and followed.

Soil fertility

The most important of all the basic principles is soil fertility. The old saying that 'you only get out of the soil what you put into it' is still as true today as it was when Man first began to cultivate a patch of land. To achieve and maintain a fertile soil is purely a matter of applying a reasonable balance of natural, organic manures or composts, together with concentrated organic or inorganic fertilisers. Regular, annual applications of such nutritional elements keep the soil fertile, retentive and active, as well as capable of supporting good, strong growth.

Pest control

The Edible Garden has dealt with a number of the pests and diseases that may beset vegetables during growth. It should be stressed that plants grown in rich, fertile ground are better equipped to withstand pestilence than are those struggling along in poor soil. By virtue of their hybrid vigour, F.1. hybrids also have an inherent resistance to pest attack and they should be used whenever possible.

Nevertheless a few vegetable pests and diseases are extremely persistent and once present, they are difficult to eradicate. The cabbage family, the brassicas, are particularly prone to pest problems and as they represent a very important section of our all-the-year-round vegetables it pays to take precautionary measures before sowing and planting these crops. Fortunately we now have at our disposal, highly effective soil pesticides that provide total protection against soil-borne pests such as carrot fly and cabbage root fly. Their annual use as preventative measures is very strongly advocated. Similarly, a whole range of systemic insecticides and fungicides provides effective deterrents against common pests such as greenfly, whitefly, blight, mildew and many others.

But one fungal pest still soldiers on with immunity – the club root disease of brassicas. Bearing in mind that this is a soil-borne disease, always grow your cabbage and related plants from seed. Never accept plants from well-meaning friends and neighbours and never buy them either. For gardeners who already have club root in their vegetable plots, two independent and experienced sources have verified the efficacy of the following

tip; a moth ball put into each planting hole as you plant will, it is claimed, eradicate the disease.

Crop rotation
As indicated, pest control is not merely a matter of using chemical pesticides widely and indiscriminately. Robust plants have greater resistance to pests and also the practice of crop rotation plays no small part in keeping them at bay. A crop rotation system is quite simple. Divide your vegetable plot roughly into three parts – A, B and C. In the first year, part A is limed and planted with brassicas, part B is planted with peas and beans and part C is for everything else including onions, root crops and salads. In the second and subsequent years the crop groups are moved from A to B, B to C and C to A. In this way no group of crops is grown in the same piece of ground more often than once in every three years.

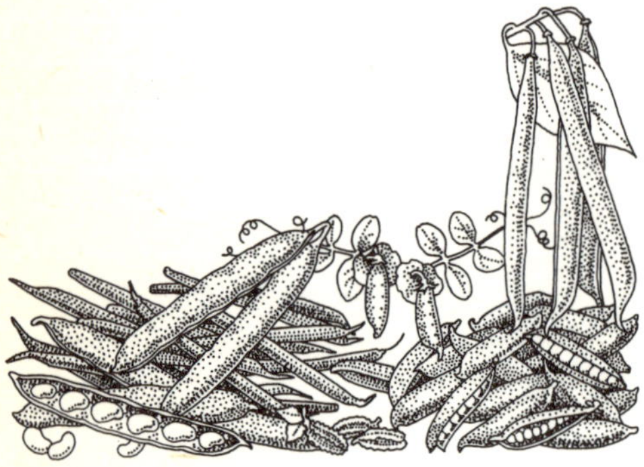

The advantages of this simple crop rotation are twofold: firstly, moving the crops around reduces the danger of a build-up of soil-borne pests, many of which infect their host plants in the summer, then overwinter in the ground to reinfect the new plants in the following year. Secondly, different crop groups require and use different quantities of the three essential plant nutrients – nitrogen, phosphate and potash. Root-crops for instance are hungry for phosphates, while leafy crops use up more nitrogen than other crops with comparatively small leaf areas. In addition, all members of the pea and bean family, the legumes, actually manufacture a proportion of their own nitrogen fertilizers. The process occurs in the nodules on the roots and at the end of the season a fair amount of nitrogen is left in the soil to benefit subsequent crops. Crop rotation therefore ensures that residual nutrients, remaining in the ground after one crop group has been removed, are available for use by a following group that can utilize them to their full advantage.

The well-planned plot
Finally it must be stressed that a vegetable plot that has been well-planned, should provide at least one fresh vegetable every week of the year. In summer the crops come thick and fast, and gluts of greens are commonplace. All too often the winter vegetable plot is bare whereas it should be stocked with leeks, kale, winter cabbages, swedes, parsnips, brussels sprouts and purple-sprouting broccoli. The well-planned plot will also provide vegetables that may be stored and used during the winter months.

Onions grown from seeds or sets are lifted in early autumn (August) and if properly dried and ripened they will keep in perfect condition for several months. Beetroot and carrots are forked up in late autumn (October). After lifting, their leaves are cut off and they are placed, in layers, in boxes of sand or slightly moist peat. The boxes should be kept in a cold but frost-proof place where rats and mice cannot get at them. Given these conditions the roots will keep firm and delicious until the following spring.

Don't forget that the planning of the following year's cropping programme can profitably be done during the long winter evenings; order your seed catalogues, sit down with them and make a careful selection of crops and varieties to suit your tastes and space.

The growing season can be extended by the careful use of cloches and cold frames; seed can be given a good head-start if sown in a propagator or kept indoors until the ground has warmed up.

Don't miss a sowing date because you are short of stakes or nets, or because you didn't have the right fertilizer or herbicide. All these things can be thought out by the warmth of a winter fire.

Garden hygiene
A well-kept garden will benefit healthy crops. Winter-servicing your tools, tidying up the shed and keeping paths in good condition are all part of a successful Edible Garden.

LAWNS AND LAWN CARE

LAWN GRASSES AND THEIR USES

The standard of your lawn is largely determined by the grasses growing in it. The most effective way of ensuring that it is of a high quality is to choose the seed of grasses that will suit not only the intended uses of the lawn, but also the situation, soil and conditons already existing in your garden.

In a country like Britain, where green fields still abound and the climate is favourable to the growth of grass, it might seem a simple task to find suitable grasses for your lawn. However, the gardener's needs differ from those of the farmer. The farmer wants grasses that grow quickly and provide the greatest bulk in top growth, while the gardener needs low-growing, vigorous-rooted plants producing fine-bladed leaves that are evergreen, hard-wearing, and able to withstand repeated defoliation by cutting, as well as compete with broad-leaved weeds.

GRAMINEAE, the grass family, runs to well over 8000 species, of which some 100 or so are indigenous to Britain, but less than 20 are suitable for lawn-making. It is possible to grow a lawn from one species only, but this would be impractical as the lawn would be very difficult to maintain. Good lawns come from balanced mixtures of different species, especially selected strains and varieties that have been bred to emphasize desirable characteristics of the natural species, such as dwarfness, fineness of leaf, resilience to – and recovery from – wear and tear, drought-resistance, and disease-resistant vigour.

Primarily, the choice of grasses depends on the uses to which the lawn will be put, although growing conditions, particularly the soil, will also need to be taken into consideration. Some familiarity with the characteristics and performance of different grasses is, therefore, necessary. Lawn grasses fall broadly into four groups – fescues, bents, meadow-grasses and rye-grasses.

Fescues

The fescue genus, festuca, contains the most important grasses for fine lawns, notable for their hardiness, drought-resistance, fine, tough foliage and ability to thrive in poor soil conditions. There are two groups: red fescues, botanically distinguished by the unbroken sheaths that surround the leaves near their base, and sheep's fescues, slightly smaller, and with sheaths that are always split.

Chewings fescue – *Festuca rubra fallax* (*F. rubra commutata*) – is the most widely used red fescue, with a tufted habit and upright shoots, and fine foliage that withstands wear, close mowing and drought. It grows readily on most soils, including chalk, but prefers rather light, porous and well-drained conditions. It blends well with other grasses and is essential for the fine lawns of bowling or golf green texture and quality. Cut leaves, in fine weather, and older leaves in winter, may discolour and brown a little, but in active growth, leaf colour is a rich green. Seeds come largely from Oregon in the United States, although the type species originated in New Zealand.

Creeping red fescue – *F. rubra rubra* and other varieties – and its forms have slightly longer and broader leaves than Chewings. They are also a little more lax in habit, and spread by underground rhizomes and creeping stems. With good drought-resistance, easy establishment, and ready recovery from damage, they are highly useful for play-lawns, as well as football and games pitches, and succeed on most soils. One of the best forms in Britain is Dawson, named after Dr R. B. Dawson, who bred it at the Sports Turf Research Institute at Bingley in Yorkshire. It is finer in leaf than the type, and can be recommended for lawns swept by sea spray. A fine-leaved strain is Aberystwyth S.59, bred at the Welsh Plant Breeding Station.

Aberystwyth S.58, a form of sheep's fescue – *F. ovina* – has a dwarf, tufted habit, and tillers freely. Although slow to establish, it keeps growing under low winter temperatures, and is very tolerant of acid and peaty soil conditions. It may be usefully included in mixtures for such conditions, and is good for tennis and ornamental lawns that are hard used.

Bents

Grasses known as bents belong to the Agrostis genus, but only a few are important as lawn grasses. They are more dominant and aggressive than fescues, and apt to come through adverse conditions in better shape.

Densely-tufted Chewings fescue (top) prefers light, well-drained conditions, while loosely-tufted wood meadow-grass (centre) grows in woods and moist places Above: hard-wearing crested dog's-tail

Browntop bent (top) is commonly used for fine lawns, putting and bowling greens Perennial rye-grass (centre) is found in old pastures and is a valued hay-maker, like shallow-rooting Timothy grass (above)

Browntop bent – *Agrostis tenuis* – is an exceptionally valuable grass for fine lawns. It is of tufted habit, but spreads vigorously by surface runners (known as stolons) and underground stems (rhizomes). It has fine, slightly flattened leaves, and is hard wearing and drought resistant. It prefers lightish, well-drained soil, but grows on all but the waterlogged, tending to more rhizomatous growth on drier soils, and more stoloniferous on wetter. It blends well with other grasses, particularly Chewings fescue, and mixtures of the two can give the finest of lawns. Seeds originally come from New Zealand, but Holland, and Oregon in the United States are now sources, a fact reflected in the name of two newer strains – Oregon Highland and Dutch Holfior.

Velvet bent – *A. canina fascicularis* (*A.c. canina*) is a fine-leaved, pleasing grass that spreads by surface runners or stolons to make a dense, springy sward, but for appearances' sake it is better suited to damp or partially-shaded places than to open lawns subject to hard use. The related species *A.c. montana* – known as brown bent – comes from dry heath soils, and is of tufted habit, spreading slowly by slender rhizomes or sub-surface shoots to give a dense, attractive, drought-resistant sward, that is valuable for the fine turf of bowling and putting greens, and tennis courts. Neither velvet nor brown bents are readily available separately, but they can usually be found in bent seed mixtures.

Creeping bent – *A. stolonifera* – is a native wilding (wild variety), variable in form, and giving rise to tiny, windborne seeds that frequently invade lawns and are often present in browntop seed mixtures. The grass is fine-leaved, very hardy, and well adapted to heavy soils, and wet and shady situations. It spreads by long, trailing stolons that are resistant to mowing, but which need periodic thinning out – making it hardly worth a place in fine turf. However, the species has given rise to strong-growing, selected strains such as Emerald Velvet and Red Top that are propagated vegetatively by means of stolon cuttings.

Meadow-grasses

As their name suggests, meadow-grasses – of the poa genus – are more at home in fields than in fine lawns. Nevertheless, they can be invaluable for recreational and background lawns, amenity areas, and for certain difficult situations. They lower the cost of seed mixtures for gardens where the finish of a crown bowling green is not vital, blending well with fescues and bents, and nursing along the finer, lower-growing species.

Rough-stalked meadow-grass – *Poa trivialis* – is low-growing, with tufts of smooth, flattish, bright green leaves on thin, creeping, shallow-rooting stems or stolons. It does best on heavy, moist soils, tolerates partial shade, keeps good winter colour, and although not very hard-wearing, does well under the discipline of regular mowing. Seeds germinate quickly, and seedlings establish themselves within a short period, responding rapidly to growing weather. In drought conditions, and on soils that dry out easily, the foliage tends to lose colour, turning yellow to reddish brown.

Smooth-stalked meadow-grass – *P. pratensis* – is of erect, stiffish, tufted habit, with flat leaves of good colour. Slower to establish than the rough-stalked species, it spreads by means of creeping, stoloniferous underground stems, and is not only more resistant to wear, but also to dry conditions. It is the species for medium to light soils, and gardens where summer rainfall is apt to be light. It is very useful for grassing slopes, banks, and pathways subject to much use. In the

United States, it is known as Kentucky blue-grass, and improved strains with finer leaves are under development.

Wood meadow-grass – *P. nemoralis* – is a native of shady places, and is slightly tufted, with narrow, bright green leaves and short, creeping basal stems. It may be useful in mixtures for shady situations, but should not be mown closely, nor relied upon on heavy or clay soils.

Annual meadow-grass – *P. annua* – is a dwarf weed, and persistent with its ability to flower and seed readily and escape the mower blades. It can cast a whitish sheen on a new lawn in early summer (May), and becomes a self-perpetuating nuisance in flowerbeds and borders. With good culture, however, the perennial lawn grasses crowd it out.

Rye-grasses

Perennial rye-grass – *Lolium perenne* – is a widespread native of Britain, with smooth stems and broad leaves of tufted habit, that grows freely almost all the year round. It does well on most soils, particularly moist and heavy ones, germinating and growing vigorously, and the species is often included in mixtures for landscaped areas. For ornamental garden lawns, however, one of its selected varieties, such as Aberystwyth S.23 or Kentish rye-grass, is preferable: these are more durable, and provide swards with denser, more dwarf foliage, tillering freely with much shorter stalks.

Rye-grass in a seed mixture lowers the cost, and enables a serviceable turf for such areas as cricket outfields, games pitches, and general family play-lawns to be established quickly on a wide range of soils, except the very acid. It does need good cultivation and consistent cutting to keep it kempt and perennially attractive. Where an even, true surface is needed for bowls, croquet or golf, it would not be appropriate, giving too coarse a texture, and tending to oust finer-leaved grasses.

Two other species are sometimes used in special cases. One is crested dog's-tail – *Cynosurus cristatus* – that is of tufted, erect habit with smooth, narrow, flat, darkish leaves. It is valued chiefly for its hard-wearing qualities, especially for cricket wickets, garden paths and areas subject to much foot traffic. Although it will grow on most soils, acid or not, it is particularly suited to light ones and those that dry out quickly.

The other species is *Phleum pratense* – commonly known as Timothy grass – that is a strong-growing native of Britain, and is cultivated on farms for hay. The foliage is somewhat coarse, but the plant germinates and grows quickly, thriving in wet conditions and on heavy, damp, clay soils. It can be usefully included in seed mixtures for landscape and amenity lawns, and sports fields, but the improved strain – Aberystwyth S.50 – should be specified.

Seed mixtures

When choosing a seed mixture for a particular garden lawn, be guided by the uses to which the grasses will be put. Pay particular attention to the wear and tear the lawn will take; the nature of the soil and its drainage; the location, with regard to aspect, light and shade; and the blending of species that will grow together to form a permanent, even-coloured sward.

Cost may also be a factor, but it should not be of overriding importance where a fine lawn is desired.

Unfortunately, seed mixtures lend themselves to adulteration. It is very difficult to harvest the seeds pure, and cleaning them of inferior seeds, weed seeds and chaff costs money, reflected in the price you pay. Seeds of the finer lawn grasses, particularly fescues and bents, are small and light, and the greater their proportion in a mixture, the more expensive the mixture is. It is wise, therefore, to buy seeds from firms of good reputation, known for setting high standards of purity and germination, and that specify the kinds of grass making up a particular mixture.

The finest lawns are made from simple mixtures of fescues with or without bents. The following examples illustrate the type of thing to look for, or – if you wish – to make up from seeds bought separately. Bear in mind that fescues are more tolerant of poor soil conditions than are bents.

A mixture recommended by the Sports Turf Research Institute for the finest turf of bowling green quality is (parts by weight):

7 or 8 parts Chewings fescue
3 or 2 parts browntop (highland) bent

A 7:3 mixture would be better for lighter soil conditions, and an 8:2 for richer, more loamy ones.

On the other hand, given a fairly light soil or one overlying chalk, an all-fescue mixture consisting of equal parts Chewings fescue and creeping red fescue S.59 would succeed well. The inclusion of creeping red fescue improves establishment on most soils, as well as lightening the cost a little, and it still gives a very fine decorative sward:

5 parts Chewings fescue
3 parts creeping red fescue S.59
2 parts browntop bent

The mixture can be varied for particular conditions. One alternative, designed to give a finely-textured ornamental lawn on average garden soils or loams, is:

12 parts Chewings fescue
4 parts creeping red fescue S.59
4 parts browntop bent

On a light acid or peaty soil, 2–3 parts of sheep's fescue could be added.

The inclusion of meadow-grasses and crested dog's-tail increases durability, lessens costs, and provides pleasant, good-looking swards for most garden purposes. A suggested mixture for a general amenity lawn or family tennis court would be:

3 parts Chewings fescue
2 parts creeping red fescue S.59
2 parts browntop bent
1 part smooth-stalked meadow-grass
1 part crested dog's-tail

Rough-stalked meadow-grass is very useful on heavy, clayey soils and moist, rich ones, for which a suitable mixture could be devized around the following:

3 parts browntop bent
2 parts rough-stalked meadow-grass
4 parts Chewings fescue
1 part Timothy S.50

The inclusion of rye-grass lessens seed costs, and provided one of the low-growing, leafy, indigenous strains is used, appearances are good. A fine, hard-wearing general lawn can be made from:

3 parts rye-grass S.23
2 parts Chewings fescue
2 parts creeping red fescue S.59
2 parts rough-stalked meadow-grass
1 part browntop bent

For light, drier soils, smooth-stalked meadow-grass could be substituted for rough-stalked, and 1–2 parts crested dog's-tail added.

The most difficult place to maintain a reasonable lawn is in shade, especially under trees. There is usually a dryness problem, but where the soil is suitably prepared, humus-enriched and fertilized, a good mixture could be formulated around:

4 parts rye-grass S.23
2 parts rough-stalked meadow-grass
2 parts wood meadow-grass
2 parts creeping red fescue S.59

Leaving out the wood meadow-grass, but including sheep's fescue and a little browntop bent, would give a mixture tailored to produce a pleasing, serviceable lawn quickly in the open.

For verges, banks, and places that can only be mown infrequently or in an irregular manner, a mixture of rye-grass, meadow-grasses, Timothy, and what fescues are available, will give a cheap, enduring sward.

LAYING TURF AND SOWING A LAWN FROM SEED

1

2

3

4

The most popular method of making a new lawn is undoubtedly by laying turf, for it creates an immediate effect and the area can be used as soon as the job is complete. The advantage of making a new lawn from seed (over the page) is that you can choose your grass. However, whether it is the sturdy utility grass or the more decorative fine type, it must not be neglected.

For turf to flourish and produce a successful lawn, thorough soil preparation is necessary and if possible the ground should be preparared a few weeks beforehand to allow for settlement. It is equally important to purchase good, weed-free turfs that are of the same thickness and have them delivered as near as possible to the date you intend to lay them. If they arrive 48 hours before laying, stack them without unrolling; if there is to be a longer gap between arrival and turfing, unroll each turf and lay it flat.

Marking out curved edges

There has, in recent years, been a breakaway from the traditional square or rectangular lawn in favour of ones with gently curving edges. An irregular lawn site is a bit more difficult to mark out, but the easiest method is to lay out a length of string or rope to mark the outline, then drive in canes or wooden pegs against the string at intervals of about 60–90cm (2–3 ft), and twist the string around them. You will then have quite a durable outline of the lawn to which you can work.

Preparing the site

Thoroughly dig the lawn site to the depth of a spade (single-digging), or, if the subsoil (lower soil) is compacted, to two depths of the spade (double-digging). Be careful not to mix subsoil and topsoil – keep them in their correct layers. A hard subsoil could result in a badly drained or waterlogged lawn if it is not well broken up. During digging incorporate plenty of bulky organic matter in the bottom of each trench, such as well-rotted farmyard manure, garden compost, leaf mould, peat, spent hops or even decomposed straw. This will help to retain moisture in light, sandy or chalky soil during dry weather and will encourage better drainage of surplus water in heavy clay soils.

If you have such a heavy clay soil it would be advisable to incorporate plenty of coarse sand or grit during digging to assist further in drainage of surplus moisture. A good lawn can never be achieved if the soil holds too much water in the winter. If your site does become very seriously waterlogged in winter, the only satisfactory answer is to have a proper drainage system installed, consisting of tile drains sloping into a soakaway.

Levelling and raking

Once you have completed digging it is best to allow the soil to settle naturally for a few weeks. This is a good time to carry out any general levelling that may be necessary. Then, shortly before laying the turf, final preparations can be undertaken, when the surface of the soil is reasonably dry. Never work on the site when it is wet and sticky or you will end up with a mud patch.

Break down the roughly dug soil with a fork or rake to produce a reasonably fine surface. Then firm the soil by treading systematically over the entire site with as much weight as possible on your heels. At this stage you may apply a general-purpose fertilizer or sterilized bonemeal at 135g per sq m (4 oz per sq yd), which can be incorporated into the surface during final raking.

This raking is to provide a fine, level surface on which to lay the turf, and you should take this opportunity to ensure the site is really level, with no hollows or bumps. Rake the soil from any high spots into the hollows and firm it well with your heels. The smoother and more level the site, the better the finished job will be.

Laying the turfs

The actual turfing should be done when the surface is reasonably dry. If you have a paved area with a straight edge, this is a good place to start. Lay one row of turfs along, and hard up to, this straight edge. The turfs will generally be 30cm ×

5

1 *Begin to lay the turf along one side of the lawn. Be sure the edges are straight*
2 *Turf should be cut with a sharp half-moon edging iron or a sharp knife*
3 *When filling in the turfs, lay them as close together as possible*
4 *Be sure that the turfs are level with the ground or following the slope of the chosen site*
5 *Place more soil under turfs which are too low or remove soil from under those which are too high*
6 *Tamp down the newly-laid turfs to firm them in place*
7 *A newly-turfed lawn has a brickwork pattern which later knits together*
8 *Use a stiff broom to lift the flattened grass and brush in the top-dressing*

6

7

8

1m (12 in × 3 ft) and should be laid lengthways across the site. Allow the turf to overlap your string outline so that when you finish laying you can go round the edges with a knife or half-moon edging iron, cutting them to the required shape, using the string as a guide.

When laying the second row of turfs remember that the joints should be bonded or staggered like bricks in a wall. In other words, the joints of the second row should fall in the centre of each turf in the first row. You should always work over the turf which has already been laid, so it is advisable to stand on a plank to stop your heels sinking into the new turf, especially if it is fairly moist.

Butt the turfs hard up against each other so there are no gaps in the joints. You can push them close together with the tines of a fork used back to front. If the turfs have been well cut and are all of the same thickness they will require little firming. Patting them down with the back of the fork is generally sufficient. If levelling is necessary, do it by adding or removing soil beneath the turfs during laying. Continue turfing the whole site in this way, ensuring that all joints are staggered. To achieve this bonded effect you will need to cut some of the turfs in half at the edges of the lawn.

After turfing, the lawn can be given a light roll if you have a small garden roller. If not, walk up and down the plank, moving this evenly so that the whole lawn is covered eventually.

Adding a top dressing

For a really good finish, brush in a top dressing with a stiff broom. This can be either good, fine topsoil or a mixture of topsoil, coarse sand and fine peat. Apply a 13mm ($\frac{1}{2}$ in) layer over the lawn and work it really well into the grass and joints. Remove any surplus, to ensure the grass is not smothered. This will fill in any gaps there may be between the joints and will also encourage the grass to grow and the turfs to knit together well.

Watering programme

In mid spring it will probably not be necessary to water the turfs after laying as the ground should be moist. But as late spring and early summer approach, with drier weather, you must undertake a regular watering programme. If the turfs are allowed to dry out before they become established or well rooted into the soil, they will shrink and the joints will open up, producing ugly cracks. In addition, the turf will take a long time to become established if it is not watered during dry spells in the spring and summer and it is quite likely the grass will turn brown. It will take a considerable time to recover from this, and weeds may start invading the dried-out patches.

The most thorough way of watering a lawn is to use a sprinkler on the end of a hosepipe, and leave this for at least one hour on any one part of the lawn. This will ensure the water gets well down to the roots.

To sow new lawn: **1** *remove all debris from site, then dig and manure;* **2** *break down surface with fork;* **3** *tread over to firm, then rake;* **4** *sow seed evenly, releasing slowly;* **5** *divide ground, and seed, into equal parts for accurate sowing;* **6** *rake seed in – across previous furrows*

1

2

3

Although it is far cheaper to sow grass seed than to lay turfs, you will not be able to use the lawn for a few months. Also grass seed and seedlings are prone to damage by bad weather and birds, so a good deal of care is needed in the early stages.

The best time to sow is from early to mid autumn (August to September), but late spring (April) is also suitable. In spring you will have to pay more attention to watering as the ground can dry out rapidly, resulting in poor or delayed seed germination.

Preparing the ground

So that it has a chance to settle, prepare the soil several weeks before sowing. Dig and manure the site thoroughly and level it by raking the soil in various directions, breaking down any clods of earth and removing stones, weeds and other rubbish.

If the surface is particularly rough you may have to do a more thorough job. Use levelling pegs, a straight 2·50m (8–10 ft) plank of wood and a spirit level. Hammer in one levelling peg to a suitable height and put in the others at 2–2·50m (6–8 ft) intervals. Place the plank on top of the two pegs and check how straight it is with the spirit level. Hammer the pegs in as necessary until the plank is level. Repeat this procedure until all the pegs are at the same height.

Rake the topsoil until roughly the same amount of each peg is showing above the ground. If there are bad bumps or hollows remove some subsoil from the higher to the lower areas, but make sure the topsoil always remains on top.

A few days before sowing, break down the roughly-dug ground with a fork and then firm it by treading over the entire site systematically with your heels. Apply a general-purpose fertilizer, or lawn fertilizer, at 70g per sq m (2 oz per sq yd). Next, rake the site with an iron rake making the soil as fine as possible and removing any large stones and other debris. Then firm and rake the soil again, this time working 'across the grain' of the first raking. Remove any more stones that have reached the surface.

Provided the surface of the soil is dry when you carry out this final preparation, you should now have a really fine surface on which to sow the grass seed. Just before sowing, go over the entire site in every direction very lightly with a rake, drawing it along the surface to produce mini-furrows. This will be a help when you come to cover the seed.

Utility lawn mixtures

Next choose your grass seeds: there are mixtures to suit all purposes.

If you require a utility lawn that is very hardwearing and suitable for games and a good deal of foot traffic, choose a utility-grade mixture which includes some really tough grasses. A typical mixture would contain 4 parts Chewing's fescue, 3 parts perennial ryegrass, 2 parts crested dog's tail and 1 part rough-stalked meadow grass.

Chewing's fescue is a fine-leaved dwarf grass which is very drought-resistant and is included in the mixture to help give the lawn a finer appearance. But it will eventually die out and be overtaken by the perennial ryegrass. This is a true utility grass, coarse-leaved, very hardwearing, and especially good on heavier types of soil. It will not stand really close mowing – and indeed a utility lawn should not be closely cut.

Crested dog's tail is another coarse, hardwearing species; it is good on light soils and withstands drought. Rough-stalked meadow grass is of creeping habit and clothes the soil with foliage. It is also a coarse-leaved type and is good on moist, heavy soils.

Luxury-grade mixtures

However, if you prefer a really fine lawn you must choose a luxury-grade mixture containing only fine grasses. Such a lawn is unsuitable for heavy use, but it will provide a beautiful setting for your flower beds and borders. You will have to give it much more attention and more mowing than a utility lawn. Mow it closely: this generally means mowing twice a week in the growing season (spring and summer). You must also feed and water it if you want to keep it looking really good, for it will soon deteriorate if you neglect it; the fine grasses will die out and coarser weed-grasses will take over.

For a fine lawn mixture, choose 7–8 parts Chewing's fescue and 2–3 parts browntop bent. Both are very fine-leaved grasses. Chewing's is a tufted species, while browntop is creeping and covers the surface of the soil with foliage. It is a very drought-resistant species, like Chewing's, but this does not mean that you should neglect to water it in dry weather. This mixture will produce a dense, dark-green sward.

For shaded areas

Normal grass-seed mixtures are unsuitable for shaded areas under large trees or places overshadowed by tall buildings and walls. The grass simply would not grow well and would be thin and patchy. Fortunately, however, it is possible to buy mixtures specially developed for shaded areas. A typical mixture consists of 5 parts rough-stalked meadow grass, 3 parts wood meadow grass and 2 parts creeping red fescue. Wood meadow grass is very shade-tolerant and is often found

4

5

6

growing wild on the edges of woodland and forest clearings. Creeping red fescue is an adaptable species, that is highly drought-resistant and has a creeping habit of growth.

Calculating the quantity
Having decided on a mixture, you must then calculate the quantity of seed you require. You will need to know the sowing rate. For fine lawns this is 35–45g per sq m (1–1¼ oz per sq yd); for others increase the rate to 50–70g (1½–2 oz). Measure the length and width of your site and multiply to calculate the area. It should then be an easy matter to work out the quantity of seed required: multiply the area by the sowing rate.

How to sow
Ideally you should choose a fine, calm day for sowing, when the soil surface is dry. Be sure to sow the seed evenly, otherwise you will have a patchy lawn. Divide the entire site into strips 1m (1 yd) wide by marking out each strip with string, secured by canes at each end.

Then calculate the number of square metres (square yards) in each strip and weigh out sufficient grass seed for each one. Sow half the seed up and down the strip, and the other half across it. This should ensure even sowing at the correct rate. Repeat the procedure for all the strips until the whole site has been sown.

If you wish to be even more precise you could divide each strip into square metres (square yards) by laying bamboo canes on the soil. Then weigh out the seed into the required number of small lots, sufficient for each square.

When sowing seed by hand, hold it well above the soil, say at waist height, and slowly release the seed as you walk the length and breadth of the area, moving your hand fairly rapidly from side to side. This 'broadcast' method usually ensures very even sowing.

You can also sow the seed with a fertilizer distributor, but only if the machine is adjustable. Obtaining the correct sowing rate is a matter of trial and error. Make practice runs over a sheet of polythene until you find the right setting. Measure out sufficient seed for a given number of square metres (square yards), put this in the distributor and make one run over the measured area of polythene. If the machine runs out of seed before the area is completely sown, or if there is still seed in the machine after running once over the area, then you will need to try other settings. It will only be worth your while using a distributor if you have an exceptionally large lawn; for small gardens, hand sowing is just as quick.

Care of new lawns
After sowing, lightly rake the lawn to cover the seed. Rake across the tiny furrows you made before the seed was sown. You will find that most of the seed is then covered with soil. Don't firm the surface as it may become caked after rain or watering and so inhibit seed germination.

Birds can be a nuisance as they relish grass seed. Some seed is treated with a bird repellent; otherwise discourage them by stretching black cotton between sticks over the lawn in a criss-cross fashion about 8–10cm (3–4 in) above the soil.

It is very important to water whenever the surface of the soil starts to dry out, both before and after the seeds have germinated. If the soil is allowed to become dry germination will be patchy, and the seedlings can quickly die and wither away. In fact it is essential to carry on watering throughout the summer if you are sowing in spring, or well into the autumn if sowing during early or mid autumn (August or September). Apply the water gently and evenly using a lawn sprinkler on the end of a hosepipe. Always water thoroughly; dribs and drabs do more harm than good, so stand the sprinkler on each portion of the lawn for at least an hour.

The seedlings should appear in two to three weeks if you sow in late spring (April), or within one to two weeks after an early or mid autumn sowing.

Rolling and mowing
Once the seedlings are about 2·5–4cm (1–1½ in) high lightly brush the lawn with a brush or besom to remove any worm-casts. Carry out this task when the lawn is dry. Then you can give the lawn a light rolling – using either a small roller or, preferably, the rear roller of a hand-mower. This is to firm the surface of the soil which was loosened as the seeds germinated. It also presses into the soil any small stones which might otherwise damage the mower blades. Light rolling induces the grass seedlings to produce new shoots and so speeds up the lawn-making process.

Start mowing when the grass is 5cm (2 in) high. Sharpen the mower blades well as they may tear out the seedlings or severely damage them. Set the blades high so that only the tops of the seedlings are removed.

Weeds usually appear with the new grass but annual weeds soon die out once you start mowing. You can hand-weed a new lawn, but make sure you hold down the grass seedlings with one hand while you pull out the weeds with the other, or you may also pull out the young grass.

On no account should you use the normal hormone lawn weedkillers on a new lawn as they could severely damage or kill the young grass. It is necessary to wait 12 months after sowing before starting to apply them. But there is a special weedkiller (containing the chemical ioxynil) which is suitable if applied according to the maker's instructions.

LAWN CARE
Hand mowers and tools

Whatever the size of your garden it is more than likely to contain a lawn, or at least a grass area. All grass, whether long or short, fine or rough, requires constant attention, and it is much easier if you have the right equipment for your type of lawn. In fact, when proper tools are used, producing a superb green sward really does become more of a joy than a chore.
Hand lawn-mowers and other lawn care equipment are illustrated here and we follow up with advice on power lawn-mowers and basic maintenance in an extended survey over the page.

All but the smallest lawns need to be cut with a mower, but before you decide which type to buy compare the various models and list your requirements (this also applies when buying other lawn care equipment). Certain mowers work better on short grass and edges, others on long grass, and all grass boxes are not equally efficient. Choose a lightweight model with adjustable handles if you have steps to negotiate or storage problems.

Hand lawn-mowers
Although it can be tiring to hand mow a large lawn, it is certainly very economical to use a hand machine for small and medium-sized ones. They are also considered to give a better finish than power-operated machines.

Nowadays, due to skilful engineering, cylinder hand mowers are very easy to push and operate. They come in two types: roller and sidewheel and each has its advantages.

Roller types have a small roller in front of the cylinder and a large one behind. The two rollers help to give lawns the striped effect for which many people aim. They also make it easy to cut edges and narrow strips of grass as they simply overhang where necessary. However, these roller types do not operate well if the grass is more than 5cm (2 in) long.

Sidewheel mowers have only the small roller in front of the cutting cylinder and are better for cutting long grass, but they require a balancing act to cut lawn edges, and on soft ground the two side wheels can leave track marks.

Roller mowers cost about twice as much as the sidewheel types and always have the grass box attachment in front. Grass boxes may be fitted to the front or rear of sidewheel models, according to the make. They are usually more efficient when the box is fitted in front of the cutting cylinder.

With cylinder mowers the grass is cut between the cylinder blade and a fixed blade. The effective cutting width, known as the cylinder length, is usually 25 or 30cm (10 or 12 in), although one sidewheel model is available with a 40cm (16 in) cylinder.

The cutting height adjustment and ease of altering it varies according to the model, so compare these facilities before buying. Both power and hand-driven cylinder mowers are available, but rotary ones are always petrol-driven or electrically operated.

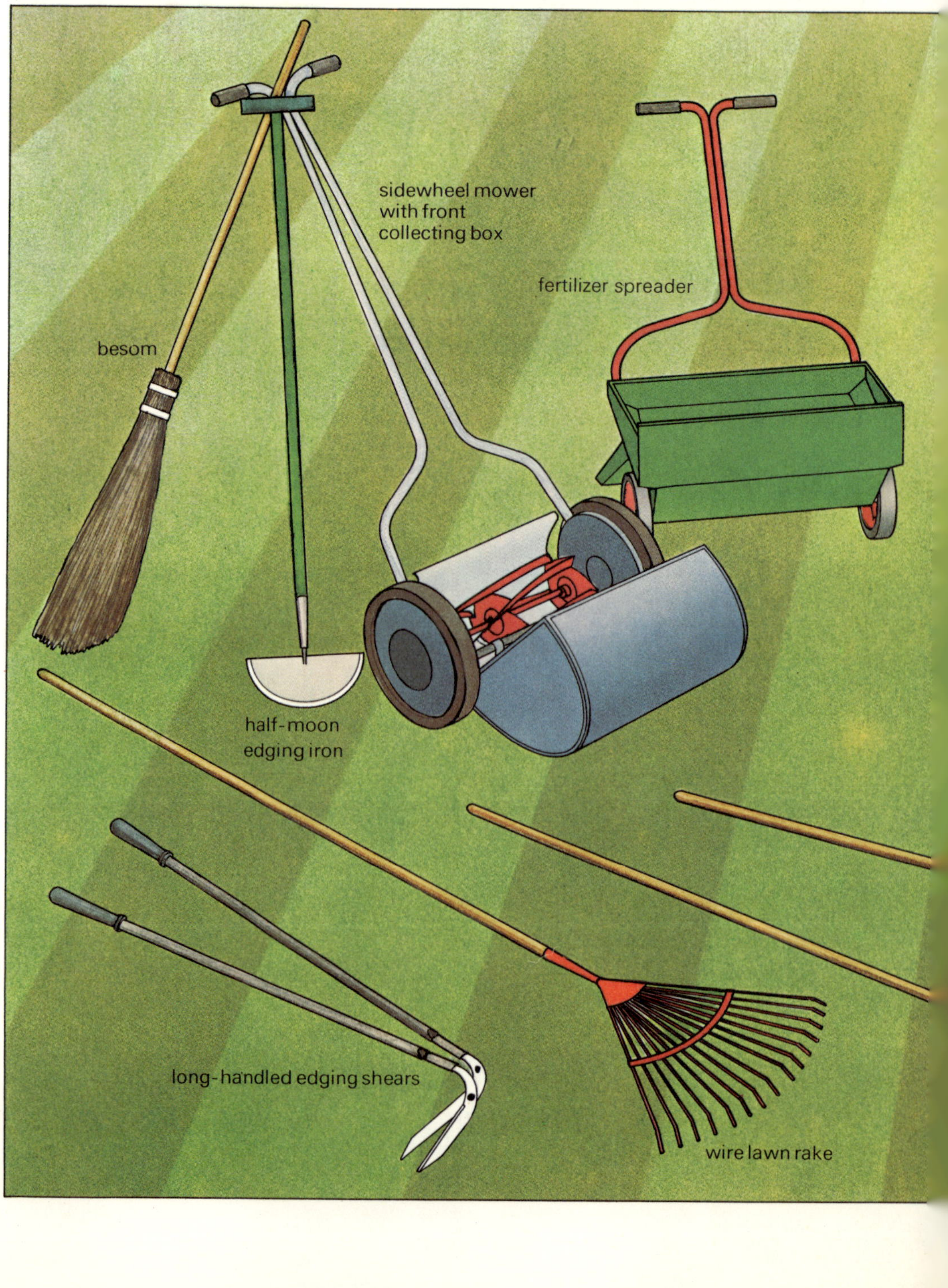

Shears for cutting
The first item for your list is a good pair of shears. There are long-handled and short-handled, edging and cutting shears. Blade sizes vary from 15–25cm (6–10 in); handles can be wooden, metal or plastic, and some models are available with rubber buffers to absorb jarring and reduce fatigue when cutting.

The traditional short-handled shears are invaluable for cutting long or short grass. To avoid having to bend, you can get the same blades attached to long handles. There are two basic models in this range, one for edging and the other for general cutting. You can also buy spring-loaded hand shears which allow for one-handed operation; one type comes with an orbital handle so that it can be adjusted to cut at any angle between horizontal and vertical.

The lawn edge trimmer, a modification of edging shears, has spring-loaded blades and you push it along to cut overhanging grass. It has a broad, non-slip rubber roller that guarantees easy guiding and balancing, even on undulating ground.

Brushing and raking
All lawns require brushing and raking to keep them looking well-groomed and pleasant to sit on. A besom, or birch broom, is ideal for sweeping off leaves, but a good stiff broom is required for getting rid of wormcasts.

Steel, spring-tined lawn rakes are essential for removing debris and for scarifying the lawn surface. You can get fixed, or adjustable, tined models, the latter being preferable as they can be used for any job from moss-collecting to leaf-raking.

There is also a lawn comb – a cross between a lawn rake and a garden rake, but it has no particular advantage over other rakes. Wooden lawn rakes are prone to breaking and so are not recommended. The traditional garden rake is best for spreading top dressing on lawns.

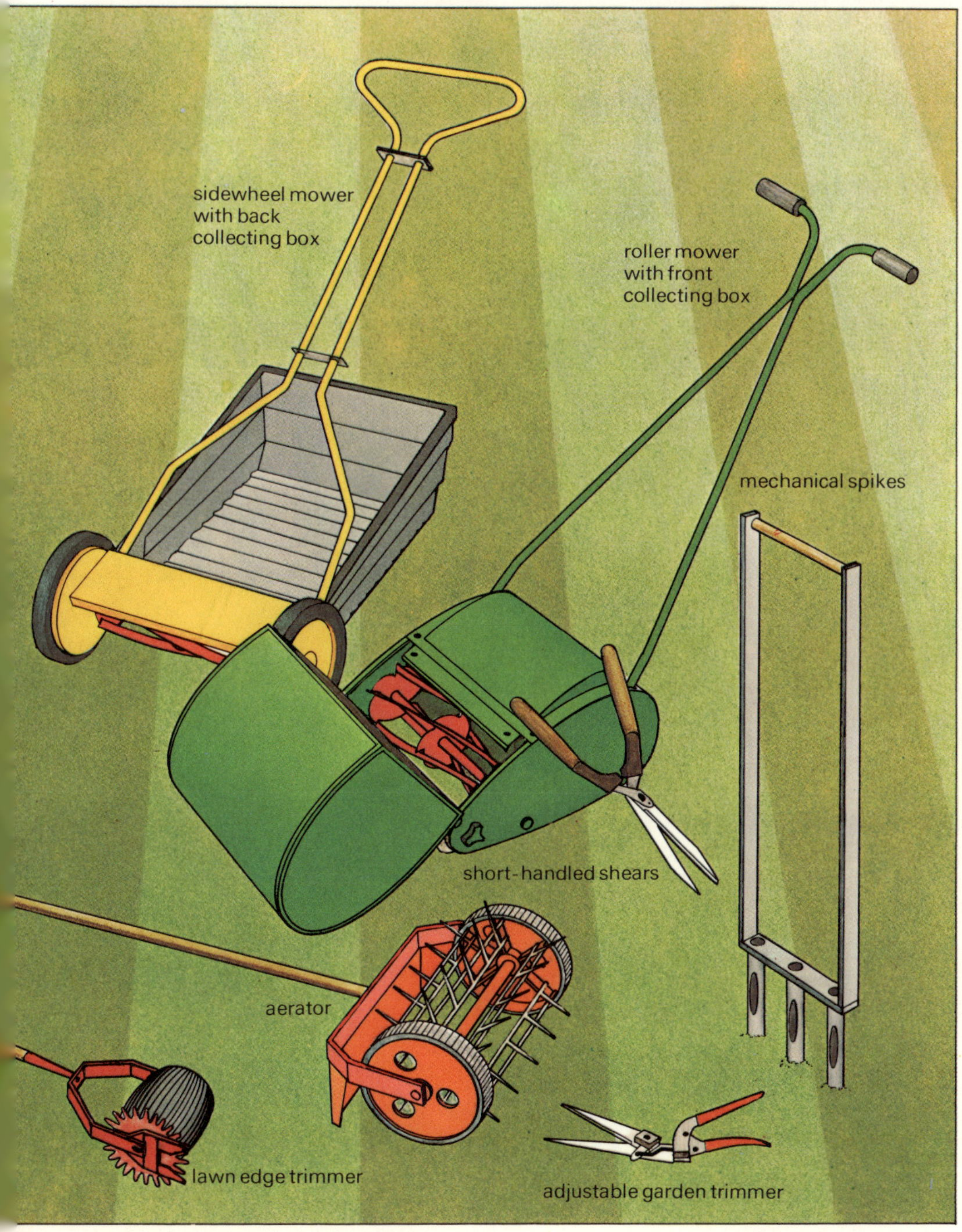

Rolling the lawn
It is worth borrowing or hiring a roller each spring to put a new face on your lawn. Winter frosts often lift the turf and rolling will consolidate the surface. It need only be done in spring. It is important to sweep off all wormcasts and debris beforehand and to roll only when the surface is dry and the soil below is damp. Don't roll when the grass is thin or wet and never use a roller weighing over 2 cwt. Bumps should be levelled out properly because rolling will not squash them down.

Tools for aerating
For this you need only use a garden fork. Push it in 7–10cm (3–4 in) deep, at 7–10cm intervals. Easier to use is a fork-like tool fitted with hollow, or solid, tines (sometimes called mechanical spikes), and it gives better results. Wedge-shaped blades can also be attached and are good for compacted areas as they prune the roots and so encourage stronger root growth. For larger areas use an aerator with spiked wheels and interchangeable tines.

Feeding and weeding
Fertilizer-spreaders ensure an even distribution of lawn feeds and lawn sands. Fertilizers and 'feed and weed' mixes come in several forms and should be applied with the spreader in strict accordance with the manufacturers' instructions.

A certain number of weeds eventually die as a result of constant mowing but a few stubborn types will remain and must be dealt with by other methods. Apply spot weedkillers from a small bottle with a squeezy-type top, or dig out stubborn weeds with a hand fork, or a long, narrow trowel.

Tidying up the edges
Finally, to ensure that your lawn never encroaches on the flower borders you should edge-up with a good half-moon edging iron at least twice a year.

POWER LAWN-MOWERS

Previously we put forward the advantages of hand mowers and other lawn care equipment. But if you really want to turn a backbreaking task into a pleasure exercise, all you need is a power lawn-mower.
You can choose between big, robust ones with horizontal, rotary cutting blades, enabling you to clear your way through neglected long grass, or well-sharpened, multiple-bladed cylinder ones that will help you to achieve the much desired 'billiard table' lawn.
Whichever model you choose, make sure it is right for you and your lawn and other grassy areas. Many of the lighter models are better for women and older people, while a strong, young enthusiast will enjoy handling a heavy, petrol-driven machine.

Power lawn-mowers are precision instruments and often have to stand up to years of rough usage, so you should always buy the best you can afford. The following guide to the various types should help you to make your choice.

Electric or petrol?
Mains-powered electric mowers start up immediately, require little maintenance, are cheaper to run than their petrol-driven counterparts, and do not make a lot of noise to upset the neighbours. Many models have TV/radio interference suppressors and standard safety equipment. However, mains-operated types (cylindrical or rotary) are not suited to large lawns or rough ground and their mobility depends on their cable length. You can also cut the power cable accidentally but with the inbuilt safety factors of modern machines this is not a danger. With battery models (only available with cylinder cutters) you are also restricted by their operating time before recharging becomes necessary.

Petrol-driven lawn-mowers, generally speaking, give more power than the electrically-operated ones (which are usually one-speed). They have variable speeds, unlimited mobility and the advantage of working well on rough ground. On the other hand, petrol mowers can be tricky to start, especially at the beginning of the season, and require a regular maintenance programme. It is surprising how many owners of petrol mowers neglect even to keep a regular check on the oil level.

Self-propelled or push-along?
All power mowers either have motorized propulsion – that is, the power source turns the wheels as well as blades (and they cost more) – or you have to push them along, in which case only the blades are powered from the engine. The power source is connected to the moving parts by belts or chains.

Cylinder or rotary?
Apart from the choice between electric or petrol power, the mower may cut by the cylinder or rotary method.

Cylinder types cut by slicing the grass between one of their curved blades and a fixed cutting plate, cutting the grass with a scissor-like action. They are good for fine lawns but not so efficient on grass longer than 5–8cm (2–3 in) high, so you must be prepared to mow at least once a week.

Rotary types have a whirling, horizontal blade (that does not require sharpening) rather like a propeller, that beheads the upstanding grass. The cut grass is thrown out of the back of the machine by the fast-moving air current. Rotary types deal better with long grass than cylinder ones and are very popular, with their emphasis on easy handling rather than achieving a striped lawn effect at all costs.

Petrol mowers (rotary)
All engines of this type have recoil starters – you need to pull a cord to start action, and many models are decompressed for easy starting. With ordinary use and regular servicing, the engines should last for many years. Two-stroke engines are slightly lighter than their more usual four-stroke counterparts and are better suited to rough spots and slopes. Having fewer parts, two-strokes should be less prone to breakdowns but they tend to be more difficult to start.

Petrol-driven rotary models are fitted with a metal or plastic grass-collecting box, or a flexible bag. On rough grass it is usual to let the cuttings fall back to the land and some models provide a better spreading pattern than others. You must beware of using this type on stony ground without a collecting box (unless fitted with a deflector correctly positioned) because stones may shoot out at high velocity as you mow. Wherever possible, sweep stones out of the way before you start mowing, and never mow with children standing nearby.

Cutting widths of most rotary lawn mowers vary from 38–60cm (15–24 in), and cutting heights from 13mm–15cm ($\frac{1}{2}$–6 in), with independent adjustment on each of the four wheels or by one central mechanism.

Some newer models have rollers fitted behind the blade to give a striped effect of a kind and they incorporate clutches and varying speeds. Most rotary types have fold-down handles for easy storage.

Petrol mowers (cylinder)
These are the popular, traditional mowers that produce well-striped lawns and a fine cut. It cannot be emphasized enough that a petrol cylinder mower is a precision tool and should be treated as such: Due respect and regular maintenance will pay dividends.

petrol rotary mower

Cylinder mowers are usually self-propelled, although some models have a switch to disengage the roller, converting it to a push-along type. On some types you can also disengage the cylinder for moving the machine from place to place. The engines tend to be four-stroke but, as the cubic capacity varies, so does the horsepower. Most cylinder types have a system of gears, clutch and a brake.

Cutting heights vary from 3–30mm ($\frac{1}{8}$–$1\frac{1}{4}$ in), and it should be easy to adjust to the one you want. You can choose from cutting widths of 30–60cm (12–24 in). Grass-collecting boxes are usually made of steel. The number of blades on the cylinder varies from 5–10, the more blades, the finer the cut, and they must be well-adjusted to ensure a clean cut.

A big roller, or side wheels, support the cylinder. Those with a large metal roller are good for fine turf and enable you to cut right to the lawn edge. Side-wheel types are better for rough spots.

Hover types (rotary)
These, such as Flymo, come with choice of petrol or electric power. They are ideal for steep banks as they are kept afloat by a current of air, gliding along effortlessly about 6mm ($\frac{1}{4}$ in) clear of the ground. But you have to rake up the grass cuttings after use.

Tractor types (rotary or cylinder)
If you have 2,000 sq m ($\frac{1}{2}$ acre) of lawn or more, you might consider a 'sit-on' petrol-driven mower. These larger machines are like small tractors and make the job very easy: you simply drive around to cut the grass. The cylinder type is more suited to exceptionally large, fine lawns.

Electric mowers (cylinder)
This type does give a finer striped finish than the rotary, and the smaller models are very easy to manipulate, rather like a vacuum cleaner. One-handed operation is all that is required for most of the time.

Most models have 5–6 cutting blades on the cylinder and operate on one speed, although there are new, larger models with 2–3 speed operation. Cylinder sizes start at 30cm (12 in) and go up to 45cm (18 in). Cutting height adjustments are easy to make with a screwdriver and the range is similar to that of petrol models. Some types have a pivoting handle that automatically adjusts to your height.

Battery-operated models, although they are obviously convenient to use, are heavier than mains mowers and slightly more difficult to manoeuvre. They are only available with cylinder blades and the battery needs re-charging overnight after each mowing.

Electric mowers (rotary)
This easy-to-use type is clean, quiet and fitted with every convenience. The main disadvantage is a tendency to burn out if used non-stop for long periods. Some models are fitted with a waterproof,

double-insulated switch that cuts off automatically if the motor overheats or stalls. When using one of these mowers, you must make sure that you do not accidentally cut through your supply cable. It pays to develop a system of walking that ensures you cut in a direction which pulls the cable rather than allowing it to go slack. Never mow down-

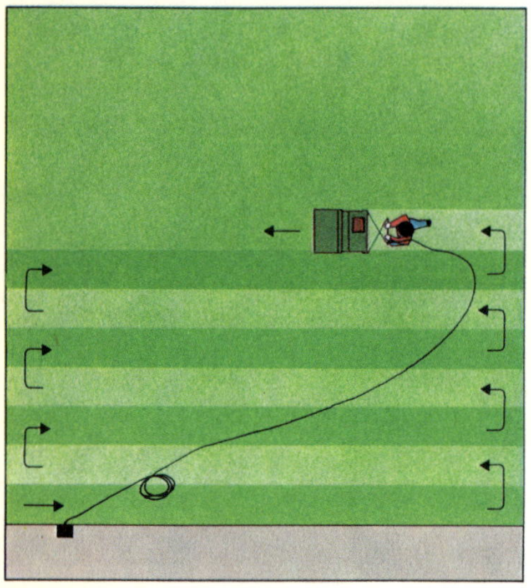

Start mowing nearest your power point so as to avoid accidentally cutting the cable

hill, or pull the machine towards you, or wear open-toed sandals. You've only got one pair of feet, so take care not to let them get under a rotary mower.

Blade sizes vary from 30–45cm (12–18 in) and height adjustment is either independent on each of the four wheels, or by one central arm on the handle which raises or lowers the whole cutting system. Adjustable handles are quite common on these models.

Most types have steel or plastic grass-collecting boxes, some with extra-large capacity that allows for more mowing time between visits to the cutting pile. There is very little to go wrong and these mowers should last for years.

Basic maintenance

For hand mowers the basic maintenance required after a season's work is fairly straightforward and service agents will do it for a reasonable fee. Unless you intend to undertake all your maintenance yourself, you should take your power mower to a reputable firm after the last winter cut, so that it will be in good shape for the first one the following spring. It may need anything doing to it, from blade-sharpening and spark plug-cleaning, to a complete overhaul. If you have a mains-operated electric machine you must be sure that both its insulation and your earthing

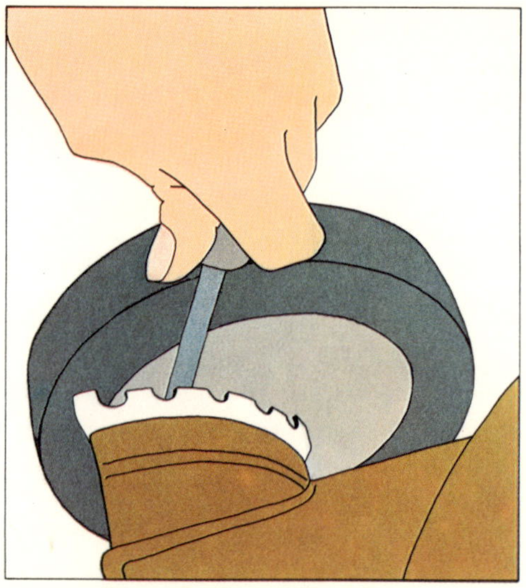

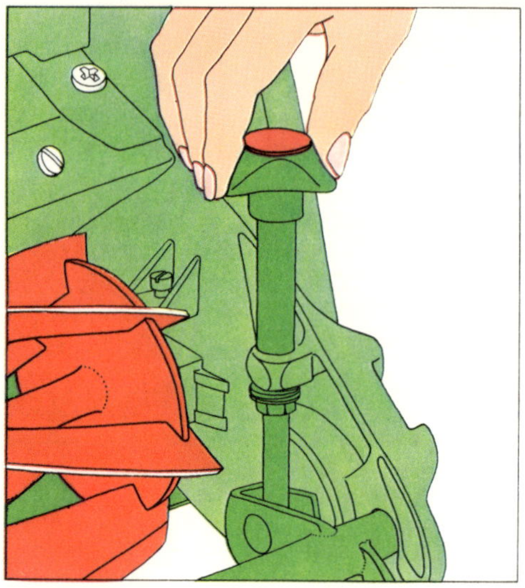

Top: on rotary mowers raising and lowering wheels adjusts the blade height
Above: on cylinder mowers lowering front rollers raises blades, and vice versa.

system are efficient, so check them regularly every year.

On a battery-operated machine the batteries should be kept fully charged throughout the non-mowing season.

In addition there are many small jobs that, if done at the proper time, will save money and ensure continuing good performance from your machine. To start with, one of the greatest enemies of the lawn mower is rust. Even if you cut only in dry weather there is still sufficient water in the grass at any time to cause rust. Wiping the cylinder and fixed blades thoroughly with an oily rag after every mowing will help to keep them keen and free from rust, and postpone the need to sharpen. At the end of the mowing season be sure to oil all blades, gears, chains and bearings. Any component with signs of rust should be removed, scraped clean, oiled and replaced.

Easy-to-handle petrol-driven rotary hover mower floats along on a cushion of air

Some screws, especially those on the fixed blade and ones that have been left for years, may prove difficult to remove. Be patient and don't get heavy-handed. First scrape away any rust, dirt and paint from around the screw and then apply some special penetrating oil. Allow a few minutes for it to seep into the threads, and then try to undo the screws with the largest-sized screwdriver that will fit (an under-sized one will just damage the screwhead). If this does not work, play a blowlamp gently over the obstinate screw or use a cold chisel and hammer. At any rate, when you replace the screws, be sure to grease them thoroughly so as to ensure easy extraction next time.

For professional sharpening, blades are removed from the machine. However, if you are going to tackle this job at home, there are a few ways of sharpening the blades without removing them. There are proprietary sharpeners available, but the cheapest and simplest method is to use coarse grade grinding paste (as for valves in a car engine), which gives a sufficiently good result. Smear it onto the blades quite thickly and turn the cylinder backwards; when you have finished, clean the blades thoroughly.

Above all, it is essential to store your mower in a dry place, not just during the non-mowing season, but all year round.

SPRING AND SUMMER LAWN CARE

You will only achieve a dense lawn of deep green grass, like the rich sward above, by regular maintenance. But spring and summer are the busiest seasons in the lawn care programme when you must mow, feed, weed, rake and water. An oscillating sprinkler of the type illustrated here is a worthwhile investment.

Regular mowing not only maintains the appearance of the lawn, but also helps to get rid of weeds. Feeding puts back into the soil the nutrients that the closely packed roots use up. Weeding is necessary to eliminate moss, clover and other plants that may take over the lawn, and raking clears and cleans the surface.

Watering is essential in hot and dry periods before the shallow roots suffer lasting damage.

How to mow

Start to mow as soon as the grass begins to grow vigorously, which can be mid to late spring (March to April), depending on the weather and the geographical location of your garden. Continue mowing throughout spring and summer, finishing in late autumn (October) when growth stops. Once a week should be sufficient in spring and autumn and during very dry summer spells, but when the grass is growing fast – in late spring and summer – you will need to mow twice a week for a good result.

If the lawn is cut less than once a week during the growing season you will find that, when you mow it, the grass will suffer the sudden loss of a large quantity of leaf, and this can very much reduce its vigour. Also, if you mow infrequently and then shave the lawn too closely, you will quickly ruin it because the fine grasses will be weakened, resulting in a thin, patchy lawn which will rapidly be invaded by weeds such as annual meadow grass, pearlwort, daisies and yarrow.

Remember that mowing does not just ensure a neat lawn, but also encourages dense, healthy growth and helps to reduce weeds and worms. So mow often, but not too closely.

For a utility lawn do not cut the grass any shorter than 3cm (1¼ in) during spring, autumn or in drought conditions. In summer, provided the grass is growing well, cut to 2·5cm (1 in). Fine, luxury lawns can, and should, be mown closer – to 20mm (¾ in) in spring, autumn or during a drought, and to 13mm (½ in) in summer if growth is vigorous.

Mow only when the grass is dry; cutting in wet conditions can pull and bruise the grass and cause mud patches. Scatter wormcasts with a broom or besom before mowing, otherwise the mower will flatten them and produce unsightly patches of mud, inhibit growth and encourage grass seeds to settle. Use a grassbox on the mower so that the cuttings do not build up on the lawn and hamper growth. During droughts, however, a little grass left on the lawn will help keep the roots moist.

If you like a striped lawn mow in parallel (mower-width) strips, slightly overlapping them so that no grass is left uncut. Mow each strip only once, turn, and mow the next in the opposite direction. Next time you cut the grass mow at right angles to the previous cut.

This controls the strong shoots of rye-grass that tend to form on the surface and also keeps down weed grasses.

Use of lawn fertilizers

Start feeding once the grass is growing well, which is generally from late spring to mid summer (April to June). The fertilizer you apply puts back into the soil important plant foods such as nitrogen, phosphorus and potash, which have been used up by the grass. You can apply another dressing of fertilizer in the autumn, but in this case use one of the special autumn lawn fertilizers.

For lush, green grass feed annually – the denser the grass the less trouble you will have from lawn weeds. The best time to apply fertilizer is when the soil is moist; if it is dry you must water the fertilizer well in after application.

There are many excellent lawn fertilizers on the market and all should be used according to the maker's instructions. Apply them evenly and at the correct rate of application. Either scatter by hand or use a fertilizer distributor (a worthwhile implement to buy), being sure to check that the controls are set correctly.

Weeding and raking

Even in the best-kept lawns weeds are bound to appear, generally the rosette-forming, perennial kinds. Unless you can control them they will compete with the grass for food and water. Some, particularly plantains, daisies and dandelions, may also smother the grass.

You can control the majority of weeds with lawn weedkillers that contain the chemicals 2,4-D and fenoprop, or 2,4-D and mecoprop. You must use them strictly according to the manufacturers' instructions, otherwise you may severely damage the grass. Apply them with a watering can kept especially for the job and fitted with a dribble bar. An inexpensive plastic dribble bar can be obtained from any good gardening shop or centre. The best time to apply weedkillers is from late spring to mid summer (April to June), preferably after an application of fertilizer when the grass is growing well. Never apply them during a drought. For persistent weeds you may need a second application about six weeks later.

If there are only a few weeds apply a spot weedkiller, or weed by hand. The best way is to dig them out using a narrow bladed trowel or knife. Try to remove the roots of the weeds without disturbing the soil too much. Fill the holes with a fine soil, firm and sow with the appropriate seed mixture.

Very coarse weed grasses (that have survived mowing) can be controlled by slashing them in various directions with an old knife; weedkillers have no effect on them.

Moss, also, cannot be destroyed by the usual preparations, but should be treated with lawn sand according to the manufacturer's instructions. (Use the same treatment for lichens and algae and also for pearlwort and clover.) Apply it in late spring (April) before you feed the lawn. When the moss has become blackened, rake it off, preferably with a spring-tine lawn rake.

While on the subject of raking, this needs to be done during spring and summer to remove dead, matted grass and other debris which otherwise could choke the grass.

When to water

Water the lawn during dry spells in spring and summer. You will often need to start watering regularly in early summer (May) to keep the grass green and help it to absorb essential plant foods from the fertilizer dressing. Water before the effects of drought are obvious – before the grass starts to turn brown – as it takes a long time to recover and regain its deep green hue.

If the lawn surface has become hard or compacted spike it before watering so that the water is able to penetrate to a good depth. Simply go over the lawn with a fork, pushing it into the soil at 15cm (6 in) intervals to a depth of about 10cm (4 in), or use mechanical spikes.

Watering once a week should be sufficient for most lawns. Increase it to twice a week during very hot, dry weather. It is no use just moistening the surface of the soil, so apply a really good quantity each time using a sprinkler on the end of a hosepipe. The ground must be soaked to a depth of at least 10cm (4 in). This means applying a minimum of 2·5cm (1 in) of water, or 25lit per sq m ($4\frac{1}{2}$ gal per sq yd).

Watering can be carried out at any time of day, but if you leave it until the late afternoon or evening, then far less water will evaporate in the sun.

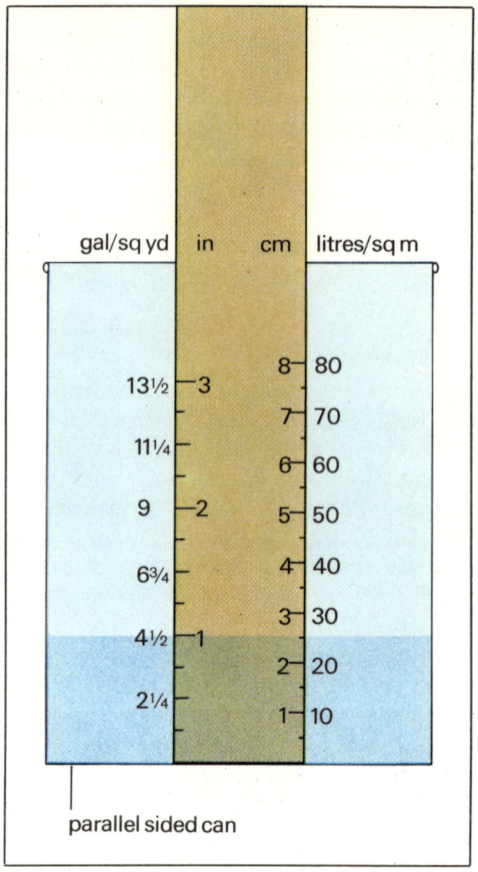

Chart for converting linear units to fluid capacity. If using a ruler (as above) you must allow for any blank space at the start

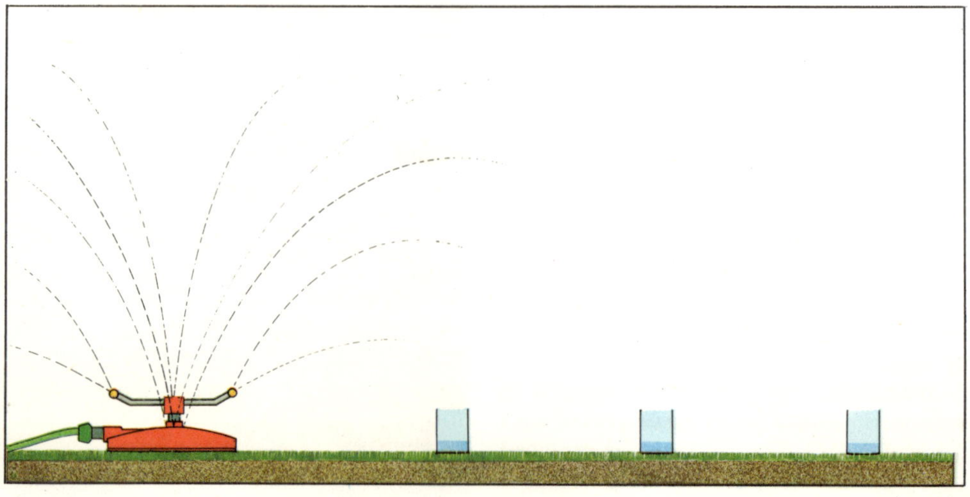

If you arrange 5–6 similar-sized cans in a row, you can easily test the sprinkling time needed for adequate watering (and evenness of distribution) by how quickly and evenly the cans fill with water. In this way you avoid over- or under-watering

LAWN WEEDS AND THEIR CONTROL

The ready availability of mosskillers and selective weedkillers means that the fine-leaved grasses essential for a high-quality lawn can now grow freely, without fear of competition from undesirable elements.

There is a wide selection of lawn weed-killers and mosskillers on the market. Here we describe the main choices, and their respective uses.

Broad-leaved weeds

The appearance of so-called 'hormone' weedkillers in the late 1940s revolutionized the control of weeds such as daisies, plantains, dandelions and buttercups. These chemicals introduced a completely new concept of control in that they were capable of killing broad-leaved weeds without damaging narrow-leaved grasses. Consequently, it was possible to weed by the simple expedient of watering them, in solution, on to the lawn.

Hormone weedkillers The first of this new class of killer was MCPA, followed soon after by 2,4-D. Later a whole series of variants were introduced, including mecoprop, fenoprop and dichlorprop. Although all these behave in a similar fashion, each has its own special virtues. Thus MCPA and 2,4-D, while very effective against daisies, plantains, dandelions and buttercups, have little effect on white clover, chickweed and pearlwort. Mecoprop, fenoprop and dichlorprop, on the other hand, give excellent results against these resistant weeds. Consequently, modern lawn weedkillers usually contain MCPA or 2,4-D combined with mecoprop, fenoprop or dichlorprop. Dicamba is another weedkiller that is available as a mixture with 2,4-D.

These chemicals all act by stimulating the weeds into deformed and excessive growth, so treated weeds at first appear more prominent. However, the killing action is quite slow and can continue for up to six weeks. If a repeat treatment is needed to obtain complete control, it should be delayed six to eight weeks after the first application.

Application Since the killing action takes the form of a growth response, the use of killers needs to be restricted to the period from late spring to mid autumn (late April to September), during which the weeds are growing actively. These treatments should not be given in cold weather or during periods of drought when weed growth is at a low level.

Weedkillers are commonly applied as solutions, using a watering can fitted with a normal rose. The rose can be replaced by a sprinkle-bar that not only makes it

Seed of the dandelion Taraxacum officinale *(above) is equipped with a plume as an aid to wind distribution*
Wild white clover Trifolium repens *(left) spreads vigorously by overground runners*

easier to apply the solution evenly, but also enables the job to be done with less water. Pressure sprayers can be used provided they are adjusted to give a coarse spray, but even then there is the risk of damage being caused to nearby cultivated plants by spray drift. Never apply weedkiller on a windy day.

It is not essential to use weedkillers in a solution. A combined granular feed/weed product, making it possible to feed and weed the lawn in one operation, is an alternative approach.

Although few lawns are entirely free of weeds, in many cases the infestation is too light to justify overall treatment. In this situation one of the proprietary aerosol spot-weedkillers provides the easy answer, producing a narrow jet of liquid that is easily aimed at individual weeds. Furthermore, some of the products are designed to cover the treated weeds with foam, making it easy to see those that have been treated.

Limitations Provided they are used as recommended, selective weedkillers have no ill effects on established grass. However, they can be very damaging to bulbs such as daffodils, and plants with grass-like leaves. So areas of lawn with naturalized bulb plantings should not be treated till the bulb foliage has died down and been mown off.

One limitation of hormone weedkillers is that, while they can safely be used on established lawns, they can be damaging to seedling grass or newly-turfed lawns. Should weeding be necessary in these areas, then the chemical to use is ioxynil; this is also effective against highly-resistant weeds such as speedwell (veronica) in established lawns, particularly if mixed with 2,4-D.

Weed grasses
Lawns are constantly subject to invasions by strong-growing weed grasses like Yorkshire fog and creeping soft-grass. These clump-forming wild grasses are readily recognized by their broad leaves and silvery, hairy appearance. Selective weedkillers have no effect on these weeds. Instead, the clumps should be cut out with a knife and the lawn level made up with fresh soil. Small areas will fill in with growth from the lawn grasses; larger areas may need to be re-seeded.

Mosses and lichens
Infestation by mosses is a recurrent problem with many lawns. These primitive plants are naturally among the first invaders of bare, undisturbed ground, and can quickly colonize bare patches caused by too-close mowing, or indeed any area where the grass is sparse. Lawns that are heavily shaded or poorly drained are particularly prone to invasion.

Moss on a lawn is usually at its most obvious in the spring. This is because it is able to continue growing during the winter when grass growth is minimal. Late spring (April) is the best time to use a mosskiller, since the grass is then able to grow into the spaces.

Lawn sand One method of controlling moss is to apply lawn sand, that consists of sulphate of iron and sulphate of ammonia, bulked out with sand. This mixture needs to be applied very carefully as it can be damaging to the grass.

Other mosskillers A modern alternative is to use one of the proprietary killers; these also contain sulphate of iron, but they have no ill effects on the grass. Indeed, these products make the lawn look more attractive by giving it a greener colour, and they also supply nitrogen, thus stimulating early growth of the grass.

In addition to sulphate of iron, there are a number of other chemicals used in proprietary lawn mosskillers. These include chloroxuron, dichlorophen, mercurous chloride (calomel) and tar oil. All these, when used as directed, will kill moss, but none of them stimulates grass to better growth.

A lichen *Peltigera canina* is sometimes found growing on lawns on acid, sandy soil. It forms brownish, leafy lobes that make dense, unsightly clumps. Mosskillers are effective against it, but the fertility of the soil should also be improved by the use of fertilizers, in order to reduce the risk of re-invasion.

The lichen Peltigera canina *(right) forms dense, unsightly clumps of leaf lobes*
Far right, above: broad-leaved plantain Plantago major
Far right, below: a profusion of moss

WAYS AND MEANS IN THE GARDEN

BASIC GARDEN TOOLS

Two of the essential tools for every gardener – whether constructing a new garden or renovating an old one – are a fork and a spade. Many other tools also give invaluable help in the garden, but whatever type you are choosing, there is one essential rule: make sure the size and shape are right for you.

Forks and **spades** have either a D- or T-shape handle. Many gardeners claim that a D handle allows for better gripping. Try them out in the shop before you buy.

Forks are usually four-pronged and are useful for winter digging, especially on heavy soils.

Spades vary in blade width, from 16–19cm (6–8 in), and blade length, from 26–29cm (10–12 in). You'll find smaller sizes easier to use on heavier soils because less weight is lifted with each spadeload. Lighter, smaller forks and spades are made for women.

A **Dutch hoe** takes the backache out of weeding, and saves time.

When making seed drills you will find a **draw hoe** invaluable. A hand version, known as an **onion hoe**, has a narrower blade and is ideal for cultivating small patches, raised beds, and plants in pots and tubs.

No gardener can do without a **hand fork** and **trowel**. The forks have long and short blades of varying widths; the long, thin ones are excellent for prizing out long-rooted perennial weeds.

You will need a **rake** for breaking down clods to a workable tilth. They range between 30–40cm (12–16 in) wide; when buying ensure that the metal rake is well fixed to the handle.

Wooden ones are wider and are recommended only for very large gardens.

Stainless steel tools cost about twice as much as others, but they are a worthwhile investment. They last much longer, are quick to clean and don't rust. They also slip easily into soil. The handles are made of polypropylene or wood, the former being much lighter.

Pruning can be done with a **pruning knife** or **secateurs**. Well-versed gardeners recommend a sharp knife for most jobs, but many people prefer to use secateurs for trees, shrubs and roses.

The knives must be made of well-hardened steel; cheap ones or pen knives will tear at plant stems and invite infection.

There are two types of secateurs: parrot-billed (scissors action), and anvil (the single blade cuts against a metal block). They should be well-made with sharp blades; blunt ones will only crush plant tissue and frustrate the pruner.

You will need a **reel** and **line** and a **measuring rod** or **tape** in the vegetable garden and for marking out borders.

Wooden or **plastic labels** are best for marking seed-sowings.

Use **gardening gloves** for heavy work and pruning roses.

Your tool shed will not be complete without a **watering can**. Get a 7–9 litre ($1\frac{1}{2}$–2 gallon) size with a rose. It is advisable to have a second can for weedkillers.

A **hose** saves time when watering plants. Invest in a frost-proof one. A **hose reel** will also cut watering time and save wear and tear on the hose.

A **bucket** will serve to carry odds and ends until you acquire a **wheelbarrow**. When you choose a wheelbarrow don't forget to consider its weight when filled and its size in relation to your garden paths.

For hedges, lawns and mixed borders you will require a good pair of **shears**. These and other lawn equipment are illustrated from page 104 onwards.

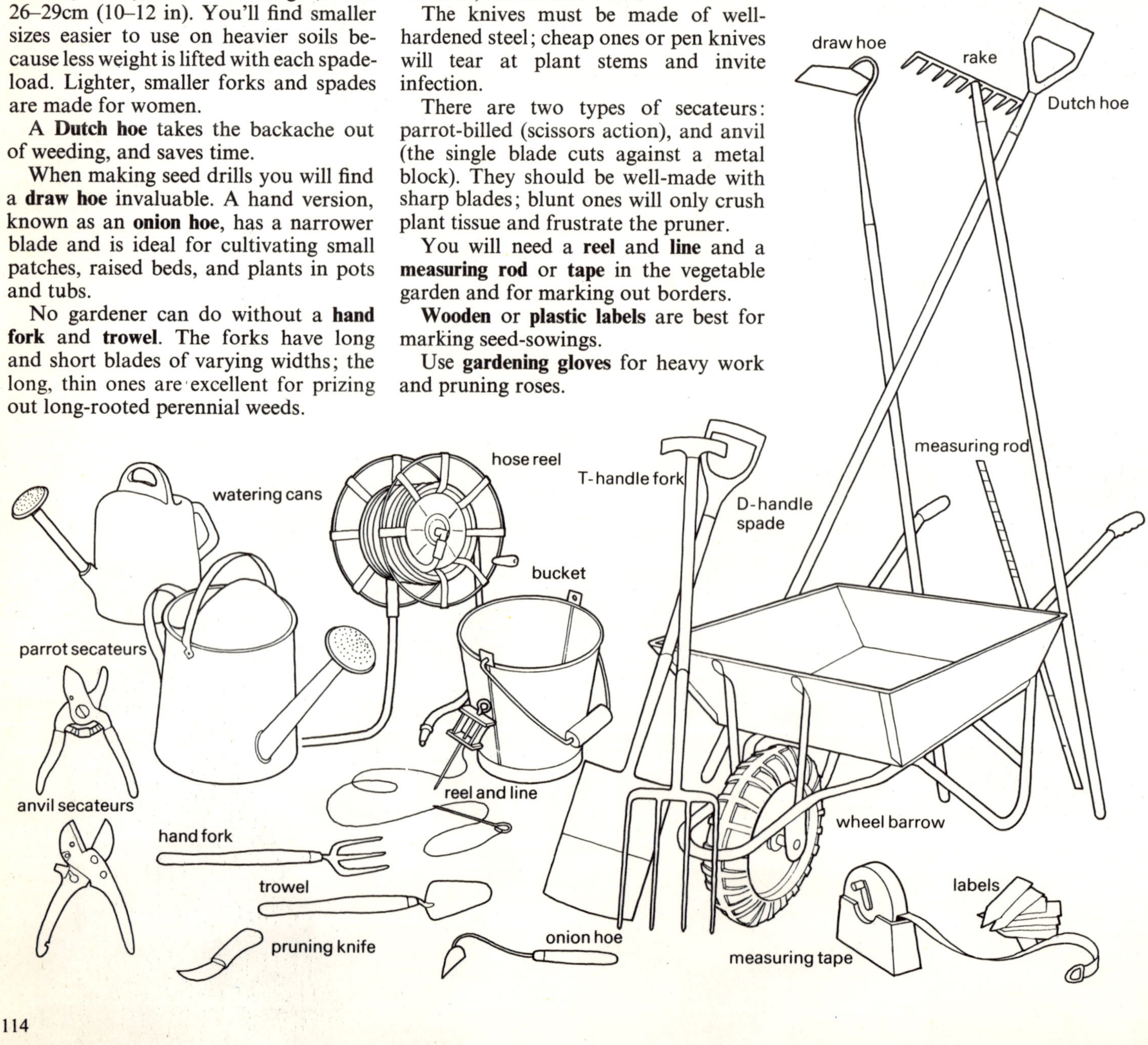

MAINTAINING TOOLS

Rust is the enemy of tools – few garden sheds or garages are totally proof against the all-pervasive midwinter damp – so before being stored away all those tools that will not be needed until the spring should be carefully cleaned, thoroughly dried and their metal parts (if not stainless steel) wiped with a thin film of oil, or even wrapped in oily rags.

It is a good practice to clean a fork or spade after every use. Hoses should be coiled and hung up and lawn mowers, especially electric ones, should be found a place off the ground. In fact tools generally are the better for being kept well above ground level, and some sort of wall rack provides the best type of storage.

This is also a time when tools should be overhauled and repaired. Replace handles and sharpen edge tools like shears, lawn edging irons, and hoes. Even spades and forks can be sharpened.

Garden shears These should be checked if they seem to have been cutting less efficiently. They may need not only sharpening but also setting. You can sharpen them – provided they are not hollow-ground – with a medium-fine file, using it on the bevel side of the cutting edges (see **1**). Hold each blade in turn in a vice and file away from the edge, that is *into* the edge. The stroke of the file should not be at right-angles to the blade but somewhat oblique to it. Work until you have achieved a clean, sharp, notch-free edge on each blade. Hollow-ground shears must be professionally sharpened.

Properly-set shears have slightly bowed blades but they should overlap fairly tightly at the tips. If the blades of your shears are not properly bowed you can bend them a little by holding the end of each blade in a vice. If they do not overlap enough you will have to file away a little of the 'heels', the flat metal surfaces down near the handles that butt together when the blades are closed. File both of the butting faces (see **2**) by equal amounts in turn.

Hoes, lawn edge irons and spades All these are improved by occasional sharpening. Hold the tool firmly in a vice and before actually sharpening it file away any notches that the edge has sustained. When the edge is smooth and free of notches start sharpening, filing away from the edge, as with the shears.

New handles Rakes, hoes and the like have a tapered metal socket to receive a new handle. These will be ready-tapered, but may need some further whittling to make them fit properly (see **3**). Tap the new handle in firmly, spike through the hole in the metal with a bradawl, then drive home a new retaining screw.

Of course, you have to get the old broken handle out first. The handles of some tools are held in with rivets and these may have to be drilled out before the old wood can be removed. Centre-punch the rivet head, drill out the head, then tap out the rivet. The new handle need not be riveted but can be fixed in place with a new round-head screw.

Spades and forks may have an integral cylindrical socket or a pair of metal 'straps'. In either case a new handle may need trimming to fit. Measure the new handle carefully against the old one (see **4**) and mark it so that you can saw off the right amount for your size.

If the old handle has broken off flush with the metal socket the old wood may be difficult to remove. The best way is to drive a large screw part-way into the end of the wood (see **5**), then hold the screwhead firmly in a vice and tap the tool-head free of the handle.

Garden hose If your rubber hose has sprung a leak you can repair it by applying a band of adhesive such as Copydex about 2–3cm (1 in) wide so that it covers the hole, and then binding a strip of cloth tightly round the adhesive. When the cloth bandage is dry cover it with a second generous coating of the adhesive.

A damaged section of the standard 13mm ($\frac{1}{2}$ in) plastic hose is best cut out and the two ends joined together with a simple patent jointing device such as the Hozelock hose-mender.

1 *Filing away from the bevelled edge (see inset) of the blade* **2** *Filing heels so that blades overlap (inset)* **3** *Tapering new handle* **4** *Measuring new handle against the old one* **5** *Tapping tool-head free of stub*

1

2

3

4
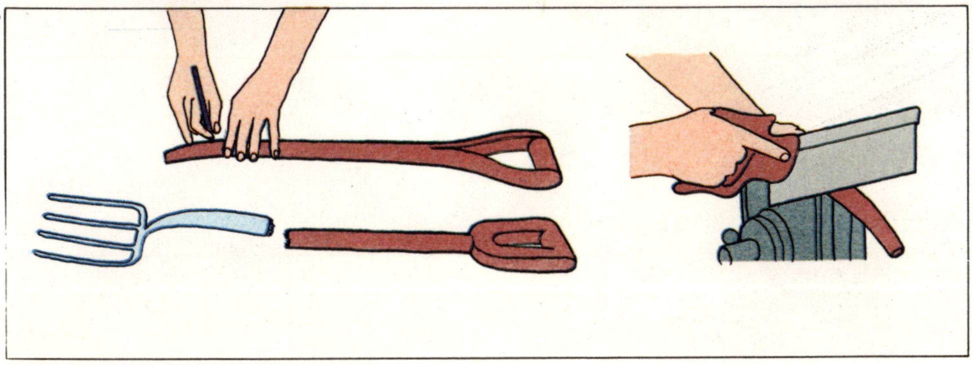

5

DOUBLE DIGGING

Digging is probably one of the most important techniques to be acquired by any gardener. And double digging can be worth all the hard work involved, especially if you have a heavy soil. Of course, if you don't feel up to it, you can always hire a mechanical cultivator.

Double digging is simply digging the soil two spits deep, that is, to the depth of two spade blades. It should improve the fertility and drainage of a heavy clay soil and is very useful where long-term crops are to be grown or an area is being given over to cultivation for the first time. As in single digging (see Week 3), the soil from each succeeding trench is transferred into the one behind it, until finally, the soil from the first trench goes into the last trench.

Digging and filling

The first step is to divide the plot into two and mark out the two sections into 60cm (24 in) wide strips. Starting at the end of the plot dig out the first strip to one spade's depth. The soil should be left next to the adjacent strip in the other half-plot.

Break up the bottom of the trench to the depth of your fork tines and then move onto the second strip. Make sure that each ensuing trench is as near as possible the same width as the one before so that the same quantity of soil is removed and a level surface is maintained. The soil from the second digging goes into the first trench, the bottom of the second trench is broken up and the process goes on until the final trench is filled with the pile of soil which has been waiting to fill the gap.

Compost and manure

If you want to apply compost or manure, it should be spread over the surface of the whole plot. As each trench is emptied, rake in the manure from the next strip and fork it into the broken-up second spit.

1

2

3

4

1 *Double digging the final trench and turning the soil into the one before.* **2** *Shovelling in the compost and spreading it evenly.* **3** *Mixing compost in with the broken-up second spit.* **4** *Filling final trench with soil left over from the first* *Right: mechanical cultivator with a rotating head helps to make double digging less back breaking. There are various fork tines for the cultivator head to deal with different types of soil*

SEED SOWING AND PRICKING OUT

Many different plants are raised from seed sown in containers in a greenhouse: summer bedding plants, flowering pot plants, and vegetables like tomatoes, lettuce, celery, cucumbers and marrows. But the techniques of sowing and subsequent care are similar.

Late winter and spring is the main period for most sowings; more precise timing is usually given on the seed packets. A heated greenhouse, or a propagator, is necessary for germination (that is, starting seeds into life).

Seed trays and pots

Seed trays, approximately 5–6cm (2–2½ in) deep, are available in either wood or plastic. Plastic ones last for many years, if well looked after, and are easy to clean. Hygienic conditions are important if you are to raise healthy seedlings, so clean the seed trays thoroughly before use.

For very small quantities of seed use plastic pots 9 or 13cm (3½ or 5 in) in diameter. These are also recommended for very large individual seeds, such as marrows and cucumbers. Again, wash all pots carefully before use.

Types of compost

Garden soil is not a very suitable medium in which to grow seedlings as it is full of weed seeds and harmful organisms, and it may not provide the correct conditions required by the seed for successful germination. Instead, buy one of the ready-mixed seed-sowing composts, the most popular being John Innes Seed Compost, consisting of loam, peat, sand, superphosphate and ground chalk.

Alternatively there are many brands of seed compost which consist only of peat with added fertilizers; these are known as 'soilless' composts because they do not contain loam. When using soilless compost you have to be especially careful with watering, for if it dries out it can be difficult to moisten again; over-watering may saturate it and cause the seeds to rot. With a little care, however, soilless compost gives excellent results.

Building in drainage

Be sure that surplus water is able to drain from all containers. When using John Innes composts it is essential to

Pricking out seedlings with a dibber

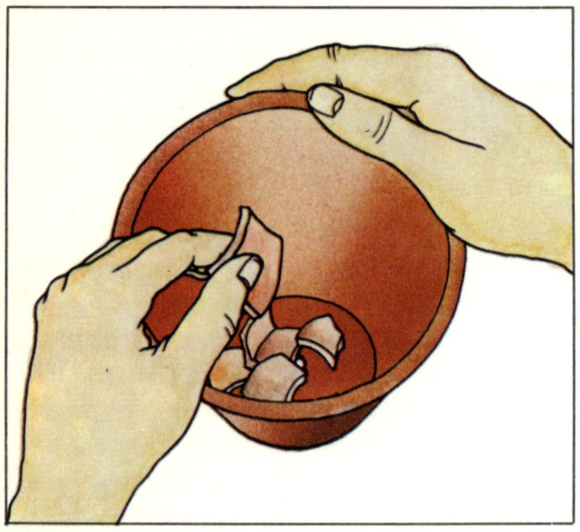

Place a layer of crocks in the bottom of flower pots to provide drainage

place a layer of crocks (broken clay flower pots or stones) at least 13mm (½ in) deep over the bottom of the pot. Cover the crocks with a little roughage, such as rough peat. If you use seed trays, crocks are not needed, just cover the drainage slits with some roughage.

Soilless compost can be used without any crocking – unless it is going in clay flower pots, in which case you must cover the large hole at the bottom with crocks.

Once you have arranged the drainage material add the compost to about 13mm (½ in) below the top of the tray or pot, to allow room for watering. Firm it gently all over with your fingertips, paying particular attention to the sides, ends and corners of seed trays. Make sure that the surface is level by pressing gently with a flat piece of wood that just fits into the tray or pot. Soilless compost should not be pressed hard but merely shaken down by tapping the container on a hard surface or lightly firming with the wood.

Very tiny seeds (like lobelia and begonia) should be sown on a fine surface. So before pressing down, sieve a layer of compost over the surface using a very small-mesh sieve. Alternatively you can sprinkle a thin layer of silver sand over the compost before sowing. Do not use builder's sand as this contains materials toxic to plants.

Water the compost lightly, using a fine rose on the watering can, before you sow.

Sowing the seeds

Seeds must be sown thinly and evenly otherwise the seedlings will be overcrowded and you will find it difficult to separate them during pricking out (transplanting). They will also have thin, weak stems and be prone to diseases like 'damping off'.

Small seed is usually sown broadcast (scattered) over the surface of the compost. Take a small quantity of seed in the palm of one hand – just sufficient to sow a tray or pot. Hold your hand about 30cm (12 in) above the container and move it to and fro over the surface, at the same time tapping it with the other hand to release the seeds slowly. If you move your hand first backwards and forwards and then side to side this will help to spread the seeds evenly. You may find it easier to hold the seeds in a piece of paper, instead of in your hand.

It is difficult to sow very small seeds evenly, some being as fine as dust, but if you mix them with soft, dry, silver sand (using 1 part seeds to 1 part sand) this helps to bulk them up and makes them easier to handle.

Large seeds, which are easily handled, can be 'space-sown' – that is placed individually, and at regular intervals, on the surface of the compost. Tomato seed, for instance, can be treated in this way.

Very large seeds, such as cucumbers, peas and various beans, are best sown at two per 9cm (3½ in) pot. If you use peat pots, they can later be planted, complete with young plant, into the final pot or open ground. When they have germinated, remove the weaker seedling, leaving the stronger one to grow on.

Pelleted seeds

This term describes seeds that are individually covered with a layer of clay which is often mixed with some plant foods. They are easily handled and can be space-sown in boxes or pots. The compost around pelleted seeds must remain moist as it is moisture which breaks down the coating and allows the seeds to germinate.

After sowing

Seeds should be covered with a layer of compost equal to the diameter of the seed. It is best to sieve compost over them, using a fine-mesh sieve. However, do not cover very small or dust-like seeds with compost as they will probably fail to germinate.

If you use John Innes or another loam-

1 *Cover drainage materials with compost, firming it gently with the fingertips*

2 *Level the surface of the compost by pressing with a flat piece of wood*

3 *Scatter a little seed into tray by tapping it gently from your open hand*

4 *With large seeds, sow two in a small pot and remove the weaker seedling*

1

2

3

1 Sieve compost over seeds; 2 Stand tray in water till surface looks moist. 3 Use a dibber to lift seedlings and transfer them to a new tray, where they will have room to grow on

containing compost the seeds should then be watered, either using a very fine rose on the watering can or by standing the containers in a tray of water until the surface becomes moist. (This latter method is not advisable for loam-less composts as they tend to float; moisten them well before sowing the seed.) Allow the containers to drain before placing them in the greenhouse.

A good, or even better, alternative to plain water is a solution of Cheshunt Compound, made up according to the directions on the tin. This is a fungicide which prevents diseases such as damping off attacking seedlings.

Aids to germination

Place the pots or trays either on a bench in a warm greenhouse or in an electrically-heated propagator. Most seeds need a temperature of 15°–18°C (60–65°F) for good germination. The containers can be covered with a sheet of glass that, in turn, is covered with brown paper to prevent the sun's warmth drying out the compost. Turn the glass over each day to prevent excess condensation building up on the inside. Water the compost whenever its surface starts to become dry. As soon as germination commences remove the covering of glass and paper, for the seedlings then require as much light as possible if they are to grow into strong, healthy plants.

Pricking out

Once the seedlings are large enough to handle easily prick them out into trays or boxes to give them enough room to grow. Generally, standard-size plastic or wooden seed trays are used that are 6cm (2½ in) deep; there is no need to put drainage material in the base. The trays are filled with compost in the way described for seed-sowing, again leaving space for watering. A suitable compost would be John Innes Potting Compost No. 1 which can be bought ready-mixed. It consists of loam, peat, coarse sand, John Innes base fertilizer and ground chalk. Alternatively, use one of the soil-less potting composts that contains peat, or peat and sand, plus fertilizers. Make sure the compost is moist before you start pricking out.

You will need a dibber for this job – either a pencil or a piece of wood of similar shape. With this lift a few seedlings at a time from the box or pot, taking care not to damage the roots. Handle the seedlings by the seed leaves – the first pair of leaves formed. Never hold them by the stems which are easily damaged at this stage.

Spacing out

The number of seedlings per standard-size box will vary slightly according to their vigour. Generally 40 per box is a good spacing (5 rows of 8). For less vigorous plants you could increase this to 54 per box (6 rows of 9).

Mark out the position of the seedlings with the dibber before commencing, ensuring equal spacing each way. Next make a hole, with the dibber, which should be deep enough to allow the roots to drop straight down. Place the seedling in the hole so that the seed leaves are at soil level, and then firm it in by pressing the soil gently against it with the dibber.

If only a few seeds have been sown in pots each seedling could be pricked out into an individual 7cm (3 in) pot. But if you have single seedlings, such as marrows, already started in 9cm (3½ in) pots, these will not need to be moved.

After pricking out, water in the seedlings (with a fine rose on the watering can) preferably using Cheshunt Compound. Then place them on the greenhouse bench or on a shelf near to the glass, as maximum light is essential. Continue to water whenever the soil surface appears dry.

Windowsill propagation

If you do not have a greenhouse, heated frame, or propagator, you can still raise seedlings in the house. Ideally the germination conditions should be as similar as possible to those which are recommended for greenhouse cultivation. Windowsills are the best places for raising seeds, and if they are wide ones you can use standard-size seed trays.

However it is usually possible to fit a few pots onto the narrowest of windowsills. For best results use trays or pots that are fitted with propagator tops. The temperature on the sill must not drop below the average room temperature and south- or west-facing sills are obviously best.

Make sure the seedlings are never deprived of daylight or allowed to get cold at night. Never draw the curtains across between the plants and the warm room air on cold nights, if necessary bring them into the room. Finally, to maintain strong and even growth, turn all pots and trays around every day.

Use a pot with a propagator top when starting off seedlings on a windowsill

TAKING CUTTINGS

One of the most exciting skills in gardening is to know how to take cuttings. When you can do this, and understand the principles behind the method, you no longer need to buy house plants, shrubs or perennials from a nursery, and you can replace elderly plants in your flowerbeds that are past their prime. And if you have friends who grow plants that you particularly covet, it is easy to persuade them to let you take a cutting. Liberality is a distinguishing characteristic of the true gardener.

A cutting is a part of a plant—a piece of stem, leaf or root—which is induced to form roots of its own and thus develop into a young plant that is identical with its parent.

Many plants can be propagated from cuttings but the type of cutting to prepare depends on the plant. A wide range from hardy shrubs to greenhouse plants can be increased from softwood cuttings. These are prepared from very soft young shoots early in the year, generally in the period from late spring to mid summer (April to June), although some may be taken even earlier than this.

Cuttings, whether softwood or any other type, must be prepared with a very sharp knife or razor blade to ensure clean cuts. Ragged cuts resulting from using a blunt knife may take too long to heal, and could eventually result in the cutting rotting instead of making roots for which it was intended.

Softwood cuttings

Hardy shrubs that can be propagated from softwoods include weigela, deutzia, philadelphus, buddleia, caryopteris, hypericum and many other deciduous kinds. The cuttings of these can be about 8cm (3 in) in length, and should be cut cleanly just below a leaf joint, or node. Such a cutting is generally known as a 'nodal' cutting.

The lower leaves should be carefully cut off as close to the stem as possible. The bases of the cuttings can then be dipped into a proprietary hormone rooting powder or liquid to encourage rapid root formation.

Softwood cuttings are liable to lose water very quickly and wilt, so they must be inserted in the rooting medium as quickly as possible. The usual compost for rooting is a mixture of equal parts of moist sphagnum peat and coarse horticultural sand.

A small number of cuttings can be rooted in pots of a convenient size, but larger quantities should be inserted in seed trays. The container should be filled with compost to within 13mm ($\frac{1}{2}$ in) of the rim and firmed moderately well with the fingers. Cuttings are placed in holes made with a dibber – a piece of wood shaped rather like a blunt pencil. In fact, a pencil makes a good dibber. The base of each cutting should be in close contact with the bottom of the hole. Firm in with the fingers and when the container is full water with a fine rose on the watering can.

Softwood cuttings of hardy herbaceous perennial plants such as delphinium, lupin, phlox, chrysanthemum, gaillardia and scabious, and of half-hardy perennials like dahlia and glasshouse chrysanthemum, are prepared and inserted in the same way. Remove young shoots when 8cm (3 in) long, from as close to the crown of the plant as possible.

Other plants that can be raised from softwood cuttings are tender greenhouse plants such as begonia, coleus, fuchsia, impatiens and tradescantia. Cuttings of fuchsia can be prepared by cutting the base between two nodes or joints—these are known as 'internodal' cuttings.

Growing conditions

All softwood cuttings need plenty of warmth in which to root, and a humid or moist atmosphere. The simplest method of providing these conditions is to enclose a pot of cuttings in a polythene bag, which should be tied at the top, or place a jam jar over the cuttings, and stand it on a windowsill in a warm room, preferably above a radiator. A more sophisticated approach is to invest in an electrically heated propagating case, which is generally placed on a greenhouse bench. This should be set to give a temperature of 52°C (70°F).

The covers should be removed for an hour or two, several times a week, to

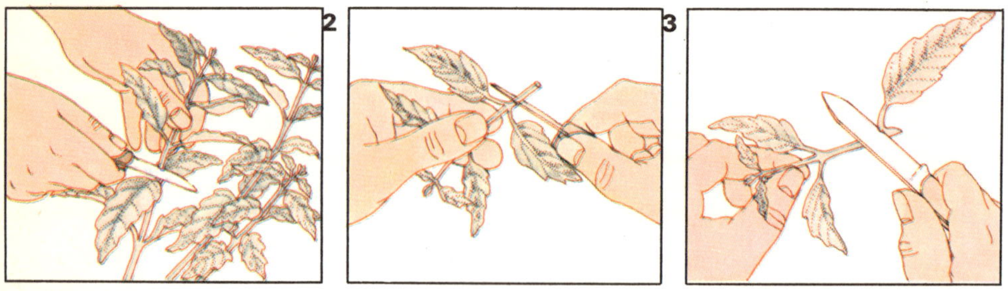

Softwood cuttings: **1** *cut shoot from plant with sharp knife or razor;* **2** *trim cutting cleanly to just below base of leaf joint;* **3** *cut off lower leaves as close to the stem as possible;* **4** *dip base of cutting in proprietary hormone rooting powder;*

5 *using dibber, insert cutting in compost, made of moist sphagnum peat and coarse horticultural sand;* **6** *firm round cutting;* **7** *water well in, using fine spray on watering can;* **8** *place in propagator or mist unit or,* **9** *put pot in polythene bag*

1

2

3

4

5 6
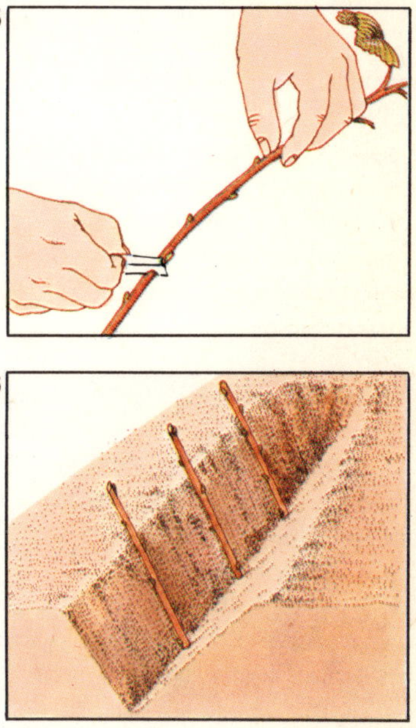

Semi-ripe cuttings:
1 *remove lower stems;*
2 *rub off lower leaves;*
3 *insert cuttings in compost*
Hardwood cuttings:
4 *cut ripe or woody shoot;*
5 *trim to four or five buds;*
6 *put cuttings in prepared, V-shaped trench, replace soil and firm well in*

allow the containers to dry off, because a great amount of condensation forms in these enclosed conditions.

The most adventurous way of rooting cuttings is to install a mist-propagation unit in your greenhouse. This provides heat at the base of the cuttings and sprays the leaves intermittently with water, which prevents the cuttings from wilting and dying. Reasonably simple and cheap units are available to amateur gardeners.

Some softwoods can be rooted simply by standing them in jars of water on a warm windowsill indoors. Plants which respond to this treatment include coleus, fuchsia, impatiens, tradescantia and zebrina – all popular house plants.

Semi-ripe cuttings

Many plants can be prepared from semi-ripe (or semi-mature) cuttings. These are prepared from shoots which are ripening or hardening at the base but are still soft at the tip. The time to take these is late summer to late autumn (July to October).

Evergreen and deciduous shrubs, heathers, conifers and half-hardy perennials like pelargonium (geranium), heliotrope and gazania, can be increased from semi-ripe cuttings.

Cuttings generally vary in length from some 10–15cm (4–6 in), but those of heathers should be only 5cm (2 in) long. These can simply be pulled off the plant, whereas cuttings of other subjects must be nodal and prepared with a knife.

1 2 3
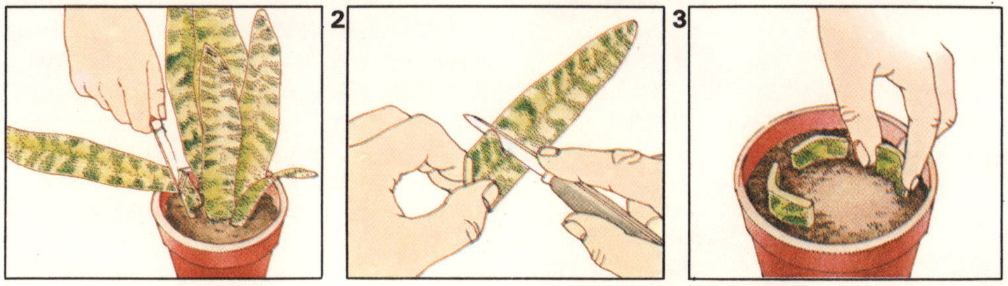

Leaf section cuttings: **1** *cut whole leaf from plant;* **2** *cut leaf into 5cm (2 in) sections;* **3** *press section (top end facing upwards) into peat and sand compost*

4 5 6

Whole leaf cuttings: **4** *cut leaf from plant;* **5** *insert whole leaf-stalk into peat and sand compost, leaving leaf-blade exposed;* **6** *firm compost round cutting*

Growing conditions

Preparation and insertion are the same as for softwoods, but less heat is needed for rooting. A cold frame makes an ideal rooting environment, but of course if you have a propagating case or mist unit then root them in these.

Hardwood cuttings

Hardwood cuttings, which are inserted in early and mid winter (November to December), need no heat at all to root. Common examples of shrubs and soft fruits raised from these are privet, willow, shrubby dogwood, Chinese honeysuckle, blackcurrant, redcurrant and gooseberry.

Choose current year's shoots which are completely ripe or woody and cut them into 23–30cm (9–12 in) lengths with sharp secateurs. Cut just above a bud at the top and just below at the base. With redcurrants and gooseberries remove all the buds except the top three or four. Dip the base of the cutting in a hormone rooting powder or liquid.

The cuttings are inserted to two-thirds of their length in a V-shaped trench made with a spade in a sheltered well-drained spot outdoors. Firm them in well. They will be well rooted by the following autumn (September).

Leaf cuttings

Some house, and greenhouse, plants are propagated from leaf cuttings in spring. With peperomia, saintpaulia, streptocarpus and gloxinia use a whole leaf with the leaf-stalk attached. The complete leaf-stalk is inserted in a peat and sand compost so that you leave only the leaf-blade exposed.

In the case of a plant like *Sansevieria trifasciata* (Mother-in-law's tongue), one of the long leaves should be cut into 5cm (2 in) sections. Each section is pressed into peat and sand compost to about half its length. Make sure you insert each section the right way up.

Rex begonia can be propagated by removing an entire leaf, cutting through the main veins in several places on the underside and laying the leaf, top side uppermost, on the surface of a tray of compost. Hold the leaf down with small stones. Young plants will form where you have made the cuts.

Like softwood cuttings, leaf cuttings need plenty of warmth and humidity to enable them to root.

Leaf-bud cuttings

A leaf-bud cutting is a portion of stem about 2·5cm (1 in) long, with an entire leaf attached at the top, and a bud in the axil (the point where the leaf joins the stem). Rubber plant, camellia, clematis, passion flower and ivy can be propagated by this method, which should be carried out in late spring (April). Insert cuttings so that the leaf only is above the compost and root in warm, humid conditions.

Eye cuttings

Grape vines and their close relations (parthenocissus and ampelopsis) are propagated from eye cuttings in mid winter (December). You will probably need a propagating case for this method as a base temperature of 52°C (70°F) is required for rooting. Use well-ripened or hardened current year's wood. Cut it into 4cm (1½ in) sections, each with a dormant 'eye' or bud in the centre. Remove a thin slice of wood on the opposite side to the bud. These cuttings are pressed horizontally into pots of peat and sand compost, with the buds uppermost, and just sufficiently deep to ensure that they remain stable. Water in and place in the rooting environment.

Pipings

Pinks are raised from a special type of cutting known as a piping. In late summer or early autumn (July or August) pull out the tops of young shoots: they should snap out cleanly just above a leaf joint or node. Each one should be left with three or four pairs of leaves, after the lower leaves have been carefully pulled off. Using a dibber, insert the pipings around the edge of a small pot containing peat and sand compost. Water well in and then place in a cold frame to root.

Root cuttings

Finally, root cuttings can be used to propagate shrubs like rhus, sambucus, aralia, campsis, celastrus, chaenomeles and rubus; trees such as ailanthus, catalpa, paulownia, robinia and elm; hardy herbaceous perennials like anchusa, echinops, eryngium, gaillardia, Oriental poppy, border phlox, *Primula denticulata*, *Romneya coulteri*, symphytum or verbascum; and the alpines *Morisia monantha* and *Pulsatilla vulgaris*.

The time to take root cuttings is when the plants are dormant, a good period being mid winter (December). Use young roots of no more than pencil thickness; the roots of some plants, such as phlox, primula, morisia and pulsatilla, will be thinner than this.

The roots can be obtained by scraping the soil away from large plants, removing a few roots, returning the soil and firming. Small plants can be lifted, a few roots removed and then replanted.

The roots should be cut into 5cm (2 in) sections with a knife or secateurs. Thick roots are inserted vertically, and to ensure that you keep them the right way up the tops of the cuttings should have a flat cut and the bases a slanting cut. The top of a root cutting is always that part which was nearer to the stem of the plant.

The cuttings can be rooted in pots or boxes of peat and sand compost. Thick cuttings should be pressed vertically into the medium so that the tops are just below soil level. Thin cuttings cannot be pushed in vertically, so are laid horizontally on the surface of the compost and covered with a further 13mm (½ in) layer. Place in a cold frame or greenhouse to root. The top growth will be produced first so do not be in too much of a hurry to lift the cuttings for planting out.

Top: pull pink shoots to obtain pipings Above: for leaf bud cuttings use a portion of stem bearing a leaf and a leaf bud

1–3 *leaf cutting using whole leaf laid on compost, with main veins cut;* **4–6** *root cuttings, using thick and thin roots*

The basic terms used in potting are 'potting off', when young rooted cuttings or seedlings are moved from trays into pots, and 'potting on', when the more advanced plants are transferred to bigger pots.

POTTING OFF AND POTTING ON

Nowadays plastic pots are generally used in preference to clay, but whichever type you have ensure that they are clean and dry before using them.

POTTING OFF

As soon as cuttings have developed a good root system they should be carefully lifted from their trays and put into individual pots about 7·5–9cm (3–3½ in) in diameter. When seedlings are large enough to handle easily they can be treated in the same way (as an alternative to pricking out into trays).

For this first potting, use a fairly weak compost, such as J.I. No 1, or an equivalent soilless type consisting of loam, peat, coarse sand, John Innes base fertilizer and ground chalk.

Allowing for drainage

Drainage material is not necessary in plastic pots as the holes are devised so that the compost does not leak. Furthermore, there is a trend towards using less drainage material in the bottom of small clay pots. When there are some drainage holes provided, place a few crocks (pieces of broken clay pots or stones) over the drainage holes and cover with a thin layer of roughage such as coarse peat or partially-rotted leaf mould. If you are using soilless compost, crocks or drainage materials are not normally necessary. Place a layer of compost over the drainage material and firm lightly with your fingers.

Transferring the plants

Hold the rooted cuttings or seedlings in the centre of the pot, with the roots well spread out, and trickle compost all around until it is slightly higher than the rim of the pot. Give the pot a sharp tap on the bench to settle the compost well down and lightly firm all round with your fingers. Make sure the compost is pushed right down to the bottom.

Some soilless composts, however, require little or no firming, so check the manufacturer's instructions first.

Remember to leave about 13mm (½ in) between the surface of the soil and the rim of the pot to allow room for watering.

After potting off, water the plants thoroughly, using a fine rose on the watering can, to settle them in further. Then they can be returned to the greenhouse bench.

Before placing a pot-bound plant in its new pot, carefully remove old drainage crocks from the base of the rootball

POTTING ON

Plants need potting on to prevent them becoming 'pot-bound' (when the roots are packed very tightly in the pot). If this happens the plants will suffer from lack of food, growth will be poor and they will dry out very rapidly and require frequent watering.

However, it is worthwhile noting that some plants, such as pelargoniums, are more floriferous (bear more flowers) when slightly pot-bound.

Plants should be moved to the next size of pot, for instance from a 9cm (3½ in) to a 13cm (5 in), from a 13cm (5 in) to a 15cm (6 in) and so on. The reason for moving only to the next size pot is that plants dislike a large volume of soil around their roots because they cannot absorb water from all of it and, therefore, it is liable to remain wet. This can result in root rot and the possible death of the plant. Small moves allow plants to put out new roots quickly.

Composts and drainage

Richer composts (those containing more plant foods) are generally used for potting on. If you prefer the John Innes type, then use No 2, which contains twice as much fertilizer and chalk as No 1. Some plants (for example chrysanthemums,

To pot on a pot-bound plant: **1** *place crocks and drainage material in bottom of larger pot, then carefully remove plant from old pot;* **2** *half-fill new pot with compost;* **3** *hold plant in centre of pot, add more compost to within 2cm (½ in) of rim;* **4** *firm all round plant*

tomatoes and strawberries for fruiting under glass) like an even richer compost, such as J.I. No 3 – particularly when they are moved into their final size of pot).

Drainage material, as described under potting off, is generally advisable when using soil composts in pots that are 13cm (5 in) or larger. A layer of crocks about 2–3cm (1 in) deep should be sufficient, plus roughage.

Repotting the plant

Remove the plant from its pot by turning it upside-down and tapping the rim of the pot on the edge of a bench. The rootball should then slide out intact. On no account disturb this ball of roots and soil, but remove old crocks, if any, from the base. Scrape off any moss or weeds on the surface with an old wooden plant label or similar object.

Place enough soil in the new pot so that, when the plant is placed on it, the top of the rootball is about 13mm (½ in) from the top of the pot. This will allow for a light covering of compost with room for subsequent watering. Firm the compost lightly with your fingers and then stand the plant in the centre of the new pot. Trickle fresh compost all round the rootball until you reach the top of the pot. Give the pot a sharp tap on the bench to get the compost well down and firm it all round.

If you are using soilless composts, follow the maker's instructions for firming. You will probably need to add more compost to reach the desired height. Finally, water in the plants, using a fine rose on the watering can.

Potting on is best done when plants are growing actively in spring and summer – or in the autumn, although growth will then be slowing down. Plants potted in spring and summer will quickly root into the new compost because of the warmer weather.

PLANT DIVISION AND LAYERING

1

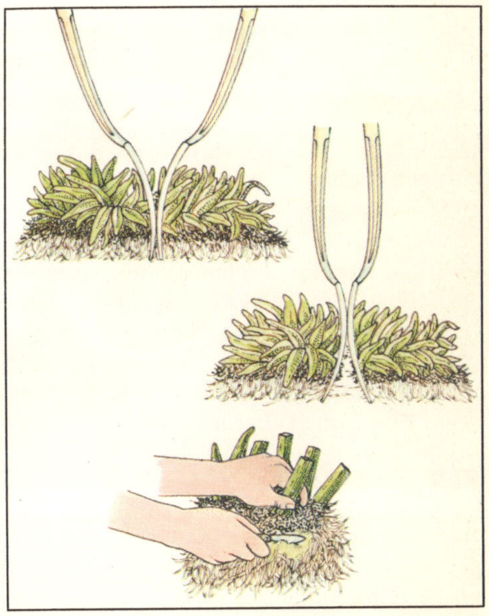

2

3

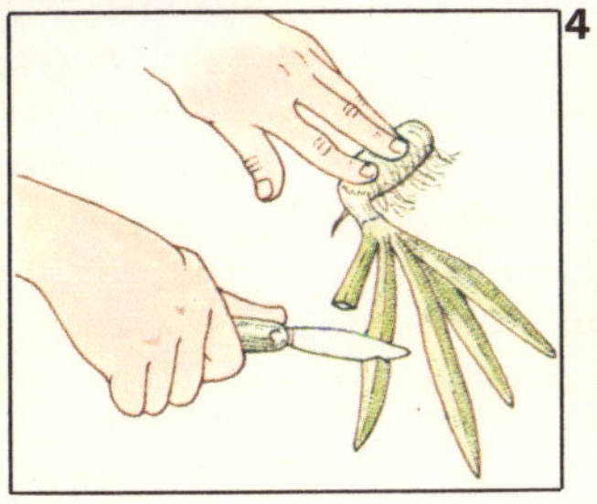

4

In nature, where plants must be able to survive all sorts of accidents, they can grow again when split into pieces, or make new roots from the point at which they have suffered an injury. Several techniques have been developed from this natural process.

The simplest method of plant propagation is division, or the splitting of plants into a number of small portions. It is the principal method of increasing herbaceous border plants and other hardy perennials; most of these need lifting and dividing every three to four years to ensure that they remain vigorous and continue to flower well. Many other kinds of plant can also be increased by division.

Perennials and alpines

The best time to carry out this operation is in mid spring (March–mid April), just as the plants are awakening from their winter rest; plants in flower should be left until they finish flowering. Lift the clumps carefully with a fork and shake off as much soil as possible. Large tough clumps can be divided by inserting two digging forks back to back through the centre and pulling the handles apart. The two portions can then be split by the same method. Discard the centre of each clump and replant only the young outer portions. Each division should consist of a number of growth buds and a good portion of roots.

Top left: preparing divided perennial plants for replanting; **1** *dividing clump of perennials with forks and trimming damaged roots;* **2–4** *cutting, trimming and replanting young rhizomes;* **5** *corm producing cormlets, and below, bubblets forming round parent bulb*

Those perennials that flower early in the year, such as doronicum, pyrethrum, epimedium, symphytum, pulmonaria and primula (including primroses and polyanthus), should be divided immediately after flowering. Some perennials are best not divided at all, as they resent being moved: these include romneya, paeony, helleborus, alstroemeria, echinops, eryngium, *Papaver orientalis*, (Oriental poppy) and Japanese anemone. Plants that grow from a single stem, cannot, of course, be divided.

Many alpine plants form mats or carpets of growth and these too can be lifted and pulled apart to provide a number of smaller plants. Thyme, raolia, sedum, gentian, saxifrage and campanula can all be split in early spring.

5

Dividing rhizomes and tubers

Some plants, of which the iris is the best-known example, form 'rhizomes', which are simply swollen stems situated at or just below soil level. There are many kinds of iris, such as the bearded iris, which is a superb border plant, and the dwarf kinds admirably suited to a rock garden.

When you divide iris—which should be immediately after flowering—each division should consist of a short portion of rhizome with some roots and a fan of leaves attached.

Many people keep dahlias from one year to another. Before planting them out in the spring, the dormant clumps can be split into smaller portions. Dahlias are best cut with a knife; make sure that each division consists of a portion of old stem with dormant growth buds at the base, and at best one tuber attached.

Bulbs and corms

Bulbs, such as daffodil, tulip and hyacinth, and corms, for example gladiolus and crocus, form offspring around their bases, and these are known as bulblets and cormlets respectively. If the parent bulbs and corms are dug up after the foliage has died down, these youngsters can be removed and stored dry until the correct planting time, which is autumn (September or October) for most, and mid to late spring (March–April) for gladiolus. Plant them fairly shallowly. Some bulbs and corms may take two or three years to flower, so be patient.

1 2 3

1 *Removing offsets from sempervivum;* **2** *lifting rooted suckers from raspberry plants;* **3** *dividing dahlia tubers*

House plants

Some house plants can be split up in spring when they start to become too large, such as ferns, aspidistra, chlorophytum, and other clump-formers. Remove each plant from its pot, shake the soil away and pull apart. Repot each portion, using fresh compost.

Offsets

An even easier method than lifting and dividing is simply to remove offsets from plants complete with a few roots attached. Offsets are small plants found growing around the parent. Carefully tease them away with a hand fork to ensure you do not damage the roots or disturb the main plant.

Sempervivum (houseleek), androsace, some saxifrages, sansevieria and many cacti and succulents form offsets.

Suckers

There are many shrubs that produce 'suckers'—shoots which arise from below ground, usually from the roots. This is one of the ways in which plants increase naturally. With some, such as raspberries, masses of shoots are produced all round the parent plants.

In the winter or in early spring (November–March), when the plants are dormant, suckers can be carefully dug up with some roots attached and planted elsewhere. Shrubs which are often propagated by this method include *Rhus typhina*, symphoricarpus, cornus (dogwood) and aralia. It is also the way to increase raspberries.

Layering

Layering is also an easy method of propagating plants. Simple layering consists of pegging down a branch or shoot into the soil, where it will form roots. It can then be detached from the parent plant and planted elsewhere. You may notice, when out in the country, that some plants, such as beech and bramble, layer themselves quite naturally without the help of man.

Almost any tree or shrub can be propagated by simple layering, provided a shoot can be brought into contact with the soil. The best time for this operation is in the spring or early summer when plants are actively growing. Choose young shoots or stems for layering as these will root quicker than older growth. The ground in which the stems are to be layered should be well prepared beforehand. Fork it over and break it down to a fine tilth. Mix plenty of moist peat and coarse sand with the soil to a depth of 15–25cm (6–9 in). Now all is ready.

About 30cm (12 in) or so from the tip of the shoot or stem it should be wounded in some way, so as to encourage quicker rooting. The easiest way to wound the stem is to grip it with both hands and give it a sharp half-twist to break some of the tissue. Another method is to cut diagonally halfway through the stem with a sharp knife, making a cut 4–5cm (1½–2 in) in length. This will result in a 'tongue' in the stem, which should be kept open with a small stone or piece of wood.

Using a piece of galvanized wire bent to the shape of a hairpin, peg the prepared shoot down where it was wounded into a 7–8cm (3 in) deep depression in the soil. Cover with soil and firm with your fingers. Tie the end of the stem protruding through the soil upright to a short bamboo cane. Keep layers well watered whenever the soil starts to become dry.

1 2 3 4 5 6

Simple layering: **1** *twist stem sharply to break surface tissue or* **2** *make cut in underside of stem;* **3** *bend stem at wound and peg to soil with wire pin;* **4** *cover pegged section with soil;* **5** *tie end of stem to bamboo cane;* **6** *when roots have formed, sever new plant from parent stem*

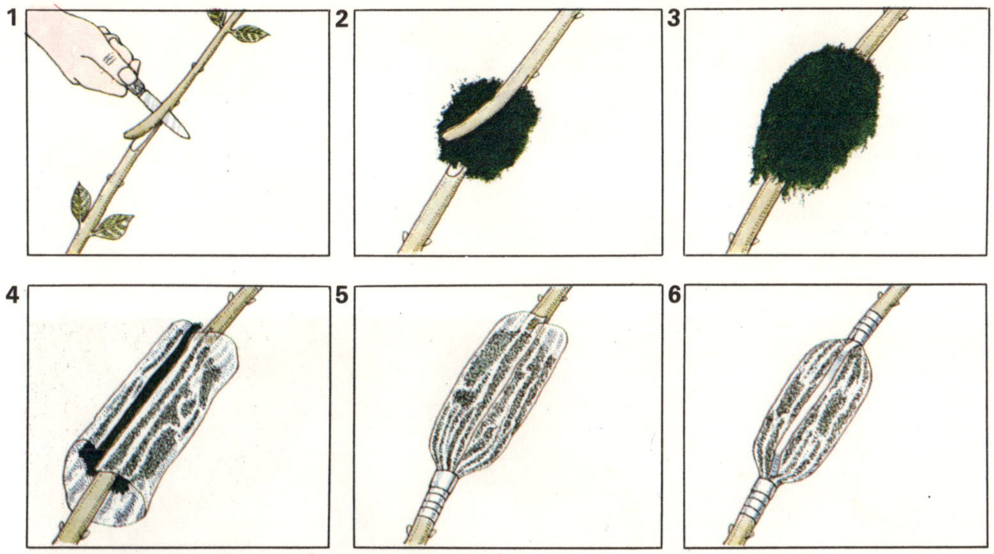

Air layering: **1** *make diagonal cut, half way through stem;* **2** *treat with hormone rooting powder and wedge open with moss;* **3** *bandage cut with moss;* **4** *wrap with polythene sheeting;* **5** *seal lower end below cut;* **6** *seal upper end and join*

Above: air layering of ficus elastica *rubber plant, showing correct angle of cut*

Some plants, such as the common shrubs forsythia, syringa (lilac), weigela, hebe (veronica), privet and philadelphus (mock orange), will form a good root system in a year. Others may take longer to root well, particularly magnolia, hamamelis (witch hazel), rhododendron, azalea and camellia. When the layers have rooted lift them carefully with a fork and sever from the parent close to the new root area. Set out as soon as possible.

Serpentine layering

This is a minor modification of simple layering, and is done with plants possessing long stems, particularly climbers like clematis, jasmine, lonicera (honeysuckle), wisteria, passiflora (passion flower) and vines. Wound the long stems and peg them down at intervals along the ground, so that you get a number of new plants from one stem. All should have rooted within a year.

Tip layering

Blackberries, loganberries and other hybrid berries are propagated by tip layering. In late summer or early autumn July or August simply bury the extreme tip of a young stem 7–8cm (3 in) deep in the soil. It should be well rooted by the following early winter (November), when it can be planted out.

Air layering

This is a useful method where stems cannot be pulled down to the ground. Again it is suitable for any tree or shrub, spring or early summer (March–May) being a good time to do it.

Use a young stem and cut diagonally halfway through it, making the cut about 5cm (2 in) in length. Make this wound about 30cm (12 in) from the tip and keep the cut open by packing it with moist sphagnum moss. You can first treat the cut with a hormone rooting powder or liquid to speed root production.

The prepared part of the stem should then be 'bandaged' with moist sphagnum moss, held in place by wrapping with a piece of clear polythene sheeting. Each end of this polythene 'sleeve' must be tightly sealed with self-adhesive waterproof tape. The overlapping edge of the polythene must also be sealed with tape.

You will know when roots have formed as they will be seen through the polythene. At this stage sever the rooted layer and plant it out.

House plants such as ficus (rubber plant) croton, philodendron, dracaena and cordyline can also be air-layered. It is done in the way described for outdoor plants, making the cut near the top of the plant. If the plant is kept in a warm place, rooting will be a matter of weeks. If the stem of the parent plant is cut hard back after removing the layer, it should produce new growth from the base.

Finally, strawberries are also propagated by layering. In the summer they produce 'runners', or stems which grow along the ground, and at intervals along these new plants are formed. To encourage these to root quickly, peg the first plantlet (the one nearest the parent) on each runner into a pot of potting compost sunk in the soil. Remove any plantlets beyond the first one. They will quickly root, and in early autumn (August or early September) should be severed from the main plant and planted elsewhere.

1 *Serpentine layering;* **2** *pegging down strawberry runners;* **3** *tip layering*

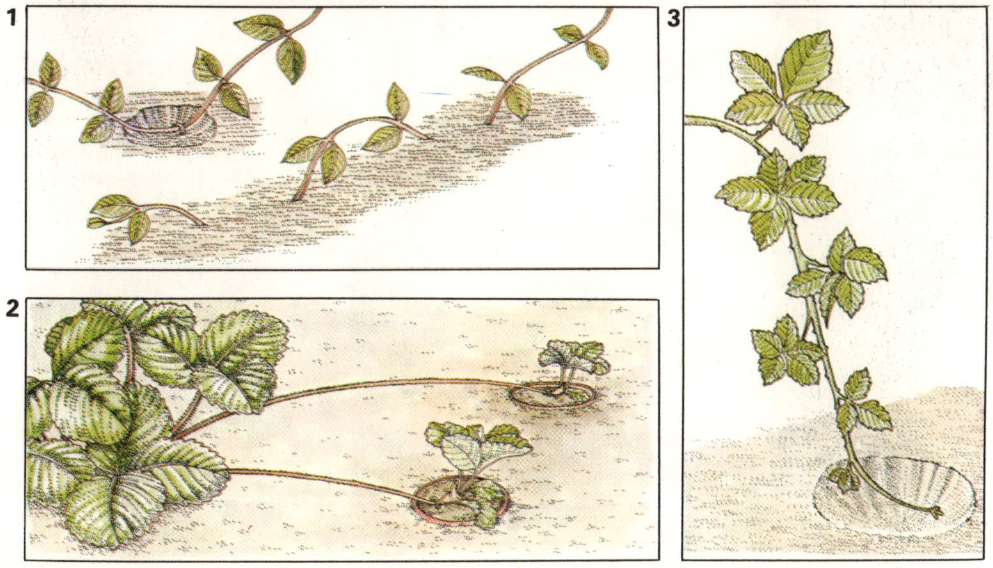

BUDDING AND GRAFTING

Without the techniques of budding and grafting we would have few varieties of rose or rhododendron, and almost no cropping or ornamental fruit trees. These two closely-related methods of propagation are easily-assimilated, and provide a fascinating and richly-rewarding addition to your range of gardening skills.

Bridge grafting stage **1** *: tree with diseased or damaged bark*

Stage **2***: cut away damaged bark before making bridge graft*

Stage **3***: make slits in bark above and below damaged area*

Stage **4***: insert scions, taken from tree, to form bridge for sap*

Budding and grafting are both ways of joining permanently together portions of two separate plants to form a complete new plant. One plant provides the root system and is known as the 'rootstock', and the other plant, which is the one we wish to propagate, provides the top-growth. A growth bud, or a piece of stem known as the 'scion', is removed from the plant to be propagated and is inserted in the rootstock, where it eventually unites with it and so a new plant develops. In all cases, it is important to make sure that the 'cambium' (the thin green layer just under the bark) of the stock is in close contact with the cambium of the scion.

Budding and grafting are generally used to propagate plants which are difficult or impossible to increase by other means such as cuttings or seed, or which would not be successful on their own roots. The rootstock generally imparts vigour to the variety budded or grafted on to it; this is usually very beneficial, especially for many roses and fruit-tree varieties which are weak if grown on their own roots. The rootstock is usually of the same species or group as the variety to be propagated. Often it is the naturally-occurring form of which the propagated variety is a cultivar.

T-budding

Budding is a method used to propagate roses and ornamental fruiting trees.

Roses You will have to plant one-year-old root-stocks of *Rosa canina*, the briar, in late autumn (October or November) for budding the following summer or early autumn (from June to early September). The buds of the variety to be propagated should be plump or well-developed and carried on current year's shoots. Remove one of these shoots with a number of buds attached. Cut off the leaves, leaving the leaf stalks (petioles). Buds should only be removed from this 'bud stick' immediately prior to inserting them in the rootstocks.

Using a really sharp horticultural knife you then cut out each bud on a shield-shaped piece of bark 2–3cm (1 in) long with a thin sliver of wood behind it. This wood should then be carefully removed from the bark. The bud is inserted in the rootstock at ground level. With your knife, make a T-shaped cut in the bark. Lift the bark with the knife blade. Hold the bud by the leaf stalk and slip it down behind the bark. Tie in tightly with raffia, making sure that the bud is exposed.

In the following spring (February or March) cut off the top of the rootstock just above the bud. Soon after, the bud will start into growth. By the autumn you will have a young rose bush.

Ornamental and fruit trees These are budded in the same way, except that the bud is inserted 15–20cm (6–8 in) from the ground. Make sure that you use the right rootstocks; Malling and Malling-Merton apple stocks for apples and crabs; Malling Quince A for pears; *Prunus avium* Mazzard or Gean for cherries; Brompton for almonds, apricots, nectarines, and peaches; and Myrobalan for plums. For other ornamental trees, use the naturally-occurring species as a rootstock.

Chip budding

Although chip budding is performed on roses and fruit trees in exactly the same way as T-budding, you are more likely to achieve successful results.

Remove a bud with a substantial piece of wood about 4cm ($1\frac{1}{2}$ in) in length. Make a cut about 20mm ($\frac{3}{4}$ in) below the bud at an angle of 20 degrees into the stem. Then insert the knife about 20mm ($\frac{3}{4}$ in) above the bud and cut down behind the bud to meet the first cut, so that the bud can be lifted out. A corresponding cut should then be made in the stock, so that the bud should exactly fit the cut in

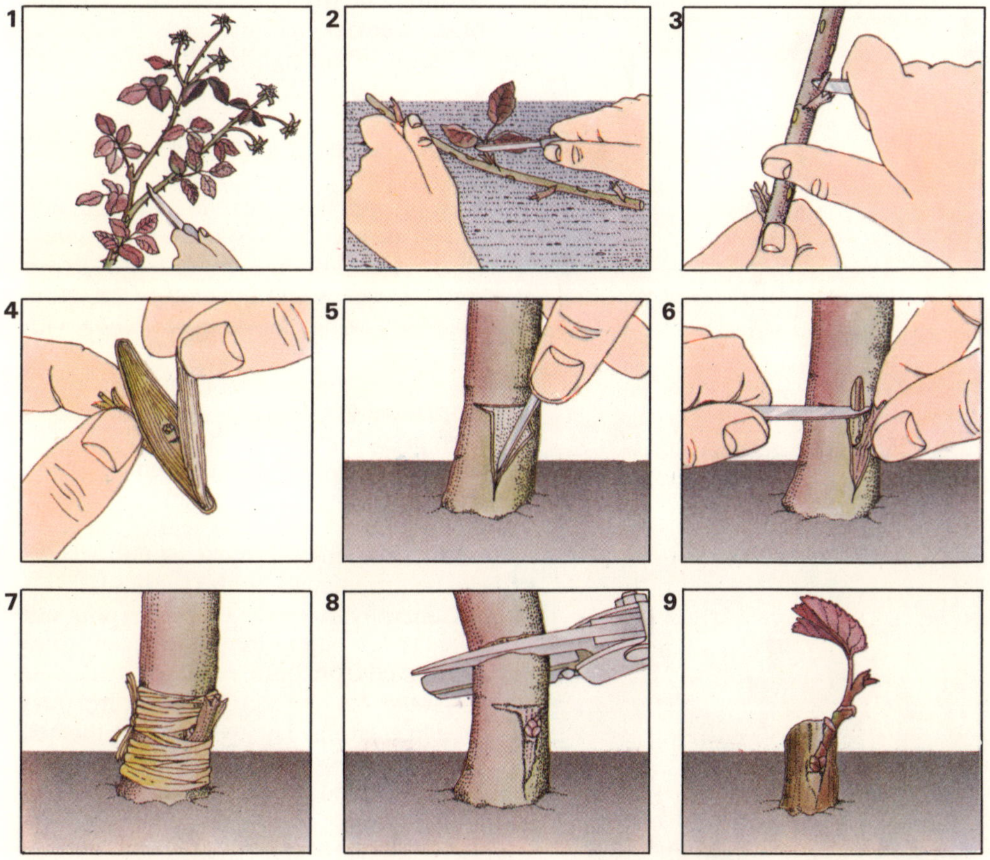

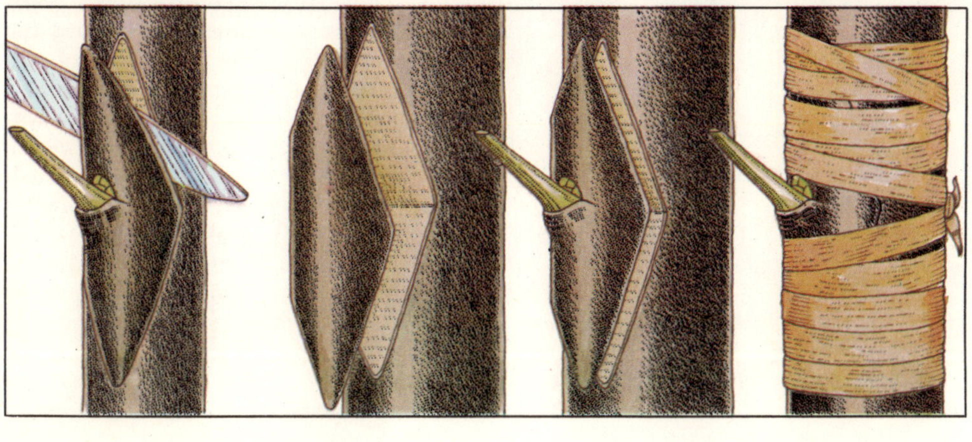

Rose budding: ***1*** *cut wood from rose to be propagated;* ***2*** *trim leaves off budstick;* ***3*** *cut bud from budstick;* ***4*** *peel away wood from back of bud;* ***5*** *make T-cut in rootstock;* ***6*** *insert bud, trimming to fit T-cut;* ***7*** *tie in place with raffia;* ***8*** *cut back rootstock in following spring;* ***9*** *bud coming into growth. Chip budding (left): remove bud; make cut in rootstock; insert bud; tie in bud with raffia*

the stock. Then tie in with raffia or plastic tape above and below the bud, making sure the ties are firm. The bud itself can be left exposed.

Whip and tongue grafting

An alternative method of propagating ornamental and fruiting trees is whip and tongue grafting, which is also carried out in spring (February and March). Use the rootstocks recommended above; plant them in winter or early spring (from November to March), and graft in the second spring (February or March) after having planted the rootstocks.

Whip and tongue graft (below, left to right): prepare scion; make tongue in scion and rootstock; fit scion to rootstock; bind with raffia; treat with tree paint

Cut the rootstock to within 10–15cm (4–6 in) of ground level. At the top make a slanting cut 4–5cm (1½–2 in) long; make a shallow downward v-shaped cut near the top of the first cut to form a 'tongue'. The scion should be four buds in length and prepared from well-ripened shoots produced the previous year. Cut the base with a slanting cut 4–5cm (1½–2 in) long with a shallow downward cut near the top to form a similar tongue. Push the tongue of the scion into the tongue of the stock and then tie in securely ('whip') with raffia, and cover all exposed surfaces with tree paint.

For the graft to be successful, all cuts must be perfectly flat and should match each other exactly, and the cambium layer of the stock must be in close contact with the cambium of the scion.

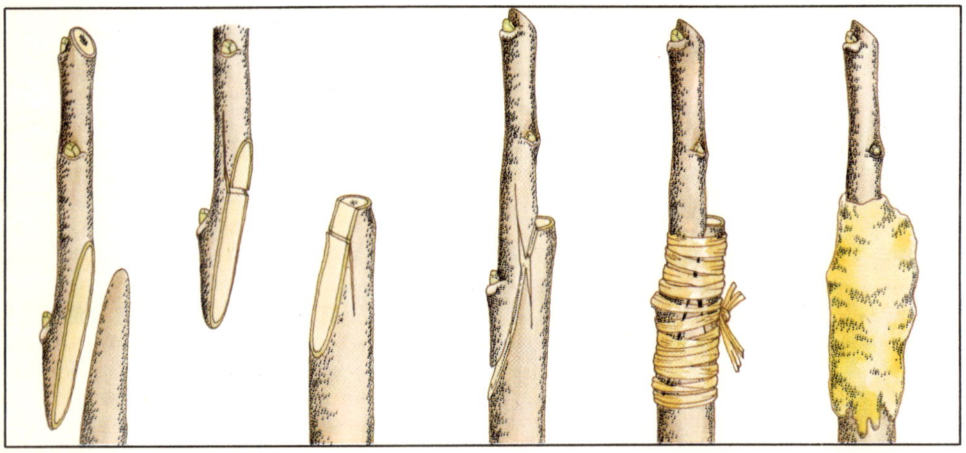

Saddle graft (above): make matching wedge-shaped cuts in scion and rootstock, tie in place and bind firmly

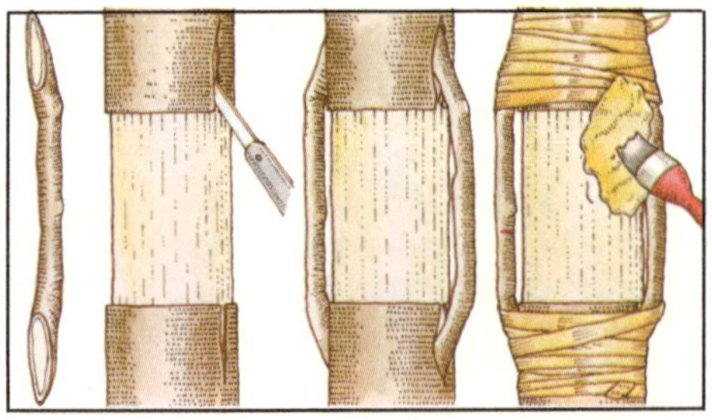

Bridge graft: use scions from tree to bridge damaged bark. Insert as for crown graft and treat with tree paint

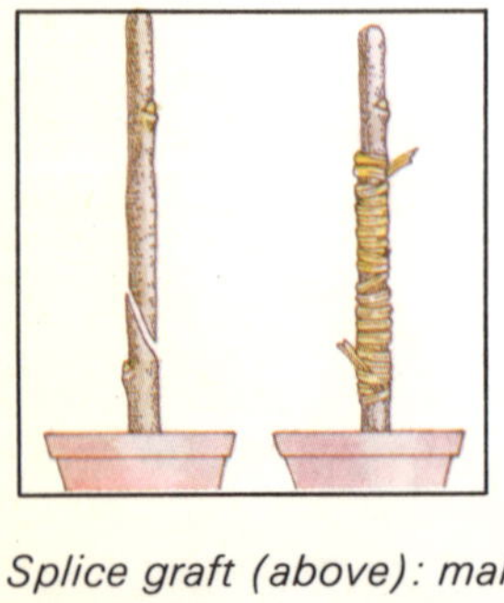

Splice graft (above): make long, slanting cuts in rootstock and scion. Bind tightly with raffia and keep under glass till scion is growing strongly

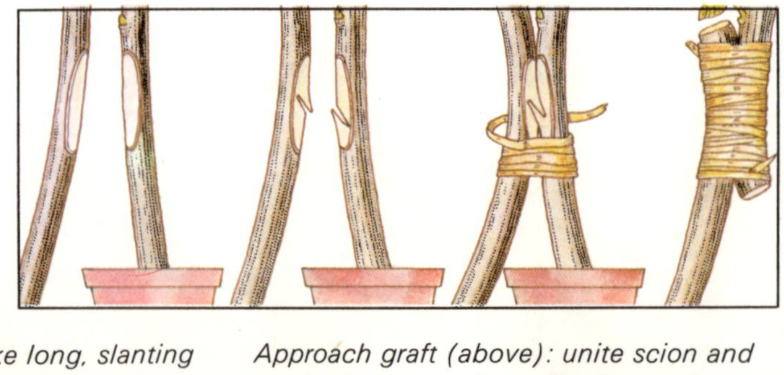

Approach graft (above): unite scion and stock without cutting scion from parent plant till graft has taken. Remove sliver from both, cut tongues and bind

Saddle grafting

Saddle grafting is used for propagating hybrid rhododendrons, and should be done in spring (February or March) in a heated greenhouse. The stock is two-or three-year-old *R. ponticum* in pots. Cut it down to 2–4cm (1–1½ in) and cut the top into a wedge shape. Cut a previous year's shoot about 10cm (4 in) long with a bud at the top as the scion and cut the base in an inverted V-shape to fit exactly over the stock. Tie in with raffia and keep under glass until the scion is growing well.

Splice grafting

Splice grafting is used for rhododendrons and also for syringa (lilac), for which you should use privet stocks. Graft in spring (February or March) under glass. Cut the stock down to 5cm (2 in) and make a long slanting cut from one side to the other. Make a corresponding cut at the base of the scion. Bind tightly with raffia. Keep under glass until the scion is growing strongly.

Bridge grafting is useful if the bark of a tree has been damaged. Use a few scions from the tree to bridge the damaged area and so ensure that sap continues to flow up the trunk or branch. Use the crown graft (see below) at both ends of the scion. Bind with raffia. Seal exposed wood with tree paint.

Approach grafting

In approach grafting, the scion is united with the stock without first removing the scion from the parent plant; then when the graft has united the scion is severed from its parent. Many trees and shrubs can be propagated by this method.

Generally, stocks are grown in pots and taken to the parent tree. A sliver of wood is removed from both stock and scion and a tongue cut in each as for whip and tongue grafting. The two cuts are pushed together and bound with raffia.

Topworking

There are various grafts that are used to convert old fruit trees to different varieties. This is sometimes necessary if the existing variety is of inferior quality or a poor cropper. First, there is the method known as 'topworking', when the branches are cut back to stumps, to which scions of the new variety are grafted, using either the crown or the cleft graft.

Crown (or rind) graft Prepare scions about four buds in length, by making a slanting cut about 4cm (1½ in) long at the base. Then cut a 4cm (1½ in) slit in the bark at the top of a stump and slide the base of the scion down behind the bark so that the surface of the cut is in contact

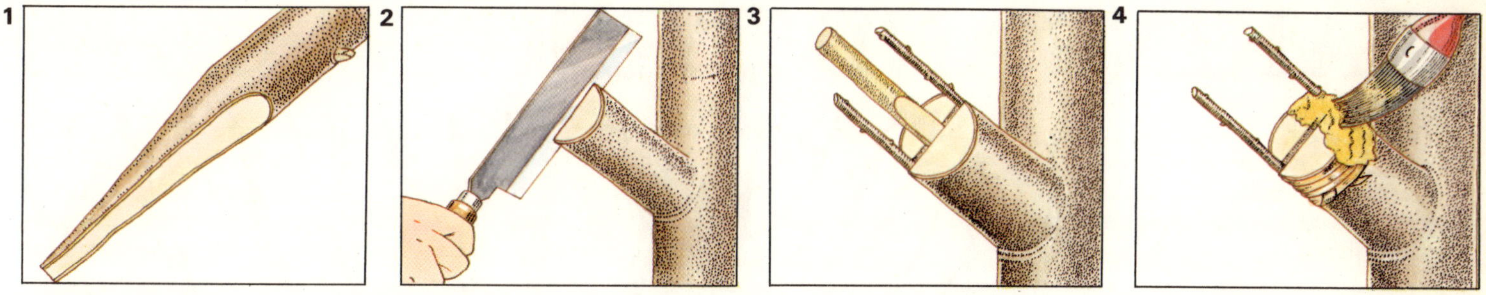

Cleft graft (above): **1** *prepare scions;* **2** *split end of stump;* **3** *insert two scions in cleft;* **4** *bind and apply tree paint.*
Crown graft (right): prepare scion and insert into slit made in bark. Bind with raffia and treat with tree paint

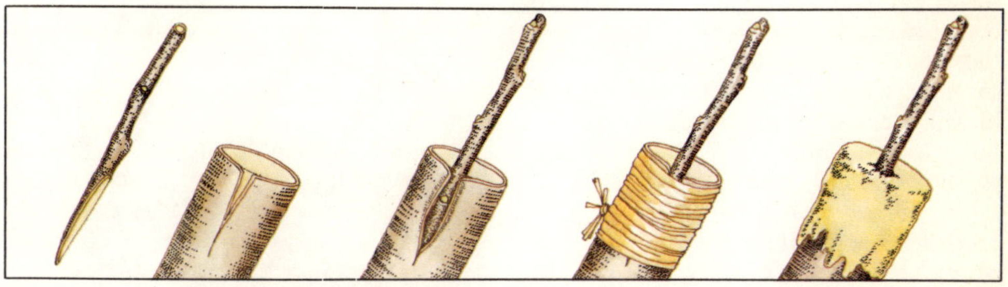

with the wood of the stump. Bind with raffia and cover graft with tree paint.

Cleft graft Cut the base of the scions into a long tapering wedge shape. Prepare the stumps by splitting the ends with a chopper. Keep the splits open with a wedge, and insert two scions, one on each side of a stump. Ensure that the cambium on one side of each scion is in contact with the cambium on one side of the stump. Remove the wedge and cover the graft with tree paint after tying with raffia.

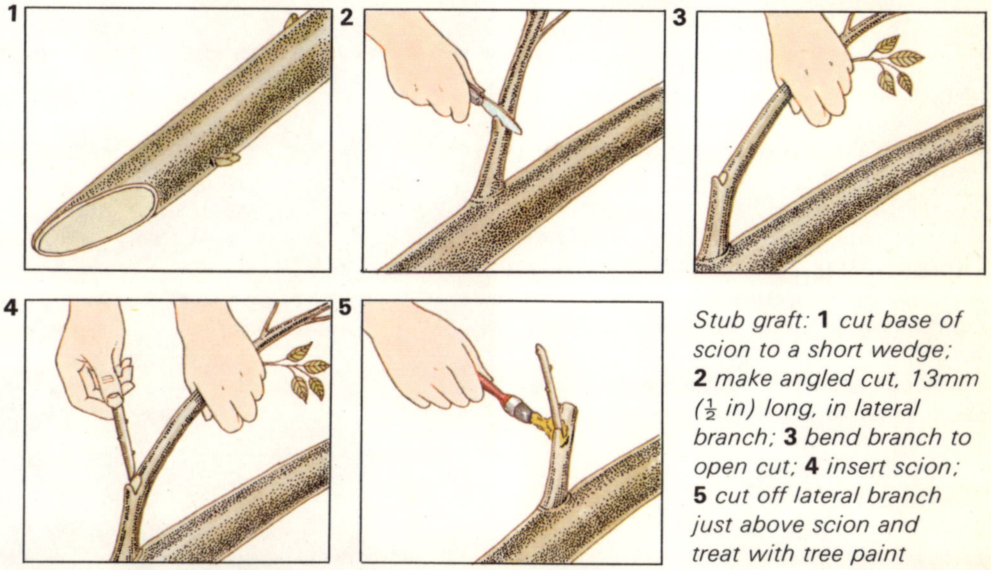

Stub graft: **1** *cut base of scion to a short wedge;* **2** *make angled cut, 13mm ($\frac{1}{2}$ in) long, in lateral branch;* **3** *bend branch to open cut;* **4** *insert scion;* **5** *cut off lateral branch just above scion and treat with tree paint*

Frameworking

Another method of converting established fruit trees is 'frameworking'. This is probably a better method than topworking because the new tree will crop sooner – indeed it may produce a good crop of fruit in the third year from grafting. The main branch system of the tree is left intact. Scions should be eight buds in length, and well spaced out all over the tree.

Stub graft Leave some side branches 6–25mm ($\frac{1}{4}$–1 in) in diameter on the tree, as the scions are inserted in these. The base of the scions should be cut to a short wedge. Make a 13mm ($\frac{1}{2}$ in) long cut at a 45 degree angle in a lateral branch; pull the branch to open the cut and slip in the scion. Release the branch so that the cut closes and grips the scion. Then cut off the side branch close to the graft and cover the wounds with tree paint.

Inverted-L graft This can be used instead of the stub graft, but all small lateral or side branches should be removed. Cut the scions as for crown grafting, then opposite this cut make another, but much shorter, so that you form an unequal wedge. Prepare the branches to receive the scions by making incisions in the bark like an inverted letter L. Lift the flap of bark and insert the base of the scion. Close the flap of bark and pin in place with a panel pin, inserted through the bark and scion and into the wood. Cover wounds with tree paint.

Inverted-L grafting is done in spring and early summer (from March to May) while crown, cleft and stub grafting should be done in spring (February or March). When you are using these grafts to convert a fruit tree to another variety, a large number of scions will have to be inserted, but once *au fait* with grafting it is a surprisingly quick operation.

Inverted-L graft: **1** *prepare both faces of scion;* **2** *cut bark;* **3** *insert scion;* **4** *hold with panel pin;* **5** *treat with tree paint*

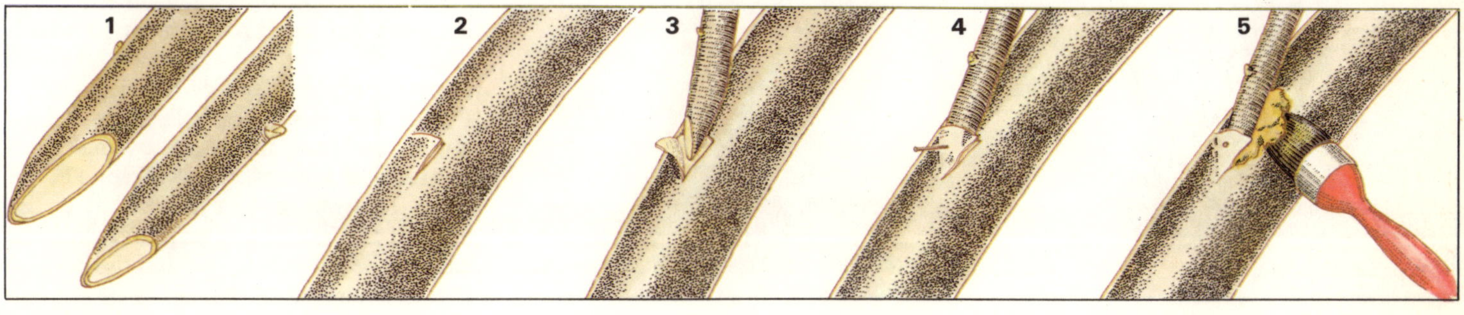

STAKING AND TYING

One of the most important tasks in the garden – and one that is too frequently left undone – is the provision of adequate support for the growing plants.

Many garden flowers and vegetables have been specially developed to grow taller than their ancestors in the wild. Deprived of their natural support, they may be blown over, or even snap off under their own weight, unless they are properly staked and tied.

Herbaceous plants

Many herbaceous plants or hardy perennials have weak and floppy stems which can easily be knocked to the ground by wind and rain. They do need, therefore, some form of artificial support.

One of the best ways to support plants with several stems is to push twiggy hazel sticks between and around them. This should be done in late spring or early summer (April or May) when the plants are just starting into growth, as the shoots will then grow up through the sticks. Of course, you need to know the ultimate height of the plants so that you can use sticks of the correct length – ideally they should be about 15cm (6 in) shorter than the final height of the plants. By the time the plants have made a good deal of growth and are ready to flower, the sticks will be virtually hidden by stems and leaves.

There are various proprietary supports for herbaceous plants that encircle the stems, but take care that these do not bunch the stems together, so giving an unnatural appearance.

Hazel twigs support bushy plants

Canes for tall plants

Wire ring supports clump of plants

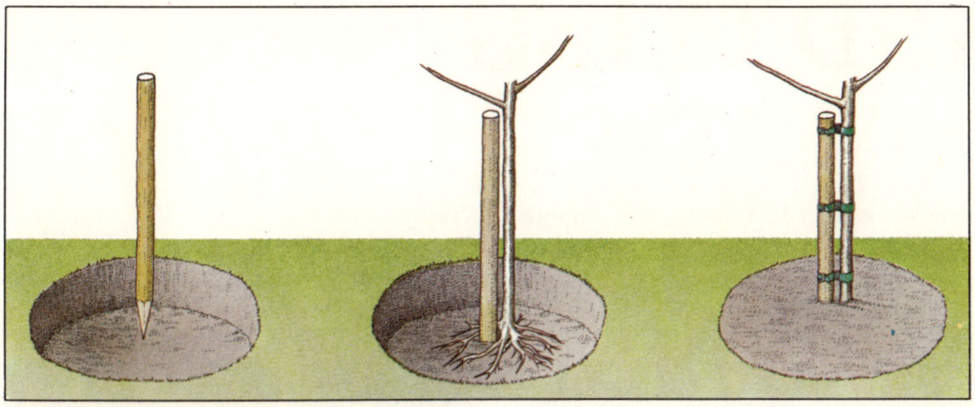

Left: when staking a tree, first knock in the stake, then position the tree and tie it to the stake with tree ties
Below left: peas supported by netting and stakes. Far left: fan-trained plum tree

Tall plants with a few stems, such as delphiniums, are best supported by providing a 2m (6 ft) bamboo cane for each stem, and tying in the stems as they grow with soft twine or raffia. Push the canes into the ground behind the stems so that they are inconspicuous from the front of the border.

Hardy annuals
Hardy annual flowers grown from seed are also invariably weak-stemmed, and benefit greatly from the support of twiggy hazel sticks. These must be inserted when the seedlings are fairly small – in the region of 5cm (2 in). Again, you can also buy proprietary supports of the type recommended for herbaceous plants.

Trees and shrubs
It is essential to provide adequate supports for trees at planting time, otherwise they are liable to be rocked about by the wind so that their roots become loose in the soil. This will prevent the trees from easily establishing themselves and if they become too loose they could even die. In addition an adequate support will ensure that the trunk of the tree remains straight.

Chestnut stakes about 8cm (3 in) in diameter are ideal for trees. Cut the base to a point and treat it with a horticultural wood preservative. Hammer the stake into the planting hole *before* the tree is inserted. It should be of such a length that the top comes just below the lowest branch of the tree after planting, with the base inserted about 45cm (18 in) in the ground.

Position the trunk of the tree 2–3cm (1 in) from the stake. When the tree has been planted it can be secured to the stake with proprietary plastic buckle ties specially designed for trees. Position one at the top of the stake and then a couple more lower down, spacing them out evenly. Ensure that the plastic buffer supplied with each tie is positioned between the trunk and the stake, to hold the tree away from its support and prevent the bark from being chafed. Trees should remain staked for a number of years, until they are really well established in the ground.

Few shrubs require staking after planting, but those that do include cytisus and genistas (brooms) and *Spartium junceum* (Spanish broom). These have small root systems and are liable to be blown over if they are not supported until well established. A stout bamboo cane of appropriate length should be adequate, provided it is inserted some 45cm (18 in) in the ground. Tie the shrub to it with soft garden twine.

Climbers
The modern method of supporting climbers on a wall is to attach trellis panels of plastic-coated metal to it. They should be secured about 2–5cm (1–2 in) away from the wall so that the plants are able to grow through the mesh. Alternatively, special galvanized nails may be used, with wire or string threaded between them.

Vegetables
Climbing vegetables, like runner beans and peas, need adequate supports if they are to grow well and produce nice long pods. Some people still use bean poles for runners, but these are becoming increasingly difficult to obtain. Insert the poles in a double row, with 45cm (18 in) between rows, so that they cross near the top. Then tie them to horizontal poles placed in the forks. The poles should be about 30cm (12 in) apart along the rows. Alternatively, a 'wigwam' of poles or canes tied together at the top can be made. Whatever system is used, allow one pole or cane per plant.

The modern method of supporting runner beans is to use special wide-mesh nylon netting ('bean netting') stretched between posts. It is generally supplied 2m (6 ft) in height and of various lengths. It is even possible to buy a special framework for bean netting which can remain in position from one year to the next and which lasts a very long time indeed.

You can support peas with twiggy hazel sticks of the appropriate height. Push these in on each side of the row when the peas are about 2–3cm (1 in) high. They will then grow up through the sticks. Alternatively, bring yourself up to date and use the special nylon pea netting which is about 1m (3 ft) wide. It should be stretched tight between wooden posts along the side of a row, or it can be formed into a tent shape over a central horizontal wire, so that the peas can grow up both sides.

All nylon netting will last for many years if looked after.

Tomatoes also need some support. Here 1–1·5m (3–5 ft) bamboo canes are adequate, tying in with raffia or soft garden twine.

Fruit
Tree fruits, such as apples, pears, plums and cherries, should be staked at planting time (see under trees and shrubs).

Of the soft fruits, raspberries, blackberries, loganberries and other hybrid berries are the only ones that need supporting. A system of stout posts, with strained galvanized horizontal wires, is needed for these crops. The topmost wire should be about 2m (6 ft) above soil level. The other wires can be spaced about 30cm (12 in) apart below this to within 60cm (2 ft) of the ground. Each end post should be braced with another post driven in at an angle of 45 degrees and nailed firmly to the main post.

If you grow trained fruit trees, particularly cordons, espaliers and fans, these can also be supported by a system of posts and wires, and bamboo poles.

STAKING AND TYING EQUIPMENT

Bamboo and split canes The longer the cane the thicker the diameter. From 30cm–3·6m (1–12 ft) lengths.
Chestnut, cedar or pine stakes Treat with horticultural wood preservative, if not pre-treated.
Plastic buckle ties and buffers Be sure to place the buffer between trunk and stalk to prevent chafing.
Plastic tree or rose ties These can be adjusted each year to allow for increase in girth.
Plastic or wire plant ties Paper-covered wire type only needs the ends twisting together to hold stem to stake; pliable plastic-coated wire type bends around stem and stake.
Plastic clips Ideal for quick support. Long-lasting if stored each winter.
Galvanized, heavy-gauge wire Fixed on a wall, can be used instead of trellis.
Vine eyes Hammer-in or screw-in types, useful for tying in light branches against walls with garden twine or string.
Lead-headed nails Hammer in to wall and bend round flexible arm, or use with garden twine or string.
Garden twine or string Usually green and treated for weather resistance, but can stretch under wet conditions. Tarred garden string is durable, but has an unpleasant smell.
Polypropylene garden string Tough and does not stretch in wet weather.
Raffia Good tying material. Can be torn to any thickness.
Traditional trellis Made of treated cedar, or hardwood for heavier, rustic types. Can be bought ready-made, rigid or expanding, in natural or painted finish. (See page 28 for fixing details.)
Plastic-coated trellis Rot-proof and long-lasting, rigid or expanding, usually in green or white.
Plastic mesh/nylon netting Convenient but more expensive than chicken wire; easily stored at end of season. Available in different width rolls or packs of specific sizes. Needs stretching between posts or supporting by metal or wood frame structure.

Staking and tying equipment

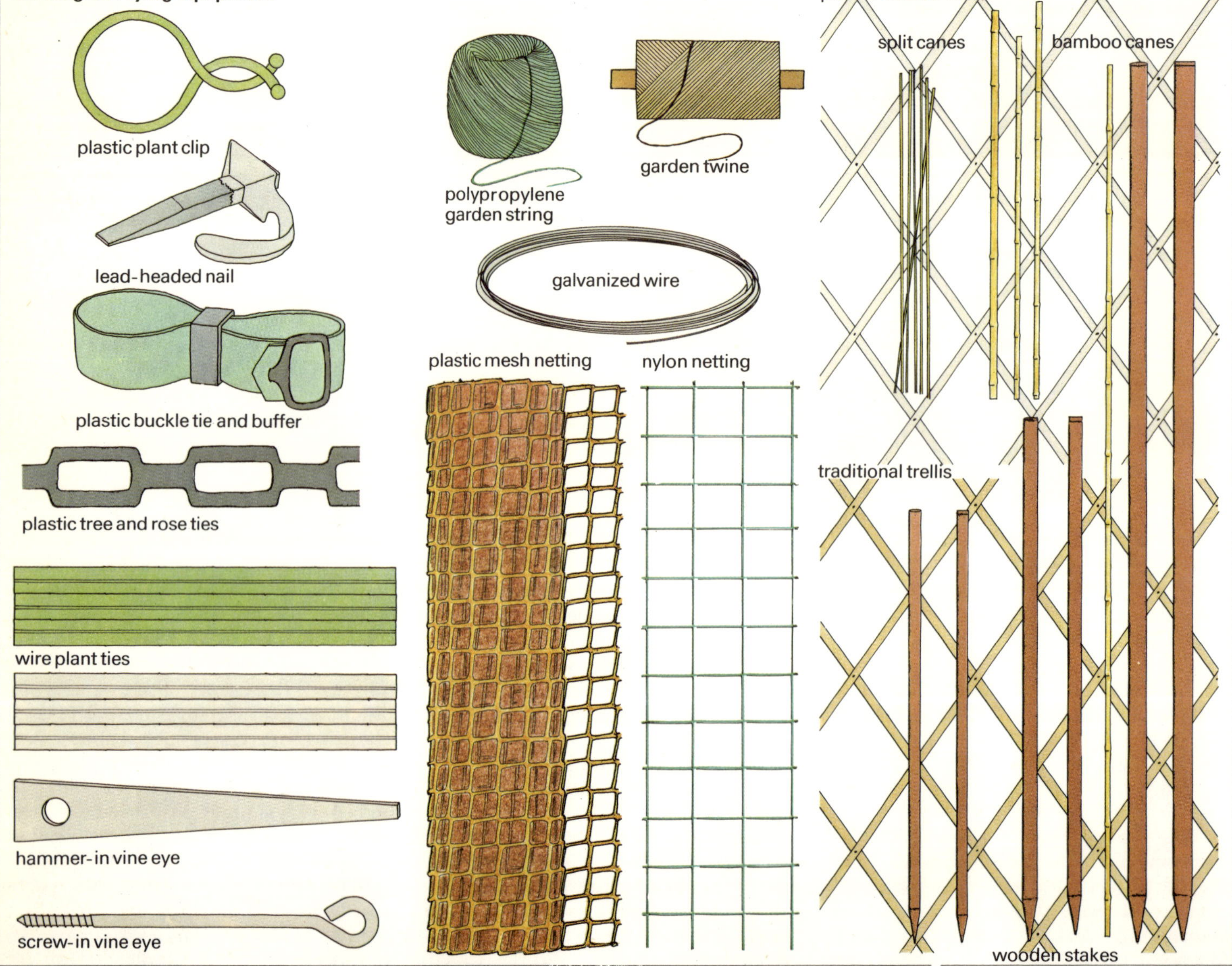

CHOOSING AND PLANTING HEDGES AND SCREENS

Most gardens have at least one hedge. You may have grown it as an attractive boundary instead of a wall or fence, or to separate one area of the garden from another. A hedge can also make an excellent background for borders and beds, with dark-leaved types showing off bright flower colours especially well.

A hedge about 1·8–2·5m (6–8 ft) tall is most often required (being a practical height for a boundary), and there are many suitable subjects for this purpose.

First decide whether you would like a formal or informal hedge. A formal one is usually clipped to a regular shape, while informal types need little or no trimming and are just left to grow naturally. Generally flowering and/or berrying subjects are used informally.

1

2

3

4

To prepare ground for hedge, double dig well in advance, mixing in compost with second spit, **1***, then turning over first spit,* **2** *and using it to cover compost,* **3***. At planting time, dig trench,* **4***, after letting soil settle and adding fertilizer*

Formal hedges

The common hornbeam (*Carpinus betulus*) is used extensively as a hedging plant and makes a thick hedge if planted 30–45cm (12–18 in) apart. It is suitable for clay or chalk soils. Clip it annually in late summer (July), but not for the first two years after planting. Common beech (*Fagus sylvatica*) is similar to hornbeam (except for its smoother leaves) and is cared for in the same way. The foliage persists throughout the autumn and winter at which time it is a beautiful golden-brown colour. Beech, like hornbeam, makes a good background for borders. You may prefer a coloured hedge, in which case you could use the purple- or copper-leaved varieties.

There is probably nothing better for a formal, evergreen hedge than the common box (*Buxus sempervirens*). Planted 45cm (18 in) apart, it makes really dense growth that stands clipping exceptionally well. It thrives on chalky soils, and its dark-green foliage makes it a good background hedge. Another dense, impenetrable hedge is formed by common holly (*Ilex aquifolium*) with its deep green leaves. Plant 45–60cm (18–24 in) apart and trim annually in early or mid autumn.

Privet is a very common hedging plant; the golden-leaved variety *Ligustrum ovalifolium* Aureo-marginatum is, perhaps, more interesting than the green-leaved type. It is semi-evergreen, and will tolerate almost any soil and situation. Plant 30cm (12 in) apart and clip as necessary in the summer.

The Chinese honeysuckle (*Lonicera nitida*) is an evergreen shrub with tiny,

5

dark green leaves – like those of the box. It forms a really thick hedge if plants are spaced 30cm (12 in) apart. As it is a fast grower it will need trimming several times during the summer.

Laurels make attractive hedges with their large, glossy, evergreen leaves. The common (or cherry) laurel is *Prunus laurocerasus* that thrives in almost any soil. Plant 45–60 cm (18–24 in) apart and prune with secateurs (to avoid cutting the large leaves in half) during the spring. The Portugal laurel *P. lusitanica* has smaller leaves but is treated in the same way as common laurel.

There are various evergreen conifers that are used for formal hedges, the most popular at the present time being the Leyland cypress (*Cupressocyparis leylandii*). It is the fastest-growing conifer in Britain and has good, deep-green foliage. Plant 45–60cm (18–24 in) apart and clip in late summer.

The Lawson cypress (*Chamaecyparis lawsoniana*) is a similar hedging plant although it is not such a fast grower. A good deep green variety is Green Hedger.

The common yew (*Taxus baccata*) is a very adaptable evergreen plant and makes a good dark background for shrub or flower borders. It grows very well on chalk. Plant 45–60cm (18–24 in) apart and clip in late autumn.

If you want a dwarf, formal hedge – perhaps to surround a bed or a border or to edge a path – then a good plant is the edging box *Buxus sempervirens* Suffruticosa, that will grow only 60cm (24 in) in height, but can be kept lower by clipping in summer. Plant 30cm (12 in) apart.

Informal hedges

There are many attractive shrubs suitable for planting as informal hedges up to a height of 1·8–2·5m (6–8 ft). Berberis (barberry) forms very thick, prickly hedges and is particularly suitable for boundaries as it will keep children and animals out of (or in) the garden. The most popular ones are *B.* × *stenophylla* with yellow flowers in spring and *B. darwinii* with deeper yellow flowers. Both are evergreen. They are best not trimmed very much (this applies to all flowering hedges) otherwise flowering will be affected. A dwarf berberis hedge can be formed with *B. thunbergii* Atropurpurea Nana, that has deciduous purple leaves. Plant all 30–60cm (12–24 in) apart.

Evergreen escallonias are very popular, especially on the coast, and should be planted 45cm (18 in) apart. They may be lightly trimmed after flowering. *E. macrantha* and *E.m.* Crimson Spike (both crimson) are excellent for hedging.

Lavenders make fine low-growing hedges (up to 1m or 3 ft) and should be planted 30–45cm (12–18 in) apart. Trim off dead flower-heads. *Lavandula spica* (old English lavender) is most popular.

Pyracantha (firethorn) makes good, informal, evergreen hedges, and produces heavy crops of orange berries in the autumn that last well into the winter. The best is probably *P. coccinea* Lalandei. Plant 45–60cm (18–24 in) apart.

When to plant

Buy bare-root hedging plants whenever possible, as they will be much cheaper than container-grown plants. Many nurserymen grow plants especially for hedging at reasonable prices. The time to plant them is from early winter to mid spring (November to March).

If you buy container-grown plants, you will be able to plant your hedges at any time of the year. And you will find that certain subjects (for instance Leyland

Position first plant at correct depth and firm in, **5**. *Space out second plant at correct distance,* **6**, *and repeat procedure*

6

cypress and hollies) may be offered in containers rather than as field-grown plants to avoid root disturbance.

Preparing the ground
When preparing the ground, first ensure that it is free of perennial weeds; once your hedge has been planted these will be almost impossible to remove. So treat the site with a suitable weedkiller well before planting time. Once the ground is clean – and free from weedkiller (which can take several months) – you should dig a strip about 1m (3 ft) wide. Double digging (to two depths of the spade) is desirable to ensure that the roots of the hedging plants are able to penetrate deeply; this will give you a stable hedge. Dig in organic matter such as well-rotted farmyard manure or garden compost, at the same time.

Allow several weeks for the ground to settle before planting. Then, just prior to planting, apply a general-purpose fertilizer at 135g per sq m (4 oz per sq yd) and lightly prick it into the surface of the soil. Break down the soil to a reasonably fine tilth that is suitable for planting, and firm it by treading with your heels. Now the site is ready to take your hedge.

7

8

7 Tread in newly-planted shrubs before watering. **8** *With correct care and attention, the finished product will soon flourish*

How to plant
As hedging plants are planted close together in a line, the easiest way to plant is to mark out a straight row with your garden line and take out a trench. Space out the plants at the correct distance apart in the trench and then replace the soil around them, firming it really well with your heels. Make sure the roots of bare-root subjects are well spread out. If planting container-grown specimens, do not disturb the rootball, just carefully remove the container from around it.

After planting, water well in if the soil is dry, and thereafter keep well watered during dry weather. It is a good idea to mulch a young hedge to conserve soil moisture. Use rotted manure, garden compost or peat laid 5–8cm (2–3 in) deep along each side of the hedge. Spray evergreen subjects with an anti-transpirant (such as S. 600) to prevent excessive water loss from the leaves until the plants start rooting into the soil. Use the product carefully, following the manufacturer's instructions.

Trimming hedges
Most formal hedges need trimming regularly to keep them shapely and well clothed with foliage. Start by trimming the sides of a hedge in the early stages and allow it to reach the desired height before trimming the top. Formal hedges can be trimmed to various shapes, but a wedge shape is very practical as it easily sheds heavy falls of snow. It can be flat-topped or round-topped. A wedge-shaped hedge should be about twice as wide at the base as at the top.

You can keep the top of a hedge straight while trimming by stretching a garden line, at the height you wish to cut, on each side of the hedge. Then cut to these lines, taking care not to go below them.

Tall screens
So far nothing has been said about screens, which are really very tall 'hedges' used to hide unsightly views. They are only suitable for the boundaries of very large gardens as generally they are not cut but left to grow to their natural height. Screens need the same ground preparation and aftercare as hedges, but should have a wider spacing when they are planted. Set the plants 2m (6 ft) apart.

TRIMMING HEDGES

If you have a garden, then it is more than likely that you have a hedge. It may be carefully shaped and formal, or free-growing and informal, depending on the shrubs that were originally chosen to form it. When you come to trim them, formal and informal hedges have different requirements, so don't wade in regardless with shears or secateurs.

Formal hedges are trained to a particular shape, generally square-topped, round-topped or wedge-shaped. To maintain their shape and neat appearance they are trimmed regularly during the growing season. Frequent trimming of formal hedges also ensures a dense hedge, well furnished with foliage. Informal hedges (including trees used as tall screens) should be allowed to grow as naturally as possible and not be trained to any particular shape.

Different types of hedges

Typical examples of plants grown as formal hedges are: privet, yew, box, beech, Chinese honeysuckle, Lawson cypress, holly and hornbeam.

Flowering and berrying shrubs are often used for informal hedges; close and regular trimming would result in great loss of flowers or fruits, which are their main attraction.

There are a few flowering shrubs, however, that could be grown as semi-formal hedges, in which case not too much flower is lost. For example, lavender can be lightly clipped and still smother itself with a mass of mauve or blue flower spikes. It must not, however, be cut back hard or it will die.

You will find that any type of hedging plant can be grown informally if desired, and of course some flowering and berrying shrubs (such as *Rhododendron ponticum* and pyracantha) will make excellent formal hedges, although you will lose most of the flowers and berries.

The frequency of trimming formal hedges depends on the habit of growth. For example privet and Chinese honeysuckle are very fast growers and you will need to trim them two or three times in the growing season if they are to look neat. Slower-growing hedges, like beech and hornbeam, generally need trimming only once a year.

Top: formal use of Buxus sempervirens *(box); top right: mixed hedge of beech, copper beech, yew, box and hornbeam; top, far right:* Chamaecyparis lawsoniana *(Lawson cypress), a fast grower*
Above: trim privet two or three times during growing season. Right: tall hedging for shade, Taxus baccata *(yew)*

How to trim

Before starting to trim a hedge lay some hessian, polythene sheeting or an an old sheet on the ground to catch the trimmings as they fall. They can then be collected with ease and placed on the compost heap.

Centre: trim laurel hedge with secateurs to ensure leaves are not cut in half
Above: cut back old flowered wood on forsythia to just below lowest flower

To keep a formal hedge perfectly straight and level, use a garden line as a guide. When trimming the sides, place the line along the top of the hedge to the required depth of cutting. When trimming the top, the line should be placed along one of the sides to the required height of cut.

Informal hedges are generally trimmed once a year. Often you will only need to remove over-long or straggly shoots and any dead wood with a pair of secateurs.

Flowering informal hedges usually require that the old flowered wood be cut back immediately after flowering each year. This encourages the growth of strong, new flower-producing shoots from lower down the stems. The time of trimming different kinds of hedge varies tremendously, and suggested times are included in our chart (see next page).

If formal hedges (or indeed informal types) become out of hand they may need cutting back hard into the old wood. This spoils their appearance for a while as you will have removed a lot of foliage, leaving bare stems. But this is only a temporary

GUIDE TO TRIMMING HEDGING PLANTS

Botanical name	Common name	Time	Frequency (per year)	Cutting shape
Aucuba	spotted laurel	late spring (April)	once	formal or semi-formal; use secateurs
Berberis	barberry	after flowering	once	informal or semi-formal; not too hard
Buxus	box	early autumn (August)	as necessary	formal
Carpinus	hornbeam	early autumn (August)	once	formal
Chamaecyparis lawsoniana	Lawson cypress	early to mid summer (May to June)	once	formal
Crataegus	hawthorn	mid summer to early autumn (June to August)	as necessary	formal
Cupressocyparis leylandii	Leyland cypress	early autumn (August)	once	formal
Cupressus macrocarpa	Monterey cypress	late spring (April)	once	semi-formal or informal; dislikes too much, or hard, trimming
Escallonia	escallonia	after flowering	once	informal or semi-formal
Euonymus japonica	euonymus	mid summer to mid autumn (June to September)	as necessary	formal
Forsythia	forsythia	after flowering	once	informal or semi-formal; cut back flowered shoots
Fagus	beech	early autumn (August)	once	formal
Ilex	holly	early autumn (August)	once	formal
Laurus	sweet bay	mid summer to mid autumn (June to September)	as necessary	formal; use secateurs
Lavandula	lavender	mid to late spring (March to April)	once	informal or semi-formal; remove old flowers
Ligustrum	privet	early summer to mid autumn (May to September)	as necessary	formal
Lonicera nitida	Chinese honeysuckle	early summer to mid autumn (May to September)	as necessary	formal
Prunus laurocerasus	cherry laurel	late spring to late summer (April to July)	once or twice	formal; use secateurs
Pyracantha	firethorn	late spring (April)	once	informal or semi-formal
Rhododendron ponticum	rhododendron	mid to late spring (March to April)	once	informal or semi-formal; use secateurs
Viburnum tinus	laurustinus	late spring (April)	once	informal or semi-formal; use secateurs
Taxus baccata	yew	early autumn (August)	once	formal

situation, as new shoots and foliage will soon hide these stems. Do this hand pruning in early spring just before the plants start into growth. It is amazing how old wood will quickly produce new growth after hard cutting back. However, for ordinary trimming *never* cut into the older wood but always leave a thick covering of leaves.

For small-leaved hedging plants like privet, beech and Chinese honeysuckle (indeed the majority of subjects) use a good pair of hand shears for a really neat finish. An electric trimmer is more practical if you have a lot of hedge to trim.

Large-leaved shrubs, such as laurels, rhododendrons, sweet bay and aucuba are best trimmed with a pair of secateurs to ensure that the leaves are not cut in half. If this occurs, then the cut leaves turn brown and make the hedge look most unsightly. So although it will take longer to trim these hedges with secateurs (as each shoot has to be cut out individually) it is time well spent.

Young hedges

It is sometimes recommended to let young formal hedges grow unchecked for the first few years to attain the required height. However, you will probably find if you do this that your hedge has a bare base. Instead, cut out the tops to ensure that the plants start branching low on the stems and produce foliage right down to ground level. Remember, though, that hornbeam and beech must not be cut for the first two years after planting.

Pyracantha (firethorn) hedge in flower

FEEDING PLANTS

Plants, like people, need a regular supply of food if they are to survive and grow well. The main ways of feeding your plants are by applying fertilizers and bulky organic matter (like manure) to the soil.
Manure supplies some nutrients, but its most important function is to improve the soil structure by adding organic material. This turns the soil into a healthy medium in which plants can thrive. Fertilizers provide some, or all, of the basic plant foods (nitrogen, phosphates, potash and trace elements) in concentrated form.

When digging, particularly in late autumn or early winter, it is wise to incorporate in each trench well-rotted farmyard manure, garden compost, seaweed or hop manure. These materials will supply bulky organic matter and a variable amount of plant food. None of them, however, supplies adequate nutrients for the plants to make optimum growth; therefore fertilizers will have to be added at planting time to ensure that the plants have sufficient food.

The organic matter is digested by bacteria in the soil and turned into humus. This humus is like a sponge; it holds water and prevents rapid drying-out of light soils. It also helps to break up sticky clay soils by improving drainage. Organic material is, therefore, essential because it improves the soil's structure.

MANURES

Never apply manure at the same time as lime (calcium). This is because the lime can liberate any available nitrogen in the form of ammonia, which may then be lost through evaporation. Also, never grow root crops on ground where fresh manure has been used, for your vegetables may well produce deformed roots.

Seaweed as manure

If your garden is near the coast, use seaweed as a manure. It is excellent for digging – wet or dried – into the soil in the autumn. Seaweed is one of the oldest manures known and contains many plant foods. It is now possible to obtain specially refined seaweed manures from gardening shops. Use these carefully, according to maker's instructions, as they are rather concentrated.

Manure for mulching

Rotted manure or garden compost makes a good mulch for established plants such as trees, shrubs, top and soft fruit, vegetables, roses, dahlias and chrysan-

Above left: Ascophyllum nodosum, *'egg' or knotted wrack, exposed on the rocks at low tide and ready for collection – it can be used wet or dry*
Top: fronds of sea belt Laminaria saccharina, *left on the beach at low water*
Centre: shoddy, or animal hair, laid around the base of a shrub – it is useful as an organic form of plant food
Above: spreading top-dressing of dry fertilizer around the base of the shrub in summer months with a balance of nitrogen, phosphate and potash mixed to suit the particular plant

themums. Place a layer of mulch, 5–8cm (2–3 in) thick, around the plants in spring. It will then provide some food and humus and help prevent evaporation of moisture from the surface soil.

FERTILIZERS

Bulky organic matter is not capable, by itself, of supplying all the foods the plants will require, so fertilizers must also be added to the soil.

As a general rule, dry fertilizers should be applied to moist soil, or else well watered in after application if the ground is dry. Always apply them evenly, and discard or break up any lumps; these can 'burn' roots. Apply all fertilizers carefully and according to maker's instructions. If you exceed the recommended rate of application you may seriously injure your plants.

Before sowing or planting, the usual procedure is to rake in a dry fertilizer which contains the major plants foods (nitrogen, phosphates and potash). There are many of these 'general-purpose' or compound fertilizers on the market. Probably the best known is National Growmore, which is available under numerous brand names. This is suitable for all vegetables, fruit and flowers. You can also apply it as a top dressing in spring or summer by lightly raking it into the soil surface around any of your established plants.

Special dry fertilizers for specific crops (such as roses and tomatoes) are available. These contain the correct balance of nitrogen, phosphates and potash suited to the particular plant.

Lawn fertilizers

There are several proprietary lawn fertilizers which make the lawn 'green up' quickly and grow well due to the high proportion of nitrogen they contain. Feed your lawn once or twice during spring and summer to ensure a lush, deep-green sward. Autumn lawn fertilizer, which is applied in mid autumn (September), contains more potash; this helps to 'ripen' the grass and make it more resistant to hard winter weather.

'Straight' fertilizers

You can also apply 'straight' fertilizers to plants, especially as a supplement to the ready-mixed, general-purpose kinds applied earlier in the growing season; but you must be aware of specific food requirements of individual plants before trying out these fertilizers. Be sure to handle them carefully and accurately.

Sulphate of ammonia and nitro-chalk supply nitrogen which encourages plants to make lush, leafy growth. They are quick-acting fertilizers and should be used very sparingly. They can be used on lawns and also on green vegetables such as cabbage, kale, broccoli and spinach. Apply them in spring and summer only.

Sulphate of potash and muriate of potash both supply the potash (potassium) essential for the production of fruit and flowers. It also helps to ripen the stems, which is necessary for the successful overwintering of all hardy plants. Potash can be applied in summer or early autumn. Wood ashes contain potassium and, once they have weathered for 3–6 months, can be dug into the soil during autumn digging or raked into the surface.

Superphosphate of lime supplies phosphate (phosphorus). This is also essential for good root production and all-round growth. It is usually applied in spring and summer at the rate of 3g per litre (½ oz per gal) of water and applied to the soil around plants about once a week. Avoid getting it on the foliage.

Liquid fertilizers

Use liquid fertilizers in conjunction with powdered or granulated fertilizers – not as a substitute. They should be considered as supplementary feeds to boost the growth of plants. They are generally used in the summer when plants are in full growth. Being liquid, they are quickly absorbed by plants and stimulate growth.

Dilute liquid fertilizers according to maker's instructions, and apply them to moist soil. Use them as frequently as once a week and on all kinds of plants in the house, greenhouse and garden. You can apply them most easily with a rosed watering can.

There are many brands of liquid fertilizer on the market, some of which are formulated for specific crops.

Foliar feeding

Foliar feeding is a fairly recent technique of applying liquid fertilizers to plants. The fertilizer is sprayed or watered onto the leaves where it is quickly absorbed by the plants and circulated in the sap stream. The nutrients are made immediately available to plants. This makes them particularly useful to transplanted plants before their new roots have become established.

You can buy special foliar feeds from gardening shops. Alternatively you can apply any liquid fertilizer to the foliage and it will be quickly absorbed.

Sulphate of ammonia can be dissolved at the rate of 3g per litre (½ oz per gal) of water and applied to leaves to promote growth of foliage. Likewise sulphate of potash will encourage fruiting and ripening of growth.

LIME

Lime is another plant food and this is applied on its own, generally in the winter after autumn digging, in the form of dehydrated lime. It is mainly the vegetable plot that will require lime and an application every two or three years will be adequate.

Lime lowers the acidity of the soil, and as many plants (especially vegetables such as brassicas) do not thrive in an acid soil, liming enables you to grow a wider range of plants. But do not lime if you have a naturally alkaline or limy soil with a pH of 7 or above. Hydrated lime is the type generally used.

Left: adding rotted manure to a trench
Above: applying chemical fertilizer by spoon in small measured quantities
Above right: sieving leaf mould into a wheelbarrow for use as compost
Right: fertilizer spreaders give even results
Far right: applying lime by hand

TOP DRESSING, MULCHING AND HOEING

'Top dressing' is the term for any plant food or soil conditioner that is applied to the soil surface.
'Mulch' usually refers to top dressings that are composed of bulky organic materials – such as compost or manure. Mulches help to suppress weeds, so if you are not applying a mulch then hoeing will be necessary, and must be done correctly.

TOP DRESSING

A top dressing may be left scattered on the surface of the soil or raked into the topsoil. Lawn top dressings are often brushed into the topsoil with a stiff broom.

A good general-purpose fertilizer, such as Growmore, is very useful for all kinds of plants and is probably the top dressing most used by gardeners. Put down such a fertilizer (used according to maker's instructions) before applying a mulch. Top dressings of lime, applied during winter or early in spring, are of great value to the vegetable garden – especially where brassicas are being grown.

When applying soluble chemical fertilizers, take great care to follow the maker's instructions exactly; too strong a solution can cause damage to plant roots. With many top dressings it is also important to keep them well clear of plant stems and leaves.

MULCHING

A mulch, whether it be a layer of organic matter or polythene sheeting, is usually placed over the soil in the root area of plants. Organic materials that can be used for mulching are well-rooted farmyard manure, garden compost, leaf mould, peat, spent hops, rotted grass clippings, straw, pulverized bark and rotted sawdust. Peat, straw and bark supply very little in the way of plant foods but are used for moisture conservation and weed suppression.

Reasons for mulching

One of the most important reasons for applying a mulch is to conserve moisture in the soil during dry weather, by helping to prevent its evaporation.

Mulching also prevents the growth of annual weeds, and some perennial weeds can be smothered with a polythene mulch. Furthermore, by placing an organic mulch between rows of vegetables and fruits you can avoid making the soil surface hard and compacted as you walk between the rows. An organic mulch may also supply plant foods – though not all materials will supply nutrients.

When to mulch

The best time of the year for putting down a mulch is in the spring and early summer (between March and the end of May). Apply it to moist, weed-free soil over a top dressing of fertilizer. An organic mulch should be spread around the plants, or between rows of crops, to a depth of 5–10cm (2–4 in). Obviously the greater the depth, the more effective it will be. Spread it evenly and ensure it covers the plants' root area.

What to mulch

In the fruit garden it is well worth mulching black, white and redcurrants, gooseberries, raspberries, blackberries, loganberries and rhubarb, as these fruits thrive on a good supply of matter and moisture. The ideal is an annual mulch of well-rotted manure or compost. With strawberries the usual practice is to give a mulch of straw, after danger of frost has passed, to prevent the fruits from coming into contact with the soil and getting mud-splashed or eaten by slugs.

Top fruits, such as apples, pears and plums, can be lightly mulched with manure or compost, about every two or three years. Too heavy a dressing of manure or compost to fruit trees may result in over-vigorous growth at the expense of fruiting. Instead, use material with a low food content, annually, to conserve moisture and help to prevent weed growth.

All vegetables, particularly peas, beans, cauliflowers, tomatoes, marrows, celery and lettuce, benefit from a

Above: black polythene sheeting may not look very elegant, but here it provides potatoes with a useful inorganic mulch

moisture-conserving mulch, though one that supplies plant nutrients as well is obviously the best.

Mulch the flower garden to keep the soil moist and minimize weeding. Use manure around trees and shrubs, applying a light dressing every two or three years. An annual application of peat, leaf mould, bark or spent hops can be given in the 'in-between' years; again the idea is to avoid over-lush growth. All surface-rooting shrubs, such as rhododendrons, azaleas and heathers, appreciate a mulch of peat or leaf mould each year to keep their roots cool. The same principles apply to herbaceous border plants.

Give roses an annual mulch as they require plenty of feeding. Apply a deep layer of well-rotted farmyard manure or garden compost.

Dahlias and sweet peas need moist soil and benefit greatly from a straw mulch if they are being grown in their special beds. This also prevents the soil surface from becoming trodden down as a result of the regular attention these plants need.

Remember that all newly-planted trees and shrubs should be mulched after watering to prevent the soil drying out rapidly; drying out can have a serious effect on the plants if they have not yet established fibrous feeding roots.

If you have to water mulched plants, apply it in good quantities, because an organic mulch can absorb a great deal of water. Unless you water heavily, it may never reach the roots of the plants.

Inorganic mulches

Rock gardens can have a layer of stone chippings or shingle placed over the entire soil surface to keep in moisture and prevent too much annual weed growth. The rock plants will grow much better under these conditions.

Black polythene sheeting is another useful inorganic mulch and it is possible to buy strips specially for mulching. Place it over the soil to prevent weed growth and evaporation of moisture. It can be used in all the areas described above, with the exception of rock gardens. Its only drawback is that it can look rather unsightly.

To hold the polythene in position, first make v-shaped nicks in the soil, with a spade, on either side of the strip to be mulched. Then tuck the edges of the sheet into the nicks and firm the soil with your feet. You can then make slits in the polythene and plant through them.

HOEING

If you do not mulch plants then you will have to hoe around them to keep weeds in check – unless you prefer to use chemical weedkillers. Regular hoeing is necessary to catch weeds in the seedling stage. It is much easier than hoeing out large weeds that may well root into the soil again if left on the surface. It is important to work the hoe shallowly so as not to damage any plant roots that may be growing near the soil surface.

The best time for hoeing is on a warm day when the soil surface is dry. The weeds will then quickly shrivel up and die. When you hoe try to achieve a nice, fine loose tilth on the surface. The layer of dry, loose soil will act as a mulch, conserving moisture in the undisturbed soil below.

In the vegetable or fruit garden, where footprints do not matter, you will probably find a draw hoe much quicker, working in a forward direction and walking over the hoed ground. But in the ornamental area use a Dutch hoe, moving backwards. The double-bladed push-pull type of hoe is popular and speedy.

Brussels sprouts like a fortnightly dose of fertilizer (left), while an onion hoe (below) helps keep them free of weeds

WATERING THE GARDEN

Plants need water for many reasons. Seeds will not germinate without water and plants can only use the nutrients in the soil if they are in soluble form. Water gives the plant its shape and stiffness; without it the plant becomes limp. If the water loss becomes too great the stomata (holes) in the surface of the 'skin' close and the basic plant processes come to a halt. You must, therefore, ensure that plants always have enough water for all their needs.

During dry weather you must give your plants the water that nature has failed to provide. Too often, however, the mistake is made of watering irregularly and in insufficient quantity. It is essential to give enough water to penetrate the soil down to the layer where the plant roots are growing. If you only sprinkle the surface, the water will simply evaporate in the heat of the sun.

How much water?

Apply sufficient water to penetrate the soil to a depth of at least 15cm (6 in) – preferably more. This means applying at least 2–3cm (1 in) of water, depending on the soil type. The lighter and more sandy the soil, the deeper this amount of water will penetrate. If you are using a sprinkler, you can measure the amount of water being applied by placing a number of tin cans over the area being watered. When there is 2–3cm (1 in) of water on the bottom of the tins you will know it is time to turn off the sprinkler. (See diagram in Spring and Summer Lawn Care section.) If you water with a hosepipe then you will have to dig down into the soil with a hand trowel to see how far the water has penetrated.

Start watering before the soil dries out to any great depth; a good guide is when the top 2–5cm (1–2 in) is becoming dry. In hot, summer weather you may have to water at least once a week.

It is usually best to apply water in the evening, as then none will be evaporated by the sun and it will penetrate the soil to a good depth.

Many people do not realize that wind is a major drying agent (especially in spring and early summer), so watering will be necessary after windy weather.

Sprinklers and hoses

Applying all this water will be very time-consuming if you have to rely on a hosepipe alone. It is therefore a good idea to attach a sprinkler of some kind to the end and let it distribute the water.

There are many types on the market to suit all pockets. The cheapest are those with no moving parts (mini-sprinklers), but which produce a fine circular spray from a static nozzle. Often the base of these is equipped with a spike which you push into the ground to hold the sprinkler firmly.

Rotating sprinklers are slightly more expensive. They have two adjustable nozzles on an arm which is spun round by water pressure, giving a circular pattern. These are probably the most popular for private gardens.

The more sophisticated oscillating sprinklers apply water in a square or rectangular pattern. A tubular bar with a row of nozzles (non-adjustable) moves backwards and forwards, watering a very large area. It is worked by water pressure. Some can be adjusted to water a small or large area.

Sprinkler hoses are perforated plastic hoses of various kinds which are connected to the main hosepipe and produce a gentle spray of water along their complete length. One of these can be laid along rows of crops, or between plants.

You will, of course, want a good reinforced plastic or PVC hosepipe; a 13mm ($\frac{1}{2}$ in) diameter hose is a suitable size for general use. Illustrations of sprinklers and hoses will be found over the page under Watering Equipment.

Above right: use a fine rose for watering cuttings and seedlings
Below: a perforated hose sprinkler, handy for long borders

A rotary type sprinkler that waters in a regular circular pattern

Oscillating sprinkler that will deliver an even spray into a corner

Watering vegetables

Most vegetables benefit greatly from regular watering, especially crops like runner, French and broad beans, peas, marrows, lettuce, radish, cucumbers and tomatoes. Vegetables such as cabbages and other greenstuff, and root crops like potatoes and carrots, can get by without regular watering, although their yields will not be so heavy.

All newly-transplanted vegetables must be well watered in if the ground is dry and then kept moist until established. You can water these individually with a watering can.

Germinating seeds

Seeds must be kept moist to encourage them to germinate. This is especially true of the modern pelleted seeds, which will fail to grow if they lack sufficient moisture.

Fruit trees and bushes

Fruit trees, provided they are well established, will not come to much harm if you do not water during dry spells, but the fruits may be smaller than normal. However, black, red and whitecurrants, raspberries, strawberries, gooseberries, blackberries, loganberries and other hybrid berries really do need watering in dry weather if they are to crop well.

Flowers in beds and containers

It may not be possible to water everything in the garden, especially in a very dry season when there may be restrictions on the use of sprinklers in the garden. If this is the case, the flower garden must take third place – after fruit and vegetables, which you will be growing to supplement the family budget. However, flowers in containers (such as tubs, troughs, hanging baskets and window boxes) will soon die if not watered regularly. These dry out rapidly in hot weather and may well need watering twice a day – in the morning and again in the evening.

Watering the lawn

Lawns rapidly turn brown in dry weather, although they will green up again once the rains start. To keep a lawn green in the summer you will need to begin watering before it starts to turn brown and continue at weekly intervals, or more frequently, thereafter. Remember also not to cut a lawn too short in dry weather – so raise the mower blades.

Mulching the soil

There is a method of conserving moisture in the soil which will enable you to cut down on watering. It is known as 'mulching' and consists of placing a 5–8cm (2–3 in) layer of organic matter around and between plants – covering the root area. Use garden compost, well-rotted farmyard manure, leaf mould, spent hops, straw, grass mowings or sawdust.

Another method is to use black polythene sheeting. To anchor it to the ground, bury the edges in 'nicks' made with a spade in the soil; then place a few stones or bricks on top. You can buy rolls of special black mulching polythene.

All plants benefit from being mulched, for moisture is conserved and so they do not dry out so rapidly. If you have to limit mulching, however, then concentrate on your vegetables and fruits, rather than on your flowerbeds.

Left and below: mulching trees and shrubs with compost will conserve moisture

WATERING EQUIPMENT

Even the newest of gardeners will soon find that a watering can, or two, is not enough and that a garden hose is a worthwhile investment – even though you may have to pay an extra water rate charge for running one.

Garden hose These are made from PVC in varying qualities and standard lengths are 15m (50 ft), 18m (60 ft), 30m (100 ft) and 36m (120 ft). Choose the length for your needs, either two shorter ones or one long one.

Regular ribbed PVC in black or green, or 13mm ($\frac{1}{2}$ in) bore, 1·50 or 2mm thick, is the cheapest to buy per length. This quality is liable to crack in severe weather, during hard frosts and especially if you left water remaining in it. Once kinked, it will never straighten out and you must also beware of running over it with heavy machinery or your car.

Clear, higher-quality PVC, 13mm bore, may be ribbed for extra durability. It is very flexible, will not kink permanently and you can leave it out in all weather conditions without it cracking. It also resists pressure of car wheels.

The best hoses are made of pure PVC, 13mm bore, with a nylon cord reinforcement. These have all the features of the clear PVC types as well as withstanding extreme water-pressure without rupturing.

Hose reels If you want your hose to last, store it at all times on a hose reel (a steel wheel rotating on a central axis) that can be fitted to a wall or door, free-standing or on wheels for pushing around the garden. Some of the mobile types have polythene rollers for easy moving across your lawn. The through-feed type reel (with stand or wall bracket) has a length of hose leading from the tap to a central revolving joint that feeds the incoming water into the main hose while you pull out as much length as you need. A simple wall bracket device (as for a hand-mixer) holds tools and the hose.

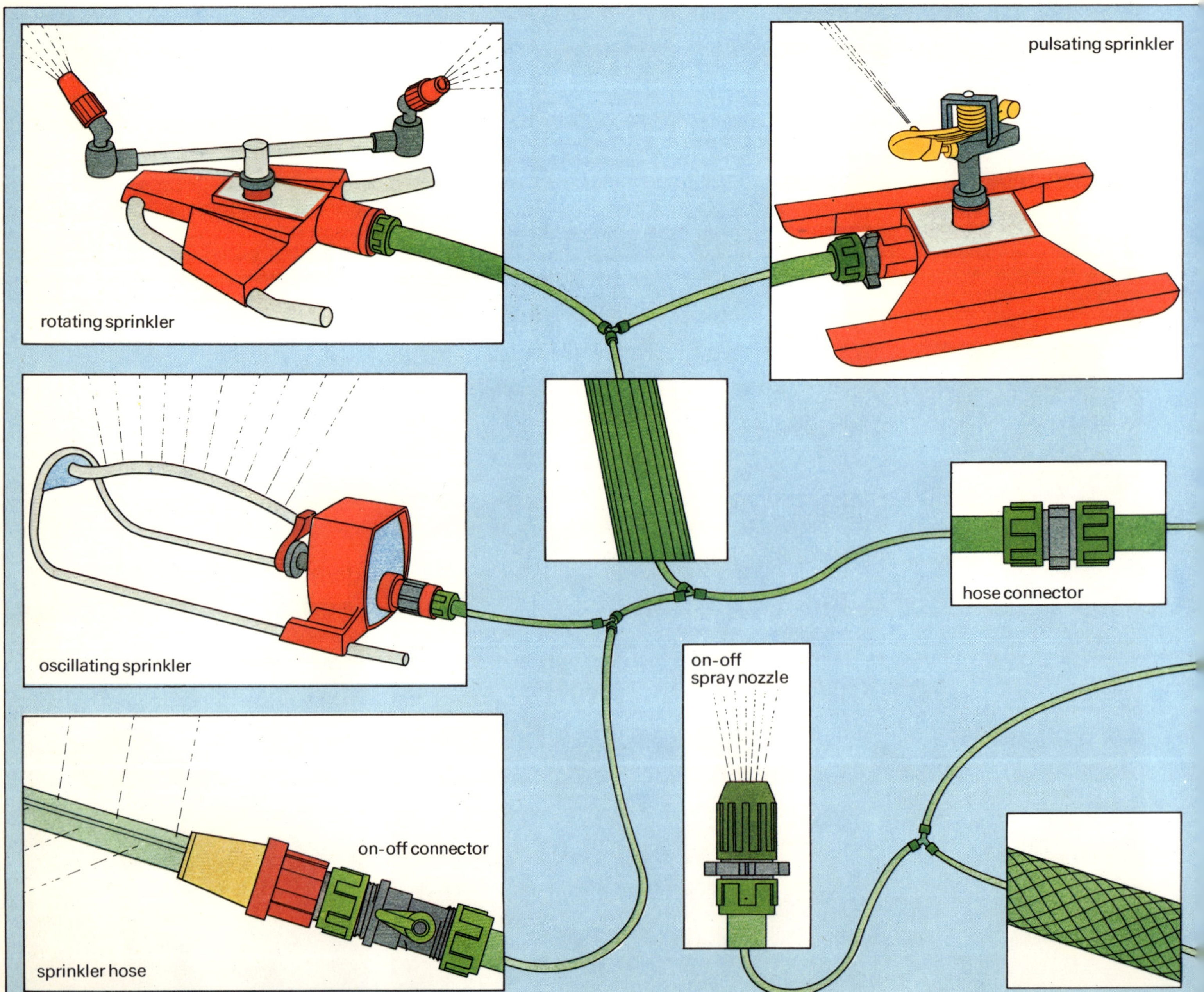

Pipeline system To save moving your hose you can install a pipeline for your lawn. Although it is better to fit this underground network before laying turf or sowing seed, it can be done later without causing too much upheaval. The pipe ends are capped and when water is required from any of the various outlets it is simple to flip back the lid of the housing, unscrew the cap, connect your attachment and turn on at the mains. Depending on your situation, it is sometimes possible to leave the pipeline above ground.

Sprayer attachments Adjustable spray nozzles are operated by turning a rotating plastic sleeve by hand to vary jet length, width and spray-droplet size. A spray gun version works by trigger pressure.

Sprinkler attachments The most thorough method of irrigation is by sprinkler, and the coverage area of different models depends on water pressure and hose size. Most sprinklers are made of plastic, where possible, but may incorporate lightweight, non-rusting metal parts. There are two basic types – rotating and oscillating.

The circular spray pattern may come from a small peg-like sprinkler (mini-sprinkler) that will irrigate up to 35 sq m (400 sq ft). Some rotating sprinklers will water up to 13m (42 ft) radius, covering an area of up to 500 sq m (5000 sq ft). Pulsating sprinklers are a variation on the rotating type and give an even larger coverage. For really large areas, around 1860 sq m (20,000 sq ft), you can use a travelling rotating sprinkler in conjunction with various automatic or water-activated timers so that it may be left unattended for long periods. These are quite complex bits of machinery and are available only from larger garden machinery outlets.

Oscillating sprinklers do not give an exact circular spray pattern. They cover areas up to 280 sq m (3200 sq ft). An adaptation of this type is the sprinkler hose, which is a length of hosepipe perforated with holes at regular intervals to emit a fine spray of water along its length when in operation.

Hose connectors For taps, couplings and water stops, repair connectors and pressure regulators. If the newer plastic fitments don't fit your system, use traditional worm drive (Jubilee), or thumb screw, hose clips.

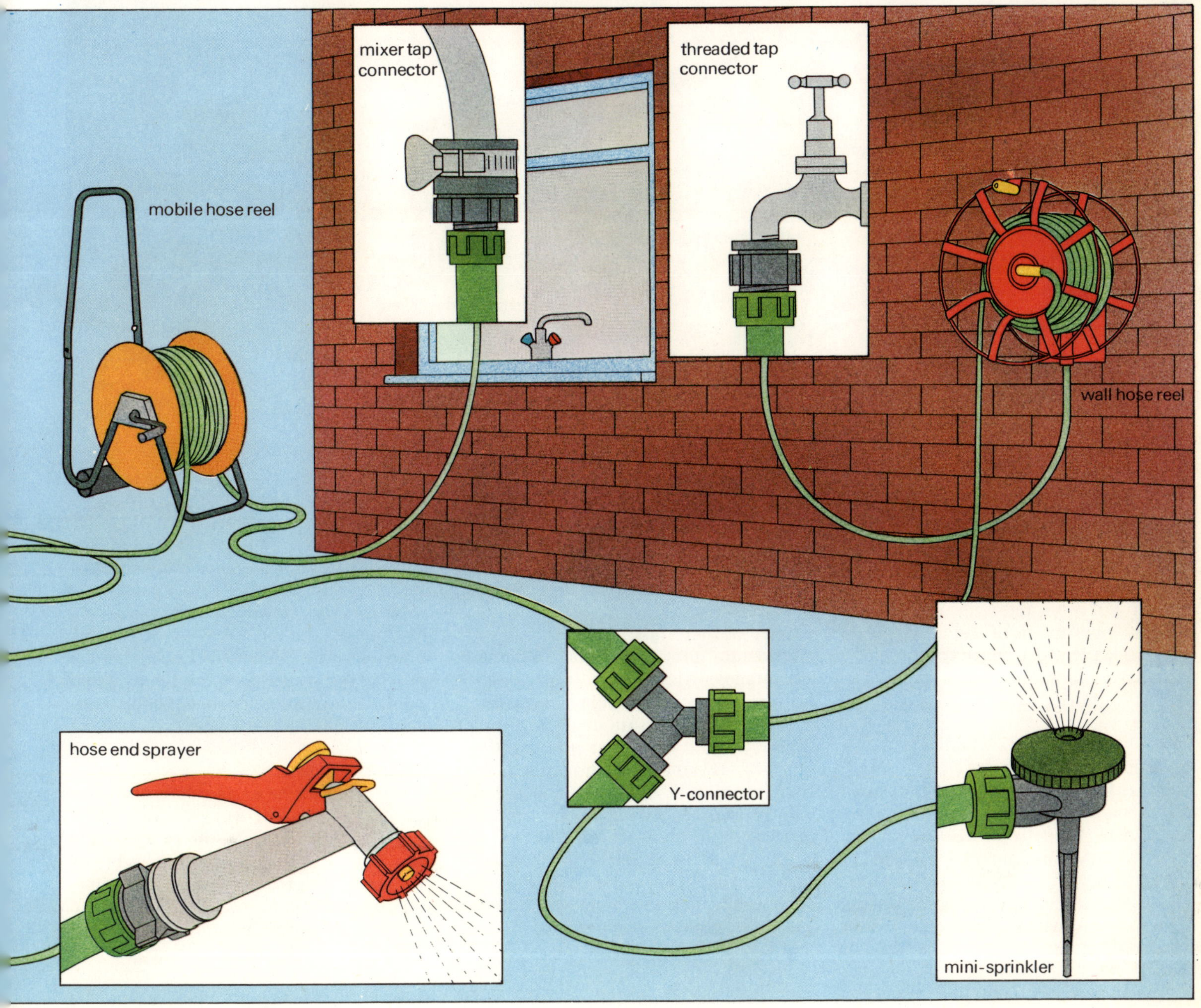

CHOOSING FRAMES AND CLOCHES

A large glass-to-ground frame, with aluminium-alloy framework, being used to house trays of seedlings and plants waiting to be transplanted

A frame – or two – costs little to buy, or make yourself (see page 66), and can be fitted into most gardens. Nearly everything you grow in a greenhouse can also be grown in frames, allowing for the restrictions in height and size.
Even if you have a greenhouse, frames can take over much of the work to leave more space for decorative plants and those demanding full greenhouse height.

First you must decide whether to buy a ready-made frame or make one yourself from a frame kit of glass-to-ground design with timber or metal sections. An all-glass frame is suitable unless you want extra warmth for propagation, or for growing cucumbers or melons.

Lids, known as 'lights', can be bought separately and you can place these over your own timber or brick-built sides, or even set one over a pit dug in the ground, adding to it as required. The lights can be easily stored away in the summer, when not in use.

Modern frames are often fitted with sliding glass sides, to give access or for added ventilation, and lights that slide aside as well as lift up so that they can be removed completely for easy working.

Choice of material

Aluminium alloy framework has many advantages: it is long-lasting, requires no maintenance and, being lightweight, is ideal for moving about. If you prefer timber, choose wood that is noted for its weather resistance, because frame sides are likely to come into contact with damp soil for long periods. Avoid soft woods treated with creosote as the vapour continues to be harmful to plants for some time. Green Cuprinol is suitable, but before using any other preservative check the maker's literature to be sure that it is safe for plants.

Plastic, instead of glass, for garden frames is light, easily portable and obviously advisable where small children are using the garden. From a gardener's point of view, however, glass has many advantages (see the section on Choosing a Greenhouse overleaf). You must use glass if the frame is to be heated, and would be advised to do so in windy areas as plastic can blow away.

Siting the frame

If you use a frame as an adjunct to your greenhouse (and it has vertical sides), you can push the frame close up to one side. This helps to reduce warmth loss from both the greenhouse and the frame.

If using a frame for greenhouse and pot plants, put it in a shady place – against the north side of your greenhouse is ideal. But most vegetable crops, and those alpines which you may be housing

in frames when not in flower, prefer a bright, open position.

With many frames it is often convenient to set them back-to-back, or alongside each other in rows. To obtain more height, stand your frame on a base of bricks or concrete blocks, or place it over a pit (providing you make sure that water does not collect in it).

Electric soil-warming cables

Frames do not have to be 'cold'; you can heat a large one with a small paraffin lamp provided you take great care to see that there is always ventilation. But installing electric soil-warming cables is by far the best method. Lay them in loops across the floor of the frame, making sure that they do not touch each other. Place a little sand on top and keep it moist: this will hold the cables in place and conduct the warmth more uniformly. Use only about 2–3cm (1 in) of sand, then a thermostat can be installed above the sand level to control the frame's temperature.

If you need extra warmth (as for pot plants) run cables round the frame sides as well. With glass-sided frames, fasten the cables to wooden battens with cleats and thrust the battens into the ground.

If you are growing plants to be rooted into a deep layer of compost (such as salad crops, cucumbers and melons) site the warming cables near the bottom of the compost. In this case a thermostat of the rod type should be thrust into the compost. Temperature can also be controlled manually or by a time switch. The considerable bulk of compost will hold warmth over the periods when the electricity is off.

Wattage depends on the size and purpose of your frame; decide after you have consulted the suppliers of such equipment.

You can use small heated frames inside the greenhouse for high-temperature propagation, or for housing a small collection of low-growing tropical plants. An aluminium framework, glass sides and top, and 2–3cm (1 in) or so of sand over the cable, are recommended. The wattage required is usually about 20W per 1000 sq cm (20W per sq ft) of frame floor, and a thermostat is essential.

Frame cultivation

If possible, avoid using soil. Instead, line a trough or pit with polythene sheeting, slitted here and there for drainage, and fill it with a proprietary potting compost. You can grow excellent, high-quality salad and other crops with little risk from pests or diseases.

Where you are moving pots or other containers in and out, firm the floor and cover it with polythene, over which is spread coarse sand or shingle. If you keep this damp, it will moisten the air in the frame; the polythene will help to keep out soil pests.

Grow house plants, and pot plants like cineraria, calceolaria, primula and cyclamen, in frames until the decorative stage when they are ready to transfer to the house, conservatory or greenhouse. Use frames to raise bedding plants and for many forms of propagation from cutting and seed. You will also find them especially useful for crops like lettuce, radish, beet and carrots that you want in the kitchen even before winter is over.

Keep plants like dormant fuchsias, chrysanthemums and pelargoniums (that are used for summer garden or greenhouse decoration) in frames during the winter when they often look far from attractive. Store dormant tubers and bulbs there to leave the greenhouse less cluttered. Some crops, like strawberries and violets, lend themselves particularly to frame culture.

Above left: timber-sided frame, with glass lights, shelters bedding plants prior to planting out. Above: rows of barn cloches protect lettuce that are almost ready for cropping

Keep glass frames (and cloches) as clean as possible to admit maximum light and discourage plant pests and diseases. Remove any mud splashes by careful use of a hose, if necessary.

CLOCHES

Early cloches were of glass and often held together by clumsy wires that were difficult to manipulate. Modern designs are simpler and often make use of plastics, which are very suitable for this purpose as cloches are frequently used only for weather protection, high temperatures being rarely necessary.

Select your type

There are tent, barn and T-shaped cloches, and a flat-topped 'utility' one. These are usually held together by special metal or plastic clips. Some cloches can be opened for ventilation or for watering, others have perforated tops to allow the rain to enter. Plastic ones with a cellular structure give greater warmth retention.

You can make simple and effective tunnels, ideal for protecting rows of vegetables, by sandwiching lengths of polythene between wire arches at intervals along the row, or by aligning ordinary cloches end-to-end. Anchor your plastic ones carefully in windy areas as they can easily blow away; use stones, bricks, wooden or metal pegs, or some special cloche fitments.

Cloches are most useful from autumn to late spring for providing protection from excessive wet and cold. Set them in place to dry and warm the soil before you dig and fertilize it, in preparation for sowing or planting.

Top: tunnel cloches of polythene sheeting are versatile. They can be cut to any length, depending on whether you want to cover one plant or a whole row. Above: corrugated plastic cloches are used here to cover strawberry plants; being lightweight these cloches need to be anchored against the wind with wire hoops. End pieces can be added to give the plants greater protection

Cloche cultivation

Use individual cloches for protecting isolated tender plants (such as fuchsia) in beds and borders, and protect groups of hardy and half-hardy annuals until they become established. You can also root cuttings directly into the ground of a nursery bed if you use cloches to cover them.

Many flowers grown for cutting benefit from cloche protection, especially low-growing bulbs in pots or bowls. Other favourite cloche flower crops are anemones, hellebore (Christmas rose), lily of the valley, violet and polyanthus. You can harden off bedding plants under cloches if frame space is not available. Also use them to protect sweet peas in the early stages.

In the vegetable garden, cloches give you year-round cropping. If you plan carefully you can move them from one crop to another as needed, thus putting a limited number to maximum use.

Working with cloches

You do not need to remove cloches for watering; the water that drains off them will seep into the soil provided that it has been well prepared. It should be porous and moisture-retaining, but well-drained. Work in plenty of humus-forming material, like peat or rotted garden compost. To avoid the wind rushing through your cloche tunnels, block the ends. This also applies to individual cloches used as miniature greenhouses to cover single, or small groups of, plants. When the weather permits ventilation, move the cloches along to leave a small gap between each one and remove the ends of tunnels.

Leave plenty of room between rows for comfortable access and keep the soil along the sides of the cloche rows well hoed to allow water retention. Soluble fertilizers can also be applied along the outside edges of the cloches.

Store glass cloches, and plastic tent and barn types, on their ends and stacked inside each other. For this purpose put down some clean boards (or lay a section of concrete) in a corner of the vegetable plot, and cover it with roofing felt for glass cloches.

CHOOSING A GREENHOUSE

Greenhouses come in all shapes and sizes – and today no garden need be without one, however small, for there are many simple and easy-to-erect models as well as more elaborate and decorative ones. For those of you contemplating buying a greenhouse for the first time, we give the basic facts about the various types available and some of the equipment you need to run them well.

The acquisition of a greenhouse opens up an exciting new area of gardening, where you don't have to worry about extremes of weather or damage from cold, wind or excessive rain. You can regulate the amount of water your plants receive and, because fertilizers are not washed away by rain, you can feed them correctly.

Temperature and ventilation can be adjusted and, by applying shading, even the light may be altered to suit plant preferences. Pests and diseases are easier to combat and the plants are protected from damage by birds and small animals.

Which type?
Most greenhouse styles offer the choice of a glass-to-ground or a base-wall design. The glass-to-ground type allows very efficient use of space for growing. When staging is fitted, there is enough light beneath for the accommodation of a varied selection of plants. The all-glass house is also ideal for tall subjects like tomatoes and chrysanthemums. By arranging your space carefully you can

A gardener's dream – an extensive greenhouse full of flowering plants

grow many different kinds of plants together. For example, you can grow tomatoes along the south side, followed by chrysanthemums – putting the pots on the floor. Your staging can then run along the north side, providing a surface on which to grow a variety of pot plants, with some space below for plants that like a certain amount of shade (as do many house plants). On the end wall you can train climbers bearing either beautiful flowers, or edible crops like cucumbers.

But for some purposes a greenhouse with a base wall of brick, concrete or timber boards (usually called a 'plant house') is preferable. Plants liking deep shade can be grown below the staging. This design is more economical to heat artificially and therefore is preferable when the greenhouse does not get much sun. It is also a good choice where high temperatures have to be maintained for propagation or for tropical plants (many of which do not demand much light). Greenhouses with a base wall at one side and glass-to-ground at the other are also available. These should be oriented east-to-west, if possible, with the base wall on the north side.

Planning ahead
Before buying your greenhouse, make sure that you are not infringing any rules or regulations by erecting it in your garden. If you are a tenant you should seek your landlord's permission; should you move, you can take the greenhouse with you. If you are a freeholder and wish to have a permanent structure (like a lean-to against the house wall) you will almost certainly require planning permission from your local council.

You must also do some advance thinking about the foundations of the greenhouse. You can lay old railway sleepers or concrete footings, or build a low, cemented brick wall on which the greenhouse can be free-standing or screwed into position. Do have a path of concrete, brick or paving stones down the centre of the house, for dry feet and clean working.

The best positions
Freestanding, rectangular greenhouses get most benefit from the sun if you orientate them east-to-west, with the long sides facing north and south. The 'high south wall' greenhouse *must*, in fact, lie this way to catch as much winter light and sun as possible. Staging, if used, should run along the north side.

With a lean-to, you may have no choice in the siting, but what you grow in it will depend on which way it faces. An east- or west-facing lean-to is usually fairly versatile since it gets some sun and some shade. If north-facing it will be very shady and is best devoted to pot plants (such as cinerareas, cyclamen, primulas and calceolarias) and house plants for permanent decoration. A south-facing lean-to can become very hot in summer and, unless you want to install shading, you should choose sun-loving plants like cacti and succulents.

Types of material
You should consider the cost of subsequent maintenance as against initial outlay when choosing your materials.

Glass or plastic? Glass has the unique property of capturing and retaining solar warmth. It also holds artificial warmth better. Polythene has a limited life and for long-term use a rigid plastic (like Novolux) is the wisest choice. Plastic surfaces are easily scratched by wind-blown dust and grit, causing dirt to become ingrained and a loss of transparency over a period of years. Plastic also becomes brittle with weathering and may disintegrate.

However, plastic is advisable if the site is likely to be the target for children's games or hooligans out to break glass, or where quick erection or portability is desirable, or where temporary weather protection is all that's necessary. Moulded fibreglass greenhouses are also available, but tend to be expensive and the fittings have to be free-standing.

Aluminium frames Aluminium alloy (often white-coated) is now tending to replace timber for the frame as it has many advantages. It is lightweight yet very strong, and prefabricated structures are easily bolted together. Sophisticated glazing, using plastic cushioning strips and clips instead of messy putty, means that the greenhouse can easily be taken apart for moving. There is no fear of rot, warp or trouble from wood-boring insects, or need for maintenance, like painting or treating timber.

Timber frames These may look better in a period-style garden. Select one of the more weather-resistant timbers such as cedar, teak or oak, but remember that all timber needs painting or treating with a wood restorer or preservative from time to time.

A 'vertical-sided 'barn' or 'span' model (far left) with timbered base walls on three sides. The 'Dutch light' house (left) is always a glass-to-ground structure; it has sloping glass walls which are designed to trap the sun's rays. Ornamental houses (right) come in many shapes and sizes, and make attractive show-cases for pot plants

Providing shade

If your greenhouse receives plenty of sun you will need shading in the summer.

Slatted blinds, run on rails over the exterior of the roof, are efficient but costly. They also have to be made to fit. Interior blinds are far less efficient in reducing temperature, since the sun's heat-producing rays have already entered the greenhouse, though they do help to prevent direct scorch.

The simplest and cheapest effective method of shading here is with an electrostatic shading paint that is not washed off by rain but can easily be removed by wiping with a dry duster. You apply and remove it like a blind.

All year round ventilation

Ventilators are usually fitted in the roof and sometimes in the sides as well, reducing excess heat in summer and controlling humidity at all times. Thermostatically-controlled units that open and shut the ventilators automatically according to the temperature inside the greenhouse are very useful, especially if you have to be away from home all day.

Types of heating

It makes sense to heat your greenhouse, if only to keep out frost, since this greatly widens its usefulness. Your heating need not be costly if you don't waste it.

Oil heaters Both oil and paraffin are easy to store and portable heaters are particularly valuable as supplementary heating in periods of extreme cold or during power cuts. Use paraffin heaters that are specially designed for greenhouses; the blue-flame design is best.

Electricity is trouble-free and gives accurate temperature control, but it can be expensive if used wastefully. Fan heating is very effective providing the fan and heat output are controlled together (preferably with a separate, rod-type thermostat); avoid a heater with a continuously-running fan. Ventilation becomes almost unnecessary with this system, and if you line your greenhouse with polythene to form a kind of double glazing you can cut fuel consumption by up to half.

Convector heaters and electrically-heated pipes are also efficient when used together with an accurate thermostat. If you decide on electricity you will need to run a cable from the house: be sure to have this done by a qualified electrician.

Natural gas There are special greenhouse heaters using natural gas, with good thermostatic control. They can also be adapted to work from bottle gas, though this makes them more expensive to run.

Natural gas, oil and paraffin, when burned, all produce carbon dioxide and water vapour. The carbon dioxide is beneficial to plants, but the water vapour can be a nuisance in winter when you will do better to keep the greenhouse dry. You will need some ventilation to keep down humidity and supply air for the fuel to burn, but this cold air does mean that some of the heat is lost.

Other types of heating Solid fuel (with the heat distributed by hot water pipes) and oil-fired boilers are still relatively cheap methods of heating. Hot water pipes, linked to a boiler, maintain high temperatures but are costly to install.

Heated propagators You will need some form of heated propagator so that you can germinate seeds without heating the whole greenhouse to a high temperature. Electrically-heated models are simple and cheap to run.

Automatic watering

There is a wide choice of equipment here. The water can be fed to the plants by overhead sprays, trickle-feed pipelines, by capillary sand benches or capillary matting. In the case of capillary watering, the sand or matting under the pots is kept constantly moist by whatever automatic system is installed.

One automatic watering system uses a photo-electric cell (connected to a special electric circuit) that registers the amount of sunlight prevailing, and controls the water flow accordingly.

Once you have installed such a system you can leave the greenhouse unattended for weeks without worry.

Artificial lighting

A paraffin lamp will give you enough light in the evenings for most jobs, but if the greenhouse has an electricity supply you can install either a lamp-holder and lamp bulb or a fluorescent tube.

A 'lean-to' can be set against a garden wall or a house wall, where it can double as a conservatory or home extension

ERECTING AND SITING A GREENHOUSE

To be the owner of a successful greenhouse, you need to spend at least as much time and thought on where to site it as on which type to choose. Equally, attention to detail when laying foundations and erecting the structure will amply reward the extra time spent.

In most cases it is wise to choose an open position for the greenhouse where it will get as much sunshine as possible. This generally means that you should try to position the unit with one of the longest sides facing south. It is a simple matter to shade the glass when you want to reduce light entry, but it is difficult to increase light without the trouble and expense of artificial lighting.

Remember that, in winter, nearly all plants will enjoy plenty of sunlight – even summer shade-lovers. Winter sunlight also means plenty of free warmth and your heating costs will be reduced.

Shady and windy sites

Avoid, where possible, a site that is near large trees (especially evergreens). Falling branches may break the glass, and spreading roots may upset the foundations. Falling leaves and exuded gums from some species dirty the glass, and you may also find that the roof is covered with bird droppings. Evergreens cast shade all year round, and many trees harbour numerous pests and diseases that can attack greenhouse plants and crops.

Small shrubs and trees are not usually a menace; these can even be planted (far enough away so that they do not cast shade) to act as windbreaks in windy areas. Strong, cold winds, usually from the north and east, can add greatly to the fuel bill. Other suitable windbreaks are fences, walls and hedges – as long as they are not too high.

Low ground and hollows

When choosing a site for your greenhouse, look carefully at the ground contours of your garden. In all cases where the site is at the foot of a hill there is a danger of frost pockets forming. Cold, frosty air can run off a slope almost like water, and surround a greenhouse that is set in a hollow. Where no other site is available, a low brick wall can help to deflect icy air currents.

In hollows and on low ground, water may collect or the ground may become very damp. These conditions are particularly unhealthy in winter when the greenhouse should be as dry as possible.

Sites near the house

Many people put their greenhouse at the far end of the garden – some distance from the house. There is often no good reason why it should be tucked away out of sight. Modern structures are rarely 'eyesores' and some designs are very attractive, especially when filled with decorative plants. There are many advantages in having the greenhouse within close reach of the house. Both water and electricity can be run to the greenhouse easily. Electricity, even if you don't want it for heating, may be needed for automatic aids or lighting; you may also wish to run natural gas from the house.

When the greenhouse is to be heated by solid fuel or paraffin, remember that the fuel will have to be carried to the greenhouse and, in the case of solid fuel, the ash carried away – yet another reason for avoiding remote sites. If you don't want to see a greenhouse from the windows of your home, you can always screen it with low shrubs or small ornamental trees.

In some cases greenhouses can be heated economically by an extension of the same central heating system used in your home. In this case the greenhouse should, preferably, come into contact with the house wall, and a lean-to is usually the best design. Where high temperatures are required it is always an advantage if the greenhouse can be set against a house wall, or a south-facing garden wall. Such a wall usually absorbs warmth from the sun during the day and radiates it at night, thus saving fuel and acting as a kind of free storage heater.

Laying the foundations

Most modern, prefabricated, amateur greenhouses are easy to erect single-handed, though with the larger sizes you may need assistance. The ground must always be firm and level, so laying a shallow foundation (by digging a trench and filling it with a fluid concrete mix that finds its own level) is often a wise move. However, some greenhouse manufacturers recommend their own base plinths and the small additional cost of these is well worth while. Some designs do not need elaborate foundations but are secured by 'ground anchors'. A separate hole is dug for each anchor and the framework is then bolted onto these before the glazing is put in.

Brick or concrete base walls, if required, are best constructed by a professional builder – unless you are reasonably expert in this sort of work. Greenhouse manufacturers always provide a detailed groundplan of the structure, so follow this closely when putting in foundations or base walls.

When erecting your greenhouse, use a spirit level and plumb line to make frequent checks on levels and verticals.

Fitting the glazing

Stand glass panes in a dry, covered place until you are ready to use them. If they get wet they are very difficult to separate and you risk breaking them. Glazing is best done when the weather is not too cold or your fingers may be too numb for careful handling. Do any metal or timber painting before the glass is put in. If you are using putty, only put it below the glass as a bed for the panes – not over the top as well, as in ordinary domestic glazing.

Plastic greenhouses

Be especially careful, when erecting and siting plastic greenhouses, to avoid possible wind damage. The suppliers usually issue special anchoring instructions and recommendations. When plastic is to be fastened to a timber framework, don't use creosote preservatives on the wood. Some plastics will become weakened by contact and all will be severely discoloured, making the greenhouse most unsightly. Moreover, creosote fumes are harmful to plants. For the same reason creosote should not be used on any timbers in close contact with plants in a confined area – such as in greenhouses or frames. Instead use one of the proprietary horticultural timber preservatives on the market.

Tending the site

The surroundings of your greenhouse should be kept tidy and weed-free. Weeds will harbour many troublesome pests; for example nearby stinging nettles may bring you an infestation of whitefly.

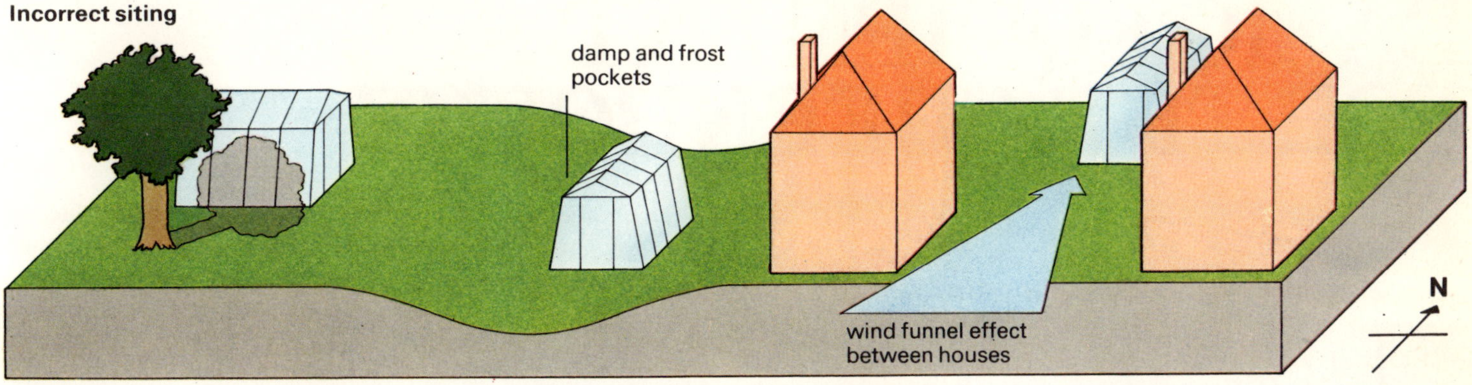

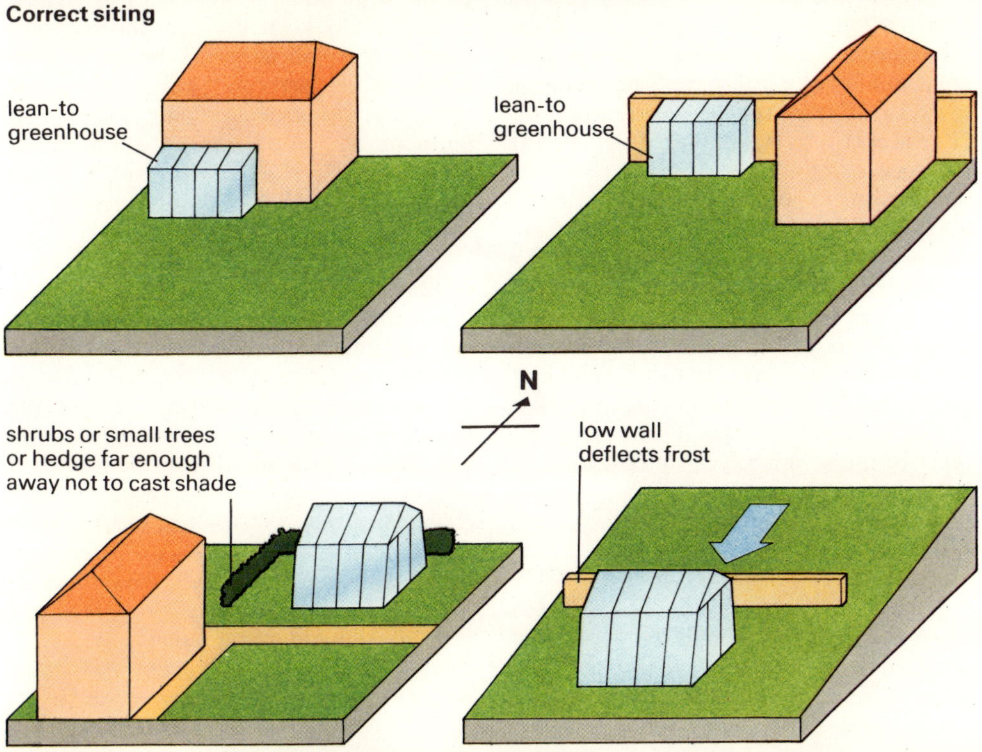

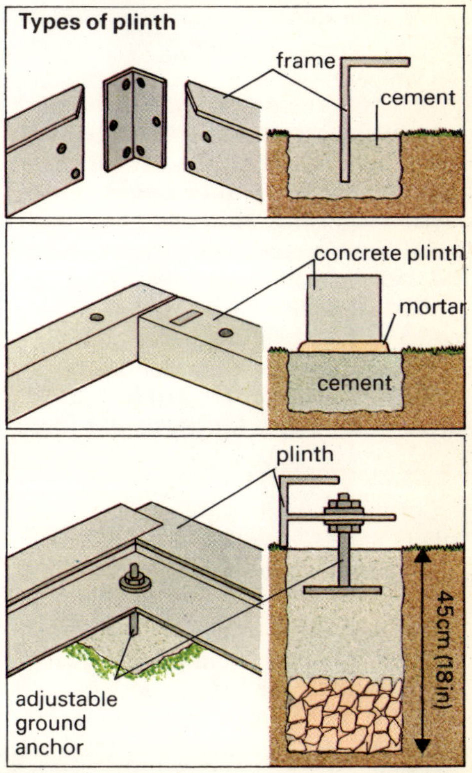

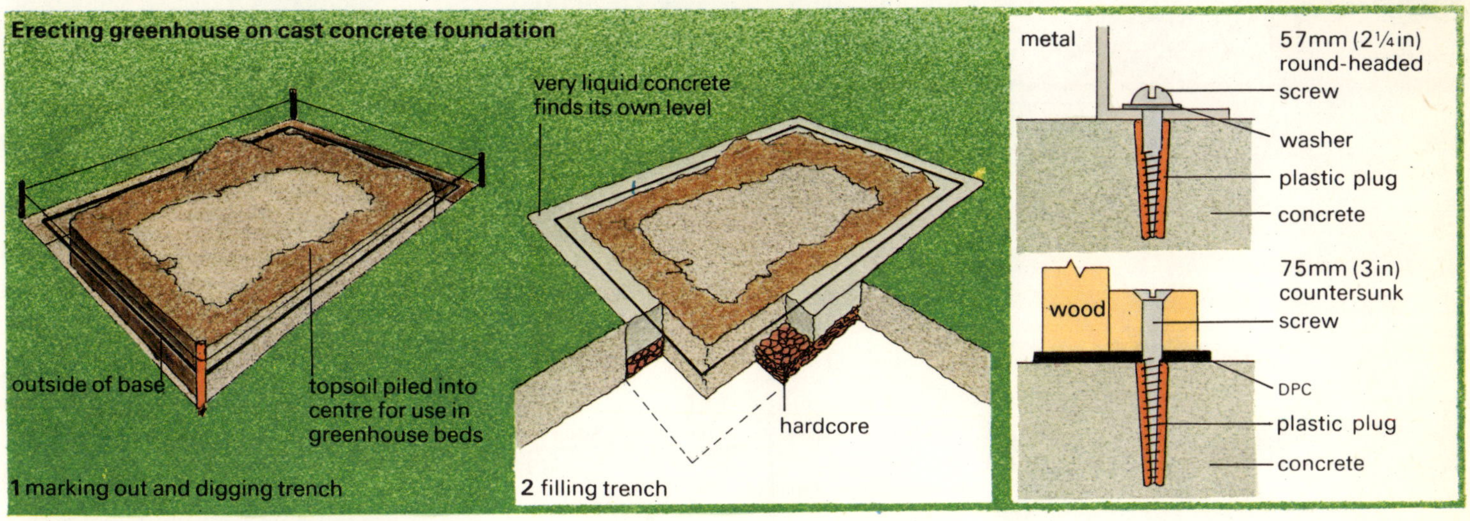

Top: avoid shade, damp, frost and wind – enemies of the greenhouse
Centre left: use house or garden walls for economical lean-to greenhouses; make use of low-growing shrubs or low walls to help protect against wind and frost

Bottom left: dig trench on a firm, level spot, remembering to place soil in centre for future use. Concrete over hardcore provides a solid base for the greenhouse that can be anchored with the right type of plugs and screws (bottom right)

Centre right: ready-made base plinths in in metal or concrete need only very very simple foundations, and are easy for the amateur to put together. The adjustable ground anchor system requires a solid concrete base

BASIC EQUIPMENT FOR THE GREENHOUSE

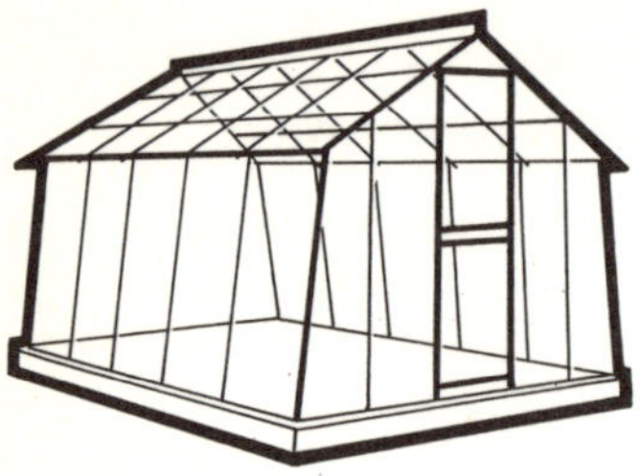

When you buy a greenhouse the price usually covers only the structure. All other items – sometimes even the ventilators – have to be bought as 'extras'. But this does allow you considerable choice of interior and exterior fittings. There are also many tools and gadgets available, in a variety of designs and price levels. Some of these are essential basic equipment and others can be bought as you need them for particular jobs.

In many greenhouses staging and shelving will be found useful at some time or other. Staging is often thought of as a permanent fixture but it need not be so. There are some small units now available that can be easily assembled and dismantled, moved about from place to place in the greenhouse, and extended to increase staging space if required. This form of staging makes the greenhouse very versatile and is specially useful in a glass-to-ground structure where a wide variety of plants of different heights can be grown.

Staging materials

Probably the most important aspect of your staging is the top surface. For most purposes a solid surface, strewn with some kind of moisture-retaining material, is the best surface for the warmer months. In winter it is an advantage if the staging top is of an 'open' nature to allow for air circulation around plants and, in warmed greenhouses, the distribution of heat; for this, slatted staging is suitable. However it is not common practice to change your staging according to the seasons, nor is it necessary. If you install open-type staging, it is a simple matter to cover it with polythene or asbestos sheeting, and then in mid spring (March) to cover this with a layer of moist shingle or other moisture-retaining material. You can then remove it all in mid autumn (September). This process helps considerably to maintain air humidity.

Instead of the conventional timber slats modern staging, particularly when constructed from metal angle strips, often has a top surface of wire or plastic mesh.

A really solid, substantial staging, made from bricks or concrete has an advantage worth noting in these days of fuel economy. Where a greenhouse receives a good amount of sunshine during the day, the bricks and concrete will store heat and evolve (radiate) it during the night. Sometimes enough warmth will be given out to keep the greenhouse frost free, and it will certainly be enough to keep the temperature more even. It is particularly valuable where rather high temperatures are being maintained for propagation or for growing sub-tropical plants, and where a relatively high warmth and humidity are needed all year.

Portable shelves

Shelving is always useful – even more so if it is portable. Depending on how the basic greenhouse structure is designed it can be fitted to the sides or suspended from the roof – or both. If buying the brackets and the shelving material separately, then

Below left: staging – ***1*** *and* ***2****, metal frames with open wood tops, and* ***3****, wire mesh stretched over wood frame, allow good air circulation, while the more solid combinations in* ***4*** *retain heat*
Below: shelving – ***1*** *suspended by metal straps from roof;* ***2*** *fixed with an angle bracket;* ***3*** *bolted-on aluminium type*

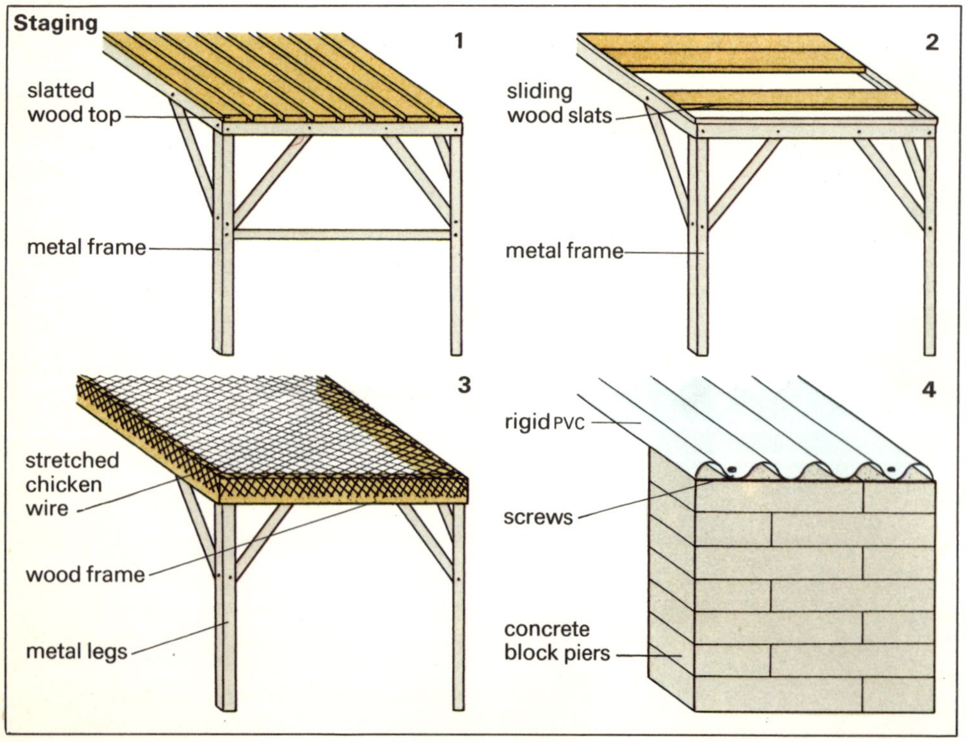

thick plate glass shelves are worth considering instead of the conventional planking or slats. Glass is a good choice if your greenhouse is very crowded as it allows more light to reach the plants below. Strips of strong plate glass can sometimes be purchased relatively cheaply as off-cuts from scrap.

Types of thermometer

Thermometers are absolutely indispensable to proper greenhouse management. You will need at least one maximum and minimum thermometer in the greenhouse interior. Others may be useful for interior or exterior frames and outside the greenhouse. In all cases do buy a quality instrument, as this will give you accurate readings and last far longer than a cheap one. Tiny temperature indicators show the highest and lowest temperatures that have been reached; these are usually set with a magnet supplied with the instrument. Designs are now made that can be gravity set, and there are also pushbutton types. You may also want a frost forecast thermometer; this is a kind of hygrometer (for measuring humidity) but it has a scale indicating the possible chance of frost. Advance warning will enable you to check heating equipment, close vents and so on.

Watering and spraying equipment

Even if you intend to install automatic watering, a watering can will be useful at some time, even if only for applying liquid feeds. Choose one with a spout that will easily reach to the back of the staging and one that's not too heavy for you to lift when it is full. Some designs have extendible spouts. If your greenhouse is fitted with a water tap, then you can use a watering lance that is controlled by a finger-operated valve. Get one with a nozzle that will deliver a fine spray for damping down, as well as a normal flow.

Ideally, you should also buy two hand sprayers. One should have a fairly large capacity for damping down or spraying foliage with water, and for applying pesticides. Another small sprayer, holding about 500cc (1 pt), is useful for treating the odd plant (when it is not necessary to make up a vast amount of pesticide). Don't forget that foliar feeds can also be applied with sprayers. A special feature to look for when buying a sprayer is a nozzle that can be directed upwards as well as downwards, and that will reach between the plants easily. This will ensure thorough coverage of the undersides of leaves when spraying pesticides; most pests first congregate under the foliage. The pump-up or pneumatic type of sprayer is convenient.

Potting benches

A very useful piece of equipment is a portable potting bench. This is a tray with one side missing that can be placed on the staging when needed. Use it for mixing compost, sowing, pricking out and potting jobs, and store it out of the way when not in use. You can easily make a bench using a sheet of aluminium (available from most do-it-yourself shops, often as off-cuts). Bend three of the edges upwards with pliers to prevent compost being pushed off the sides and back. Aluminium is one of the best materials to use because it is easy to clean and sterilize and is resistant to the hard wear caused by trowelling, cutting operations, and mixing. It is also lightweight and easily made into the shape you want.

Plastic and clay flowerpots

Keep a selection of flowerpots to hand. Plastic is easy to clean, but a few clay pots (if you can get them) are handy from time to time – some plants prefer them. The most useful sizes to keep in store for a wide range of pot plants are 8 or 9cm (3 or 3½ in) and 13cm (5 in).

Thermometers and frost detector

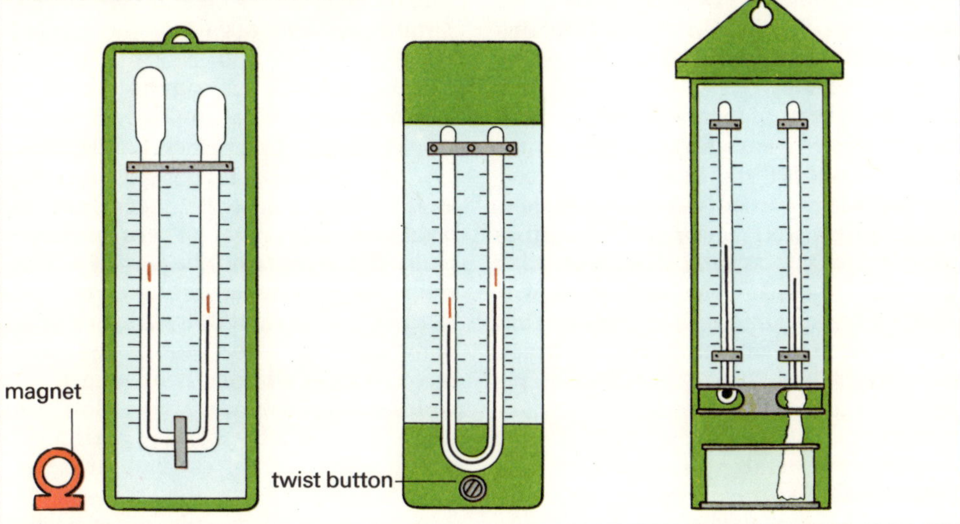

Watering equipment

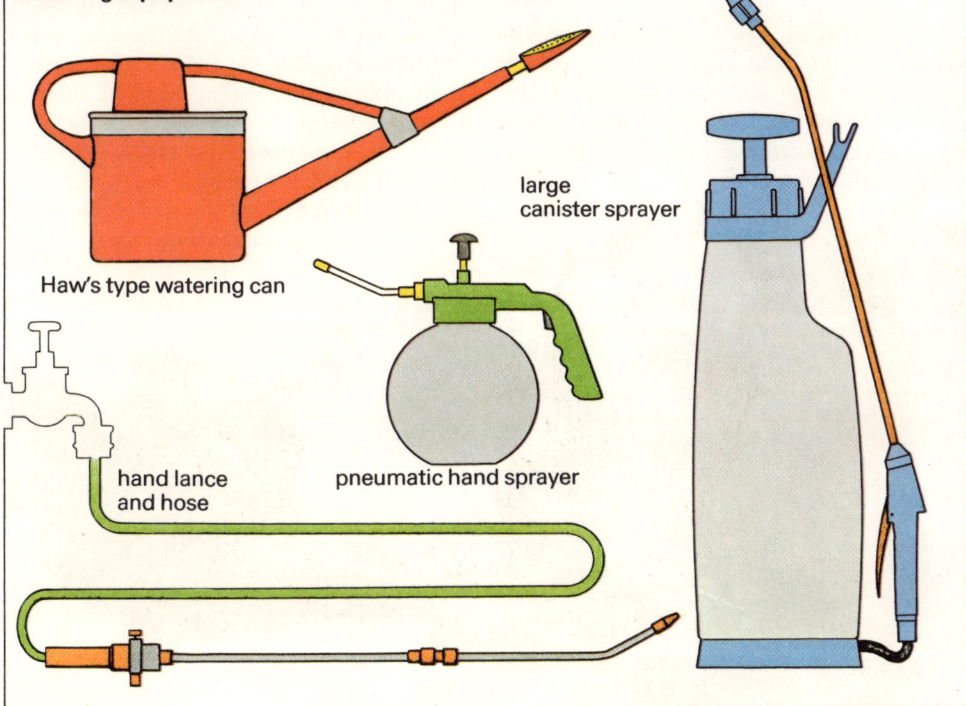

Above left: two different types of thermometer, with magnet or twist-button setting, and frost detector (similar to a hygrometer) to help give you valuable warning of a cold snap

Left: some of the basic equipment to cope with different watering needs

WEEDS AND WEED CONTROL

What is a weed? The short answer to that question is: any plant growing where it is not wanted. For instance, a grape seedling germinating in your dahlia bed is a weed – unless you want a vine amongst the dahlias. In a stricter sense, weeds are the native ancestors of our cultivated garden plants; they are undesirable because they are less attractive, generally bear smaller flowers or fruits, and are more vigorous in competition with their descendants. Weeds compete for water, nutrients and light, and often deprive cultivated plants, especially the seedlings and young ones, of their fair share of these necessities, because weeds adapt better to less favourable conditions.

There are two basic types of weeds – perennial and annual: the former are far harder to eliminate.

PERENNIAL WEEDS

Most perennial weeds are quick-growing and tenacious, often re-growing from roots or rootstocks. They are, therefore, very difficult to get rid of. Herbaceous types, such as couch grass, bindweed (convolvulus and calystegia species) and ground elder are often notoriously deep-rooted. They store food in their fleshy roots, rhizomes, stolons, tubers or bulbs. It is easy to remove the visible vegetation but difficult to eradicate the roots. With woody plants, such as brambles and ivy, it is harder to get rid of the growth above ground, but comparatively easy to eradicate the roots, which must be burnt.

Above right: the seed clock of the dandelion (Taraxacum officinale), *ready to spread a new generation over the garden. Right: daisy* (Bellis perrenis)

Manual weeding

Good hand-weeding is still one of the best ways to rid yourself of perennial weeds. Some well-timed work with a trowel will save you much time and trouble later on – providing you don't leave any of the roots in the soil.

If working near decorative or vegetable plants where you don't want to use chemical weedkillers, then manual weeding becomes a necessity. You may need to use a fork, trowel, knife or even a mattock (like a pickaxe). Be careful that you don't just carve them up; this merely helps to propagate them and makes more work in the future. Dig up the weeds, complete with roots, and then burn them or put them in the garbage bin.

When cultivating fresh ground it is essential to remove all the roots and underground storage systems; although hard work, it pays to lift them out by hand. Don't use a rotary cultivator on couch grass or dock-infested land as it will only chop up the weeds and encourage regrowth. Hoeing can have the same effect on a smaller scale unless you take care to remove the root, not just chop off leaves.

Weedkillers

Weedkillers are categorized according to their mode of action, so that you can buy whichever is most suited to your needs.

Total In an area devoid of decorative or culinary plants you can use a 'total' weedkiller, such as aminotriazole, to 'sweep the board'. A total weedkiller will kill all plants with which it comes into contact. You must take great care not to let it drift onto other plants or onto your neighbour's property. There have been many skirmishes over the garden wall as a result of misapplied weedkillers. After using it, remove and burn the debris and plant nothing in the ground for two to three months. If treatment with a total weedkiller is followed by a dose of a residual weedkiller (such as simazine) you will have a weed-free site for several months.

Another total weedkiller is sodium chlorate. It has to be used with great care as it spreads in the soil and can kill plants some distance away from the spot it was applied. Another danger is that, mixed with many other substances, it may be spontaneously inflammable, and it is therefore dangerous to store. It has a residual effect for up to a year.

Total and residual weedkillers are best for clearing paths and driveways.

Residual or pre-emergent These will not kill established weeds but they help to prevent the germination of most weeds for up to three months. There are various degrees of persistence.

Simazine has a long persistence, but it can be harmful to some shrubs (such as deutzia). Propachlor lasts for shorter periods but is less toxic and so is useful for herbaceous borders and shrubberies.

This type remains in a narrow band of the topsoil, so that any weed seeds germinating in this zone take up the chemical and die. It is possible to apply residual weedkiller where bulbs are planted, because their roots are located below the weedkiller band, and they grow quickly through it without suffering any damage. Plants such as runner beans, sweet peas, daffodils and hyacinths will all grow through the weedkiller layer after it has become inactive.

Selective Some weedkillers are termed 'selective' as they kill dicotyledons (broad-leaved plants), but will not damage many monocotyledons – such as grasses. Selective ones like 2,4-D, MCPA, 2,4,5-T or fenoprop (hormone types) kill by causing the plant to overgrow its food reserves so that it literally grows itself to death. Use this kind with great care as the slightest drift will damage crops; tomatoes are especially sensitive to them.

Non-selective The well-known paraquat and diquat weedkillers will only kill perennial weeds while they are still at seedling stage. After a few weeks they become immune and these preparations merely burn off their foliage and allow the roots to re-grow. They are de-activated immediately they meet the soil and are therefore safe to use provided they do not drift. But they must be kept away from children and animals: under no circumstances store them in old lemonade or other misleading bottles.

Methods of application

Always read the maker's instructions on the package and follow them closely; they have been based on years of research. Our recommendations give the chemical name, so when buying proprietary brands check the package label and see that it contains the correct constituents for your purpose. Keep a separate watering can for use with chemical weedkillers, and use a rose fitting or dribble-bar attachment for controlled application.

Specific treatments

Some perennial weeds are particularly stubborn and require special treatment.

Oxalis Remove these plants, which defy all chemical killers, with a sharp knife. Be sure to get up all roots and little bulbs.

Couch grass and perennial oat-grass These persistent grasses, with rhizomes, put up a fight against eradication. The only effective control is dalapon. If they are found in flower or vegetable beds 'spot' apply several doses of dalapon and then dig out the remains.

'Spot treatment' involves applying the weedkiller to the weeds only. It is done most easily by using a bottle with a pourer top or a squeezy-type container.

Docks Repeated action with dichlobenil (not easily obtainable), or spot treatment with 2,4-D, MCPA, fenoprop or mecoprop will keep the plants down. They are difficult to control because the roots, if broken on being dug out, will grow again.

Perennial nettle, bindweed, ground elder and blackberry These tend to grow near hedges or in shrubberies, and once established are likely to remain permanent residents. Apply 2,4,5-T or brushwood killer (usually a mixture of 2,4-D and 2,4,5-T) but avoid spraying onto other plants.

A good way to minimize drift is to make up a solution of this weedkiller in a container and dip the tips of the weeds in it. This will then be taken up through the plant by the sap stream – and kill it. You may need to make several applications over a few days for them to be effective. This method also works on many wild, shrubby plants such as dog rose and ivy (*Hedera helix*).

Thistles These are particularly obstinate weeds that may need pulling out by hand.

Above: bindweed (Convolvulus arvensis)

Above: couch grass (Agropyron repens)

Below: annual nettle (Urtica urens)

Bottom: creeping thistle (Cirsium arvense)

Below: dock (Rumex obtusifolius)

PERENNIAL WEEDS Guide to treatment

PLACE	TYPICAL WEEDS	TREATMENT	OTHER ADVICE
NEW LAND & WASTE LAND	Bindweed; blackberry; couch grass; docks; ivy; ground elder; nettles; oat-grass; thistles	Apply total weedkiller, e.g. aminotriazole; clear away debris and dig carefully, removing all roots, tubers and bulbous roots. Throw away or burn these.	Take care not to let the spray drift on to your own plants or over to other gardens.
LAWNS	Creeping buttercup; daisy; dandelion; plantain; speedwell	Mowing and raking; apply 2,4-D and mecoprop mixtures (ioxynil is needed for speedwell). Lever out old grass and weeds with a sharp trowel or knife.	Do not use 2,4-D or mecoprop on new lawns until the grass is at least six months old; use ioxynil for weeds on young lawns.
	Moss	Lawn sand or mercuric chloride.	Take care not to let children or animals near either of these dangerous poisons.
SHRUBBERIES & MIXED BORDERS	Bindweed; couch grass; docks; ground elder; thistles	Dig out all roots; apply a residual weedkiller to prevent fresh germination; dichlobenil kills many perennial weeds.	Check all instructions to make sure that your borders do not contain plants that are sensitive to some of the residual weedkillers.
ROSE BEDS	Couch grass; many germinating perennials	Treat couch grass with dalapon and remove by hand; simazine will prevent germination and dichlobenil completely kills many of these perennial weeds.	Take care not to let weedkiller get on to roses, especially if in leaf; apply simazine in early spring to last through most of the plant-growing season.
HERBACEOUS & FLOWER BORDERS	Many germinating and established weeds	Propachlor is a good residual weedkiller to check further germination, provided all established weeds are removed by hand or fork first.	Ensure that weather is warm and soil moist before applying propachlor.
FRUIT	Established and germinating perennials (especially couch grass and creeping buttercup in strawberries)	Use diquat or paraquat between rows to kill new weeds; dalapon for couch grass; dichlobenil for established weeds; simazine residual weedkiller around trees, bush and cane fruit.	Dig out weeds from strawberry plants as they are very sensitive to weedkillers, especially when in full leaf.
VEGETABLES	All weeds	Don't let weeds get too large before treatment. Hoe frequently to remove germinating weeds; use propachlor for some crops, but check instructions first to ensure safety of growing plants.	Hoeing is best done on warm days as weeds die from exposure and will not re-root in soil tilth; pull out any large weeds after a shower of rain.
PATHS & DRIVES	All weeds	Apply a total weedkiller, such as aminotriazole, sodium chlorate or simazine.	Avoid contact with cultivated plants in the vicinity.

Above: sow-thistle (Sonchus asper)
Below: chickweed (Stellaria media)

Wait till the ground is slightly moist, and be sure to wear gloves. Repeated doses of 2,4,5-T will help to weaken them.

Lawn weeds

The rosette-forming types (such as daisy, dandelion and plantain) are the most successful on lawns as they tend to escape the lawn-mower blades. To spot-apply weedkillers to lawn weeds use a small dropper bottle.

Dandelion, daisy, creeping buttercup, ribwort and plantain Proprietary lawn weedkillers containing MCPA and 2,4-D with mecoprop or fenoprop usually bring quick death, but must be applied in strict accordance with the makers' instructions.

Speedwell Mecoprop/ioxynil mixture is required to check this weed.

Yarrow Use repeated doses of mecoprop. Feeding the lawn with sulphate of ammonia should hasten the expiry date.

Couch grass and perennial oat-grass Two very difficult grasses to remove from lawns. Close and frequent mowing will go a long way towards finishing them off; otherwise you must dig them out with a knife. Effective weedkillers cannot be used as they would kill the lawn as well.

ANNUAL WEEDS

Annual weeds, by definition, mature, flower, seed and die within one year. 'Seed' is the operative word here, because this is the method by which they reproduce and infest the garden. It is also the key to their control; if you can remove the seed before it reaches the soil you can stop the next generation of weeds before it starts.

Many species of annual weeds grow quickly and succeed in completing several generations each year. The seeds seem to be able to germinate at any time of the year, even the middle of winter. So never assume that weeds are 'out of season'; although they may grow more slowly in winter they are always lurking.

Some of the most common annual weeds that you are likely to encounter are: chickweed, speedwell, groundsel, knotgrass, shepherd's purse, annual nettle, charlock, sow-thistle, scarlet pimpernel, goose-grass and wild radish.

Weeding by hoeing

One of the most common, and time-honoured, ways of controlling annual weeds is by hoeing. The secret of successful hoeing is to choose a day that is dry, sunny and, preferably, has a steady breeze. All these factors help to dry out the weed seedlings on the soil surface and prevent them re-rooting.

Persicaria (Polygonum lapathifolium)

Don't just decapitate the weeds when you hoe; make sure the roots are removed.

In a way, you make extra work for yourself by hoeing because you constantly bring more weed seeds to the surface where they germinate. Seeds can remain viable in the ground for years, waiting until they come near to the surface before starting to grow. Some seeds are very sensitive to the amount of daylight available and can only spring into life when they are in the topmost layer of soil. Regular hoeing, however, will keep weed seedlings under control.

Controlling with weedkillers

Most annual weeds are more easily controlled by weedkillers than their perennial counterparts. A whole range of annuals succumb to applications of dichlobenil or propachlor. Both these weedkillers are residual, but last only a few months. Diquat and paraquat are

Red deadnettle (Lamium purpureum)
also known as bad man's posies

very useful for killing germinating weed seedlings. You can spot apply these anywhere provided you take care not to let them drift onto other plants.

Unlike many perennials, annual weeds germinate within the narrow soil-surface band to which the weedkillers have been applied; therefore they die almost as soon as they start growing. So, on the whole, these weedkillers tend to be more effective against annuals. Always remember where these chemicals have been put down and make sure that no horticultural activities 'break the band' as this will allow the weeds to come through unscathed.

Special treatments

There are a few stubborn annual weeds that do not succumb easily to dichlobenil and propachlor. These usually need an application of another type (or mixture) of weedkiller.

Rayless mayweed (pineapple weed) Treat with mecoprop or mecoprop with ioxynil.

Common persicaria Several doses of propachlor or dichlobenil may be required before you eventually get rid of it.

Red deadnettle Repeated applications of mecoprop will be needed.

Annual lawn weeds

As well as the tough perennial lawn weeds, you are also likely to encounter some troublesome annual ones. One good preventive measure is to use a grass-collecting box on the lawn-mower. This will stop many weeds falling back on the lawn and propagating themselves.

Chickweed Best controlled with mecoprop which is often applied with 2,4-D as a general lawn weedkiller.

Lesser yellow trefoil Several applications of mecoprop may be needed; or use fenoprop.

Lesser common trefoil This weed often flourishes where grass is short of nitrogen. Feed the lawn with sulphate of ammonia in spring to lessen the chance of this weed getting established.

PESTS-PREVENTION AND CONTROL

The word 'pest' conjures up, for many people, a vision of hordes of greenfly on roses or blackfly on broad beans. The vision is quite justified because both are pests and both tend to infest on an epidemic scale. Agriculturists and horticulturists view any organism that interferes with crops as a pest—whether it be a virus or a predatory animal.
This section leaves aside the viruses (and fungi and bacteria) and the animals like rabbits and moles and concentrates on insects and insect-like pests, including also slugs and snails (molluscs) and eelworms (nematodes).

Insects are the largest group of creatures on earth. In evolutionary terms they are highly successful, and have proved to be man's fiercest competitors. Historically, insects have caused more deaths to mankind than all wars put together.

Insects will attack most plants, whether they live in the garden, the house or the greenhouse. Like all illnesses and disorders, prevention is better than cure and the best way to reduce your losses is to ensure that your plants are healthy when planted and then well cared for. Many physiological disorders of plants (caused, for instance, by too little water or too much nitrogen fertilizer) pave the way for attack by pests. So as soon as you notice any signs of distress or damage—act promptly.

Knowing what to look for

The pest itself may be almost invisible. Eelworms, for instance, are difficult to see under a microscope. But their size bears no relation to the damage they can do. Even visible pests may not always be sitting in full view. You may have to dig underground and study the roots to determine the cause of the trouble, or wait for night to catch such creatures as slugs.

Pests which attack leaves and flowers are the most easily identified because the damage occurs rapidly and is usually quite recognizable. Two main groups of pests attack leaves: those which have biting mouthparts (for example beetles) and those with sucking mouthparts (such as greenfly). They may hide inside or outside the leaves or, like the notorious leaf-miner, burrow between the middle layers of leaf tissue.

Larger pests (like caterpillars) are usually more noticeable but they may attack and run (or fly) away, in which case you should spray, or lay bait, against the next visit.

Fortunately there are many methods of control at your fingertips, providing you diagnose the enemy correctly and act as swiftly as you can.

Understanding the enemy

Knowing something about the life cycles and habits of pests can help you in anticipating and preventing trouble. For instance a major factor in determining how active they are is temperature; the warmer it becomes the busier they get. And up to 35°C (95°F) they breed faster too. Cold winters greatly decrease the numbers overwintering in the garden.

Day length also plays a part in controlling the breeding seasons and migration patterns of many insects. This is why they always become scarce in autumn, even before cold weather arrives. Clear away and burn garden refuse every autumn because it provides ideal shelter for overwintering pests. Many overwinter as eggs which can also be destroyed by the use of insecticides.

Use of insecticides

Most pesticides are sold under trade names, partly because the chemical names and formulae are cumbersome and difficult to remember. You can, however, be sure of getting the right product by reading the contents on the label and checking with the chemical, or proper, name given here. Full chemical names are

Left: aphides attack indoor and outdoor plants. Below left: cabbage-root fly larvae is a danger in the vegetable garden. Bottom left: onion fly, enemy of the onion bulb family. Below: cabbage white butterfly, whose caterpillars cause such damage. Below centre: cabbage white caterpillar eating brassica leaves. Bottom: the ubiquitous slug, menace of all gardens. Bottom right: potted palm showing red spider mite damage

often abbreviated, for instance benzene hexachloride is known as BHC. (It is also sometimes called gamma-BHC.)

Always use protective clothing. Rubber gloves are important and be sure always to wash hands and face thoroughly after using insecticides. Never allow children or animals to be with you when sprays are being applied, and don't let them eat anything that has just been sprayed. Also wash out all spraying equipment after use—but not in the kitchen sink.

In some cases you may be able to use physical methods of combat such as picking caterpillars off plants and burning them. These are always preferable to spraying, because all sprays have some adverse effect on the plant. This is why you must adhere strictly to the manufacturer's recommended rate of application.

How insecticides work

Insecticides kill in two main ways; first as a stomach poison, when the pest either eats it with the leaf or sucks it up with the plant sap. Alternatively, if the pest is sprayed directly, the chemical will poison through the 'skin' or suffocate the pest. The method you choose depends on several factors, such as climate, type of insect and type of plant involved.

Non-systemic ('knock-down') insecticides Many early insecticides killed either by blocking the breathing processes or by poisoning when absorbed through other exterior surfaces. But they did not persist for long and had to be used frequently in order to be effective. However, some are still very useful for certain purposes.

Pyrethrum and derris, for example, are both very effective general insecticides. They are derived from plants and do not persist for long. This means they are safe to use on vegetables—even up to the day before harvesting. Derris, however, is harmful to fish so do not use it near stocked pools.

But DDT, used by gardeners for so many years, has now been withdrawn from the gardening market as other, newer insecticides have proved to be safer and equally (if not more) efficient. Trichlorphon is one good modern substitue for DDT.

Systemic insecticides The systemics are absorbed by the plant and dispersed throughout its entire system; any biting or sucking insect will ingest them while feeding and be killed. These pest-killers remain in the plant for several days (sometimes even weeks) and they act against a wide variety of pests.

But too often spraying can result in the development of pests that are resistant to them. So spray on sighting the enemy rather than 'just in case'.

Dimethoate and formothion are systemic insecticides that control most aphides, red spider mite, scale insect, mealy bug, caterpillars and leaf hoppers. Systemic insecticides are also one of the most successful ways of killing many of the root-feeding insects, such as lettuce root aphid.

PESTS Guide to treatment

PLACE	COMMON PESTS	PLANT AREA	TREATMENT	OTHER ADVICE
GREENHOUSE PLANTS	Aphides Whitefly	Leaves Stems Flowers	Treat as for house plants or fumigate greenhouse with nicotine, dichlorvos or BHC.	Make sure all vents are closed while fumigating. Do not enter until fumes have dispersed.
	Scale insect	Leaves	Wipe off, but if badly infested spray with malathion, nicotine or systemic insecticides.	Scrape insects off where possible.
	Red spider mite	Leaves	Spray malathion, derris or pyrethrum.	Pick off and burn badly-infected leaves.
	Mealy bug	Leaves Stems	Spray with systemic or non-systemic insecticides.	Scrape insects off where possible.
	Leaf hopper	Leaves	Spray with BHC, malathion or nicotine, often available in aerosol or smoke form.	
	Leaf miner	Leaves	Spray with BHC or malathion.	Pick and burn infected leaves.
	Vine weevil	Roots	Remove and destroy grubs found when repotting plants. Drench soil of infected plants with BHC solution.	Incorporate naphthalene or paradichlorbenzene among the crocks when known susceptible plants are repotted.

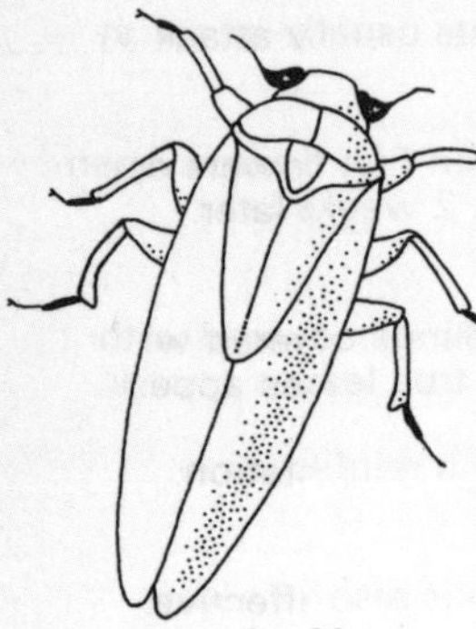

Leaf hopper

PLACE	COMMON PESTS	PLANT AREA	TREATMENT	OTHER ADVICE
HOUSE PLANTS	Aphides Whitefly	Leaves Stems Flowers	Non-systemic sprays: e.g. derris, pyrethrum, are often sufficient. For bad attacks use systemics, e.g. dimethoate.	Check all newly-acquired potted plants and eradicate any pests to prevent them spreading among your existing plants.
	Mealy bug	Leaves Stems	Spray with systemic or non-systemic insecticides, or dab with methylated spirit.	Scrape insects off where possible.
	Scale insect	Leaves	Wipe with a soft cloth dipped in soapy water or methylated spirits, or treat as for aphides and whitefly.	Place your house plants in the greenhouse when you fumigate and do both jobs at once.
	Leaf hopper	Leaves	Spray with BHC, malathion or nicotine (often available in aerosol form).	
	Leaf miner	Leaves	Spray with BHC or malathion.	Pick and burn infected leaves.
	Vine weevil	Roots	See GREENHOUSE PLANTS	

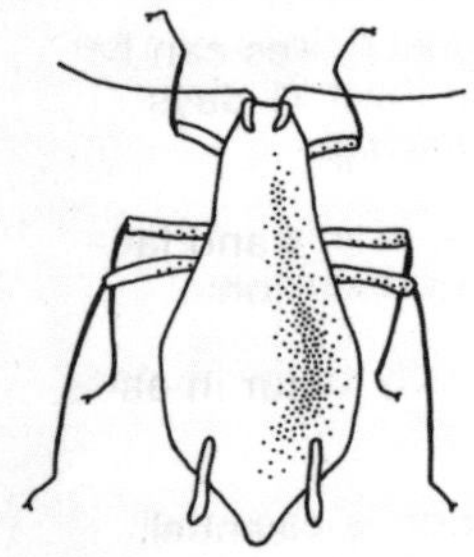

Aphid

PLACE	COMMON PESTS	PLANT AREA	TREATMENT	OTHER ADVICE
FLOWER GARDEN	Aphides Whitefly	Leaves Stems Flowers	Spray with systemic insecticide such as dimethoate or formothion.	Malathion is also effective.
	Scale insect	Leaves Stems	Spray with malathion or systemic insecticide.	Scrape off insects where possible.
	Earwigs	Flowers	Reduce populations by spraying with BHC or trichlorphon prior to flowering.	Place inverted, straw-filled flower pot traps on 1m (3 ft) canes near plants; burn resulting earwig nests.
	Capsid bug	Leaves Stems Flowers	Spray with BHC or malathion as soon as damage appears.	Prompt action is essential.

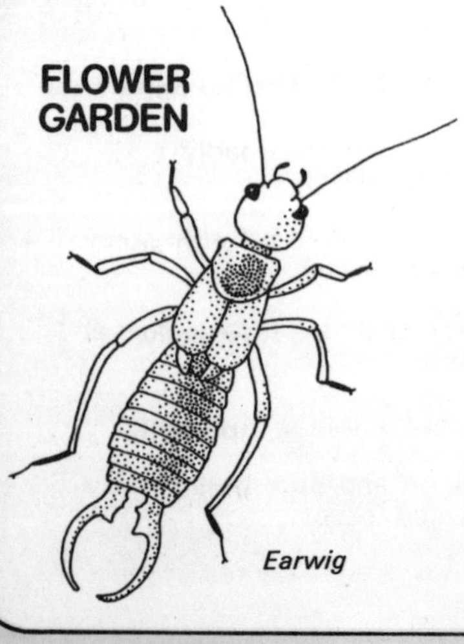

Earwig

PLACE	COMMON PESTS	PLANT AREA	TREATMENT	OTHER ADVICE
VEGETABLE GARDEN	Caterpillars	Leaves	Spray or dust with BHC, malathion or derris.	Pick caterpillars off where possible.
	Cutworm	Roots Stems	Work BHC dust or bromophos into the soil when planting.	Prevention is better than cure.
	Slugs Snails	Leaves Stems	Spray or apply pellets of metaldehyde or methiocarb.	These pests usually attack at night.
	Pea/bean weevil Grubs Thrips	Leaves Pods Peas	Apply BHC dust or fenitrion.	Apply when first flowers open and again 2 weeks later.
	Flea beetle	Leaves	Apply BHC dust when sowing seeds and at seedling stage.	Keep seedlings covered with dust until true leaves appear.
	Aphides	Leaves Shoots	Spray with systemic insecticides or malathion.	Watch for a reinfestation.
	Whitefly	Leaves	Spray with pyrethrum, dimethoate or BHC.	Malathion is also effective.
	Cabbage-root fly Carrot fly	Roots	Dust or spray BHC.	Keep seedlings covered with dust until true leaves appear.

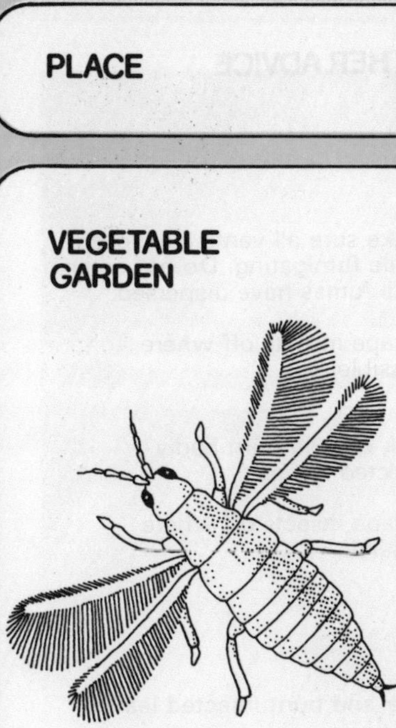

Thrips

FRUIT GARDEN	Caterpillars	Leaves	Spray or dust with BHC, malathion or derris.	Pick caterpillars off where possible.
	Aphides	Leaves Shoots	Spray with a systemic insecticide.	Watch for a reinfestation.
	Woolly aphides	Stems	Spray malathion or a systemic insecticide.	Systemic insecticides can be used, but at least 21 days before harvesting.
	Maggots	Fruits	Spray fenitrothion, BHC or derris.	Spray twice, in mid and late summer, as prevention.
	Gooseberry sawfly	Leaves	Spray thoroughly with derris or malathion.	Attacks usually occur in early summer.
	Capsid bug	Leaves Fruits	Spray with BHC or malathion as soon as damage is noted.	Prompt action is essential.
	Red spider mite	Leaves	Spray malathion, derris or pyrethrum, or a systemic.	Spray systemics 21 days before picking.

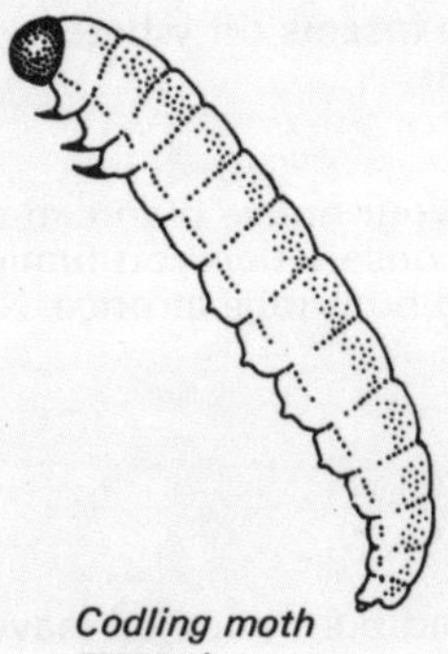

Codling moth maggot

FLOWER GARDEN CONTINUED	Caterpillars	Flowers	Spray with BHC or trichlorphon.	Pick caterpillars off by hand.
	Leaf miner	Leaves	Spray with BHC or malathion or use systemic insecticide.	Pick off and burn badly-infected leaves.
	Frog hopper (Cuckoo spit)	Leaves Stems	Spray with malathion, BHC, derris or pyrethrum.	Can be washed off with spray of soapy water.
	Slugs Snails	Leaves Stems	Spray or apply pellets of methaldehyde or pyrethrum.	These pests are most active at night.
	Thrips	Flowers	Spray pyrethrum.	Prompt action is important.
	Red spider mite	Leaves	Spray malathion, derris or pyrethrum.	Pick off and burn badly-infected leaves.

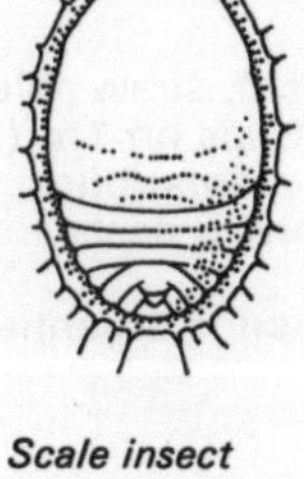

Scale insect

FUNGUS DISEASES OF PLANTS

Fungi, bacteria and viruses are the three main causes of plant disease, and of these the most important to the gardener are the fungi. Unlike insects, they can only live in and with the plant they infect, and they are common in all plants, large or small – from the tiniest seedling affected by 'damping-off' to the tall and sturdy elm tree laid low by Dutch elm disease.

Although it is quite often a simple matter to recognise that a plant is diseased – discoloration, distortion of growth, even a general air of listlessness, are all easily observed symptoms – it is usually much harder to diagnose exactly what is wrong with it. It is important, therefore, to learn to recognize the different kinds of fungal infection, so that the right remedies can be applied where possible and without delay.

Propagation of fungi

Most fungi propagate by spores (which are very similar in kind, although not in appearance, to the seeds of plants), and these can be carried from plant to plant by the wind, rain, soil or plant debris, animals and birds, and other means. Each fungus will produce many spores, and this is one of the reasons why they spread so quickly through a bed of plants, a greenhouse, or a whole garden.

Other fungi, and particularly those that attack roots, spread by means of mycelium (a fibrous growth that has much the same function as the roots or stems of plants).

The majority of fungi spread and do most damage in moist, warm conditions. To reduce the likelihood of fungal infection of roots, therefore, it is important to keep the soil well drained; and in the greenhouse adequate ventilation is essential. However, some fungi (of which the powdery mildews are an outstanding example) prefer drier conditions.

Fungus infection of seedlings

'Damping off', or seedling blight, is common when seeds are raised under unhygienic conditions. The disease is often due to a complex infection by different species of fungi, some of which are closely related. Pythium species and phytophthora species (sometimes known as watermoulds) thrive under wet conditions, and their spores are present in all soils. This is why it is essential to germinate all seed in sterilized (and therefore fungus-free) soil or compost, and to use clean pots and trays.

On sterilized soil damping-off will rapidly emerge through a batch of newly-emerged seedlings, and it is worthwhile to water with Cheshunt compound before and after germination. If the disease does take hold, watering with Cheshunt compound, captan, thiram or zineb may check it.

Plants that are growing well are less liable to attack, but even sturdy seedlings will still succumb if they are not well-cared for: over-watering and lack of ventilation are the principal cause of infection at this stage. Seedlings that have been too well nourished with excessive nitrogen may show similar symptoms.

Fungal attack of roots

The majority of species of fungus attack the leaves and other aerial parts of the plant, but there are some that spread through the soil.

Bootlace fungus The mycelium grows to look exactly like a black bootlace, but wherever it encounters dead wood it is

Above right: grey mould (botrytis) attacks many plants, especially in wet weather
Right: damping off (seedling blight) is a fungus infection
Below: bootlace fungus grows from the roots beneath the tree bark

likely to throw up a toadstool, which releases spores into the air. The 'bootlace' grows from the roots beneath the bark of the tree, where it also forms yellowish-white sheets of fungus that have given it the alternative name 'honey fungus'. A tree that is badly affected must be dug up and burnt; and the soil must be sterilized with a mixture of 1 part of formaldehyde to 6 parts of water, applied at a rate of 27 lit per sq m (5 gal per sq yd). Where infection is not too serious, a creosote-like chemical, Armillatox, may be sufficient to control the disease and allow the tree or bush to recover.

Club root Very common and attacks all members of the brassica or cabbage family (and this includes wallflowers). The plants look weak and yellow and the roots are swollen. Liming the soil helps to prevent the disease; so does a crop-rotation system. Calomel dust applied at planting time reduces the likelihood of attack, and dipping the roots in benomyl just before planting has also proved effective.

Crown gall Produces symptoms similar to clubroot, but attacks many different kinds of plant. It is favoured by wet soils: provide adequate drainage, and avoid injury to the roots. Dipping plants in a copper fungicide such as Bordeaux mixture at planting time provides protection.

Brown core Attacks polyanthus and primula roots, and the plants then become weak and sickly. Burn all affected plants and grow no others of the family on that ground for several years.

Above left: conifer gall, a white blight, may affect any conifer tree. Left: club root attacks the brassica family
Below left: roses are susceptible to powdery mildew
Below: downy mildew likes the damp

Violet root rot Affects several plant groups and is easily recognized by the characteristic strands of purple mycelium on the plant roots. Destroy all infected plants and introduce resistant crops. Violet root rot only rarely occurs in land that is in 'good heart' and so attention to drainage and soil fertility is the best means of prevention.

Black root rot Most likely to strike where plants are grown in the same place every year; it also affects pot plants. Drench the soil with captan solution.

Fungal attack of shoots and leaves

Many different fungi attack shoots and leaves, and the following are the most common examples.

Grey mould (botrytis) Prevalent in wet weather, it attacks numerous plants. Remove the infected plants to control spread of the disease, but for really effective control use benomyl, captan, thiram or zineb.

Powdery mildew Found on almost all plants, and there is often a specific species for a particular plant. This is a fungus which favours drier weather for attacks. Plants most commonly infected are roses, gooseberries, apples and Michaelmas daisies. The mildew forms a white powder on the leaves, shoots and flowers. Greenhouse plants also suffer. Cut out infected shoots on trees and shrubs the following autumn, otherwise re-infection can occur. Spray with benomyl, dinocap or thiophanate-methyl. On plants which are not sulphur-shy, sulphur or lime-sulphur sprays may be used. Many varieties of apple are sulphur-shy, for example, so it is important to make sure before using the spray. Generally the container for the mixture lists the plants and varieties for which it is unsuitable.

Downy mildew By contrast with the powdery types, downy mildew thrives in damp, cool conditions. Grey or whitish furry growths appear on leaves and spread very rapidly. Zineb is the best chemical to use.

Potato blight Related to downy mildew, and the treatment is similar. Remove and burn any plants that become very diseased.

White blister Similar to downy mildew, but the spores are liberated from blisters or pustules. The only course is to burn the affected plants, but individual diseased leaves may be removed and burnt if the infection is caught in time.

Silver leaf Affects plums, peaches, cherries and ornamental prunus, turning the leaves silvery. Cut out diseased material and treat all wounds with a protective bituminous paint.

FUNGUS DISEASES OF PLANTS
Non-systemic (knock-down) fungicides

INFECTIONS CONTROLLED	PLANTS COMMONLY INFECTED	CHEMICAL NAME	FORM AVAILABLE
Galls	Azaleas	Bordeaux mixture	Powder
Wilts	Clematis and paeonies	Lime-sulphur	Powder or concentrated suspension
Peach leaf curl	Many ornamental plants and fruits	'Liquid copper'	Concentrated solution
Blight	Tomatoes and potatoes	Sulphur	Powder
Cane spot/ spur blight	Raspberries	Several special formulations of the above are available	
Powdery mildews	Many fruit and ornamental varieties		
Scab	Apples and pears (**Caution**: do not use lime-sulphur or sulphur sprays on sulphur-shy varieties)		
Onion white rot	Onions	Calomel	Powder
Club root	Brassicas and wallflowers		
Moss and turf diseases	Grass/lawns	Other mercury-based mixtures	Mixed with lawn sand
Black spot	Roses	Cheshunt compound	Powder for solution
Leaf spots	Many garden plants	Captan	Wettable powder or dust
Scab	Apples and pears (**Caution**: do not use on fruit to be bottled or used for deep freezing)	Dinocap	Wettable powder, dust, liquid or smoke
Soil-borne infections	Many seeds and seedlings	Thiram	Concentrated solution
Grey mould/ downy mildew/ potato blight	Many plants	Zineb	Wettable powder
Rusts	Many ornamental plants and fruits in the garden	Mancozeb	Wettable powder
Spur blight	Raspberries	Several formulations and mixtures of the above are available	

Systemic fungicides

INFECTIONS CONTROLLED	PLANTS COMMONLY INFECTED	CHEMICAL NAME	FORM AVAILABLE
Grey mould	Many fruits and vegetables, growing and in storage	Benomyl	Wettable powders
Leaf spots	Many ornamental plants, soft fruit and celery	Thiophanate-methyl	Wettable powders
Scab	Apples and pears		
Powdery mildews	Roses, other ornamentals and fruit		
Black spot	Roses		

Fusarium wilt Often the cause of plants looking sickly, with yellowing leaves which appear to wilt, even in wet weather. This fungus blocks the 'plumbing' system of the plant. The spores lie in the soil for considerable periods; it can be sterilized with formaldehyde, but growing on fresh soil is often the only solution.

Apple scab Common throughout the growing season, attacking ornamental malus species such as crab-apple, pears and culinary apples. It infects leaves, stems and fruits, producing olive-green blotches on the leaves, and brown or black scabs on the fruit. Spray with lime-sulphur when flower buds emerge, but do not use on sulphur-shy varieties (see instructions on the spray container). Benomyl, captan or thiram may be sprayed from bud-burst until late summer (July). Rake up all dead leaves and burn them in the winter to prevent further spread.

Rusts Attack many plants, but hollyhocks are particularly prone. All rusts appear as orange, yellow or brown powdery masses. You can obtain resistant varieties which prevent spores germinating on the leaves. Mancozeb, zineb or maneb fungicides sprayed at fortnightly intervals should cure most rust infections.

Below: apple canker spreads along the bark, killing young shoots, and should be treated without delay
Bottom: the fruiting fungus of silver leaf appears on the bark of affected trees
Below right: rust – a mass of orange, yellow or brown pustules on the leaves
Below, far right: beware apple scab on leaves, stems or fruit in summer

Black spot Attacks roses and is probably one of the most common of fungal diseases. It starts as dark brown spots which grow up to 2cm (1 in) across. Infected leaves fall during mid summer. It also affects stems and will remain on the plant to re-infect the following season. Burn all diseased leaves and stems, and spray with benomyl, captan or zineb at the initial infection stage.

Cane spot and spur blight Affect raspberries and loganberries. Both form purple blotches; spur blight becomes mottled with black, and cane spot as it develops becomes white. Apply a copper fungicide such as Bordeaux mixture at bud-burst and, in the case of cane spot, again when the fruit has set. Thiophanate-methyl or benomyl may be used throughout the blossom period.

Stem cankers Attack many trees and shrubs. The first signs are poor, weak growth and soft patches of bark. These patches later erupt into unsightly reddish-pink pustules that spread along the bark, causing the shoots to die back. There is no chemical control for the disease, and the only solution is to cut off and burn all infected stems at once. Paint the wounds with a protective bituminous paint, such as Arbrex.

Diseases affecting tubers

These diseases can affect the other storage organ type plants as well as tubers.

Basal rot Often occurs on crocuses, narcissi and lilies. It spreads from the base as a brown rot, eventually rotting the whole bulb. It will attack at any time, even when bulbs are in storage. Cut out infected areas, dust with quintozene.

Smoulder and dry rot Attack bulbs, although smoulder is only usual on narcissus. Dry rot has a wider range and can be stopped by dipping healthy bulbs in solutions of benomyl or captan. Smoulder tends to occur in storage and a cool dry storage place helps to prevent it. If you see any signs during the growing season, spray zineb at fortnightly intervals. Other storage rots and some bulb or corm scabs should be treated in a similar manner to dry rot.

White rot and neck rot White rot is very common on spring onions and on main-crop types during the growing season. It persists in the soil and if your crop has been infected grow onions on a new site the following year. Calomel dust in the seed drills reduces the danger.

Parsnip canker Appears as brown patches and cracks on the shoulder of the parsnip, which can then be attacked by pests. The best remedy is to rotate crops or grow resistant varieties.

Fungicides

All fungicides are phytotoxic to some extent—that is, they affect the growth of the plants which they protect. It is essential that only recommended quantities and dilutions are used. Some fungicides based on lime and sulphur are particularly bad at scorching leaves if over-used. The systemic fungicides like benomyl and thiophanate-methyl are often more effective but cost more.

Removal of infected tissue will often stop the spread of a fungus and this is a point that cannot be over-emphasized. Strict garden hygiene is one of the main ways of preventing infection.

MAKING A COMPOST HEAP

Waste not organic materials from the house or garden and want not for compost is a maxim worth following. Compost, when rotted down, will improve and maintain your soil by adding humus-forming matter, plant foods and beneficial bacteria.

Compost is not difficult or time-consuming to make. Certain types of plant and household waste can be used to make it. Suitable plant waste includes grass clippings, flower and vegetable stems that are not too tough, light hedge trimmings, wet peat, wet straw and annual weeds. Leaves can be used, but not in great quantities as they are more valuable for use as leaf mould. A separate bin can be kept in the kitchen for such household waste as tea leaves, vegetable trimmings, hair, egg shells and vacuum cleaner dust. Bonfire ashes, animal manure, and sawdust are also suitable.

Not suitable for the compost heap are coarse plant material such as cabbage stems and tree prunings, diseased plants, pernicious weeds like docks, dandelions, and bindweed roots, any dead plants on which weedkiller has been used, and cooked matter, such as meat or fish.

As a compost heap is not particularly sightly, it is best situated in the working part of the garden and screened from the house. It should be protected from hot sun or cold winds, but not be against a wall or hedge. An ideal site is beneath a tree. The shape of the heap can be circular or rectangular, although most people find a rectangular one easier to cope with. The best size to aim for is about 1m (3 ft) wide, 1½–2m (5–6 ft) long, and 1–1½m (3–5 ft) high when completed.

It pays to construct the site of the heap correctly, rather than tipping the waste straight onto the ground. First dig a shallow pit – about 15cm (6 in) deep. Place the soil on one side as you will need it later. Then put down in the pit an 8cm (3 in) layer of broken bricks or stones mixed with coarse tree prunings, woody cabbage stems, straw and similar tough plant material. These will help essential drainage and allow air penetration.

When the base is prepared, begin to build up the compost heap. This should be done roughly as follows:

Layer 1: about 15cm (6 in) of organic material.

Layer 2: a sprinkling of a proprietary compost accelerator according to the manufacturer's instructions. This should supply the essential bacteria, nitrogen and chalk necessary to break down the raw matter into usable compost.

Layer 3: a 2–3cm (1 in) layer of soil, taken from the dug-out heap.

These three layers are repeated until the heap reaches the required height.

Follow these rules for successful composting:

1 Always be sure that each layer of organic material is well firmed down (but not too tightly compressed) by treading on it or beating it flat with a spade blade.

2 If using grass clippings in large quantities, mix them with other materials or they will form a soggy mass in the heap.

3 Check from time to time to make sure that the heap is moist. If it has dried out, either sprinkle water over it or, preferably, hammer stakes into the heap to make holes and then pour water into the holes.

4 To finish off the heap, level the top and put a 2–5cm (1–2 in) thick layer of soil over the top and around the sides to act as a cover.

A properly made compost heap provides material to be used either for digging into the ground or for mulching. Mulch is a top dressing layer on the surface of the soil around the plants. The compost will be ready to be dug in after about 10–14 weeks in summer or 14–18 weeks in winter. When the compost is ready for use the heap will consist of a brownish black, crumbly, pleasant-smelling and easily handled material. If the heap doesn't seem to be rotting down well in the allotted time, something has gone wrong with the construction. If this happens, it is worth the trouble of digging a second shallow pit alongside and rebuilding the first heap into that, turning the top to bottom and sides to middle and following the sandwich layer principle again. In any case, as one heap is finished, a second one should be started so that there is always a supply of essential humus-forming material ready to add to the soil.

The method of compost-making described here is simple and cheap. If, however, you have a very small garden, it may be easier for you to buy a proprietary bin compost unit, which has its own instructions for use.

If you lack the space for a compost heap as described, a bin will also give you good results. Below are three main types

Wire netting bin

Sliding plastic panel bin

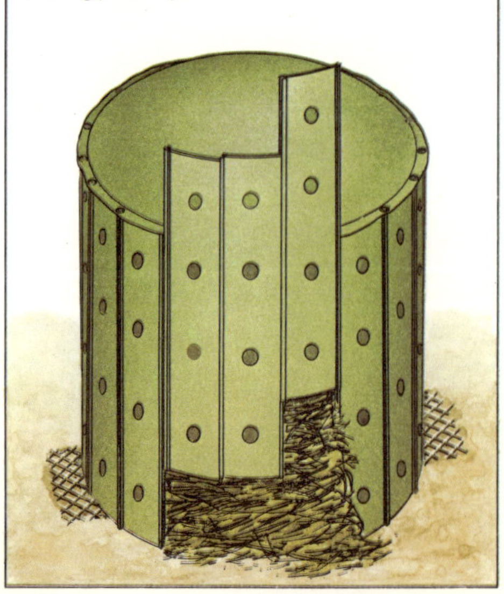

Slotted wood bin

BIBLIOGRAPHY

Gemmell, Alan *Basic Gardening* (Penguin, London 1975)

Hay, Roy (ed) *Complete Guide to Fruit and Vegetable Growing* (Ward Lock, London 1978)

Hellyer, A.G.L. *Carters Book for Gardeners* (Heinemann, London 1970)

Herwig, Rob and Schuberg, Margot *The Complete Book of House Plants* (Lutterworth Press, Guildford 1975)

Larkcom, Joy *Vegetables From Small Gardens* (Faber & Faber, London, 1976)

Lowenfeld, Claire *Herb Gardening* (Faber & Faber, London 1970)

Simons *The New Vegetable Grower's Handbook* (Penguin, London 1962)

The Gardening Year (Reader's Digest, 1968)

INDEX

Page numbers in italic refer to illustrations